CAT on A HOT TILED ROOF

Mayhem in Mayfair and Mallorca

ANNA NICHOLAS

summersdale

CAT ON A HOT TILED ROOF
Copyright © Anna Nicholas, 2008

All rights reserved.

The right of Anna Nicholas to be identified as the author of this work has been asserted in accordance with sections 77 and 78 of the Copyright, Designs and Patents Act 1988.

Summersdale Publishers Ltd
46 West Street
Chichester
West Sussex
PO19 1RP
UK

www.summersdale.com

Printed and bound in Great Britain

ISBN: 978-1-84024-683-4

A la memòria de Salvador Humbert, un mallorquí autèntic

CONTENTS

ACKNOWLEDGEMENTS

It would be churlish of me not to thank a handful of bright and bushy-tailed individuals for their pearls of wisdom on this, my latest Mallorcan voyage. These include Sari (aka Catalina) Andreu, Margalida and Margarita de Llibreria Calabruix, Guillem Puig, Joan Bolart Xarrié of Trabalenguas, Pere and Margarita Serra of the Serra Newspaper Group and Roger Katz of Hatchards Bookshop. My inestimable gratitude goes to the people of the Sóller Valley for offering my family and me safe harbour in a warm and genuine community. Last but never least, my love and thanks to Alan and Oliver.

ABOUT THE AUTHOR

As a freelance journalist, Anna Nicholas has contributed to titles such as the *Financial Times*, The *Independent*, *Tatler*, the *Daily Express* and *Evening Standard* and for the last five years has contributed a weekly column to the *Majorca Daily Bulletin*. She is a fellow of the Royal Geographical Society and has been an international invigilator for Guinness World Records. Together with explorer, Colonel John Blashford-Snell, she has also organised an expedition to carry a grand piano to the remote Wai Wai tribe in South America, which was the subject of a BBC TV documentary.

AUTHOR'S NOTE

The local vernacular used in this book is in the Mallorcan dialect. Although Mallorcan is derived from Catalan and is believed to have been spoken for more than five or six centuries, it varies greatly when written. During the Franco era, Mallorcan was forbidden in Balearic schools and this has made it an oral language, reliant on Catalan when transcribed to print because no dictionary in Mallorcan exists. Today, Catalan is the main language used in Mallorcan schools with the Mallorcan dialect being spoken in the street and in the home. The vocabulary and spelling often varies greatly from village to village in Mallorca. I have taken advice from local language experts and so hope to have accurately transcribed the Mallorcan language to print. However, I apologise unreservedly to any fervent linguists who may care to differ!

ONE

PHANTOM SHEEP

A door slams shut. Someone's clomping about downstairs. There's an intruder in the house and a damned noisy one at that. I sit frozen in my seat, momentarily distracted by the raucous croaking of the frogs in the pond beneath my window. Give it a rest, boys, this is no laughing matter. There's a sudden crash, and the sound of tinkling glass. Something dull and heavy, perhaps a wooden chair, keels over with a muffled thud. That's it. My blood's up as I hurtle barefoot out of my office eyrie with heart in mouth and pen in hand, ready to face my foe. So much for the amateur heroics, but what exactly have I in mind? Some twisted logic about the pen being mightier than the sword? Hotly, I descend the stairs, the marble reassuringly cool beneath my feet. A deep groaning rends the air and I stop dead in my tracks.

There in the middle of the *entrada* is my adversary. It's observing me dispassionately with glazed eyes, jaws caught in a sideways motion as if chewing thoughtfully on gum. I slowly level with it. There are no horns in evidence, nor a flicker of intellect for that matter, so I rightly surmise I'm dealing with a cloven-footed dumb blonde. I'm very cross.

'What on earth do you think you're doing in here?'

She averts her gaze a tad sheepishly, fleetingly surveying the damage strewn around the large sunlit hallway. A spat with an incensed Sumo wrestler might have created less havoc. Lying drunkenly on its side is a kitchen chair, its buttermilk cushion trampled and caked in mud. Spiky shards of sun-seared glass from what was once a chunky rectangular vase adorning a coffee table glint on the cream marble tiles. Toppled oak logs, until now piled neatly at the side of the grizzled old stone fireplace, have rolled under a bench, some even venturing boldly as far as the French doors. Earthy hoof marks have smeared the glass panes of the windows and clots of dry mud collect around the front doorway.

'Well?' I say, tapping my foot impatiently.

No reply. If there's one thing I've learned since living in rural Mallorca, it's that sheep really are obtuse. Try and communicate with one of these bundles of bouclé and you hit a stone wall. Amphibians are different. For the last few years, I have spent many a happy moment conferring with an ungainly toad and a chorus of musical frogs in my pond, so much so that I've come to miss them in the winter when they've gone. Of course some might balk at the idea of talking amphibians but, trust me, with a little imagination anything is possible.

The sheep now gives a little shake of her ears and clops clumsily backwards, tottering like an old girl in oversized, high-heeled shoes. Her bedraggled Rasta locks hang limply over a huge girth, the dingy white wool matted and streaked with dirt. I tut loudly to which she responds with a low rumbling expletive of an ovine kind. The wide *entrada* gives on to the kitchen where, beyond cool terracotta tiles, the back door beckons. It's flung wide open. Gracelessly, she makes a bolt for it and careers off in the direction of the swimming pool. I pad out onto the patio under the piercing scrutiny of the sun just in time to see my bulky intruder do a quick gambol around the terrace before scrambling down a stony bank into the orchard.

The Tramuntana mountain range which coils around our golden valley like a craggy grey lizard, dotted with clumps of dark pines and silver green olive trees, is pasted high in a dazzling cerulean sky. I place a hand over my eyes and watch as an eagle catches the wind and glides majestically over the terraces that lead up behind the *finca,* our old stone house. This is a not a day to be huddled over the computer in my office lair writing bits and pieces to earn a crust, but when, quite honestly, is it? Reluctantly, I slip back upstairs to my desk while trying not to focus on the mess below or the rampant sheep which is no doubt doing lumpy cart wheels across the field and baa-ing, 'You can't catch me!' to the breeze.

This is the second sheep incident this week and the novelty's wearing a little thin. A few days before, I returned from a brief sojourn in London together with Alan, my trusty Scot, and our son, Ollie, only to find the porch and terraces surrounding the *finca* covered in dung. On examining the sizeable droppings, Ollie and I hastily conjectured that this might be the trail left by some terrifying, new super-sized rodent, the likes of which had never been seen in the valley before. That was until Alan peered closer and with a dismissive shake of the head, told us they were no more than sheep offerings. We were mystified as to how any livestock had been able to enter our closed land. True, we hadn't yet got round to protecting our entire terrain with sturdy stone walls, but we had invested in several bails of cheap meshed wire from the local ironmonger's which we had wound like an untidy bandage around the exposed areas to keep out unwanted dogs and, up until now, sheep. After a quick search of the gardens we heard a loud baa-ing coming from the courtyard and raced up in time to see a woolly brown rump disappearing fast down the track. We decided that in all likelihood the fugitive belonged to our neighbour, Rafael, and that it had by now found its way back to the flock. How one of his cerebrally challenged ewes had found the temerity to trot the length of the communal track on her own, let alone break into our courtyard was a miracle in itself, but now it seemed she had an accomplice in crime, one bold enough to barge into the *finca* itself. There was nothing for it. We would have to take up the cudgel with Rafael tonight before his flock got out of hand. First, though, was the small matter of locating the whereabouts of our latest intruder, ewe number two.

Sitting at my computer, I aimlessly scan the various emails that have popped up on my screen. All of them can wait. Rather more pressingly I have an unfinished article for a magazine which has to be submitted in the morning. I glance at my watch face and realise that Alan will soon be back, having left earlier to collect Ollie from school in Palma. I can't face clearing up the clutter downstairs and besides, it seems only right to leave the evidence undisturbed for the Scotsman's return. There's a knocking on the front door. Oh, now what? Will I ever get any peace?

A small lined face is peering sightlessly through the wide glass panes of the front door. My heart softens. It's Margalida Sampol, my elderly widowed neighbour who lives at the bottom of the track. Grasping her wooden stick with her left hand, she stands patiently on the porch until I arrive to usher her inside.

'Well, well,' she sighs, speaking rapidly in Mallorcan, 'it's getting hotter, but, you know, the rains are coming. I feel it in the air.'

She pauses to mop her brow with a handkerchief while I dissect what she's just said. Slowly, with Margalida's help, I am beginning to understand the local Mallorcan dialect of Catalan, but still have to resort to Castilian Spanish for my responses. From the first day I met Margalida she explained that, with age, she found it increasingly difficult to remember Castilian vocabulary so we agreed to speak a hotchpotch of the two languages. She is hugely patient when I fail to understand what she is saying and will gesticulate and point to objects until the penny drops. Margalida is staring up at the sky. *'Sembla que vol pleure.'*

It looks like rain, she is muttering. I dread Margalida's weather predictions because they have a relentless accuracy. I lean forward and give her a peck on both cheeks. I notice that her downy white hair has been teased into small lacquered waves that bob across her scalp.

'Can I get you an orange juice?'

She squints at me with some distaste. 'Pah! You have terrible oranges. Safer to drink *vinagre.'*

Since moving to this tranquil enclave of Sóller in the mountainous north west of Mallorca, we have grown resigned to Margalida's insistence that our annual crop of oranges is an abomination to the taste buds. Why she is so vehement on this point without so much as sniffing the skin of one of our citrus orbs, I will never know. With my help, she hobbles over to the kitchen table, seemingly oblivious to the obstacles overturned on the floor, and helps herself to a sturdy oak chair.

'There's a new postman,' she suddenly announces.

This will no doubt constitute hot news in the valley. Until now, Josep, the postman, has never made it as far as our *finca*, preferring instead to dump our mail at the town post office for collection whenever we happen to be passing by. Margalida fares better because her chalet is at the mouth of the track, and does not require the tiresome, lengthy walk needed to reach our terrain.

'Good. Maybe the new one will make the effort to deliver our letters to us.'

She shakes her head in the negative. 'I don't think so. He's not a local and he has long hair.'

I dissect this information carefully. 'Have you met him?'

'*Segur*. He's given me your post this morning. That's why I'm here.'

She delves into the pocket of her vast floral overall and slaps a handful of dog-eared envelopes on the table. I've often pondered the allure of the garish polyester overalls adopted by many elderly Mallorcan women. Even in sizzling heat, these voluminous, smock-like creations are unleashed, worn either over blouses and skirts or as a stand alone fashion statement, often accompanied by pop socks the colour of workmen's tea and woolly slippers. I fan through the pile, clocking that it's mostly bills and unsolicited marketing bumph. It irritates me that junk mail has insidiously found its way to the mountains.

'I thought it was a woman at first,' Margalida is muttering. 'I called him senyora, and he laughed and said his name was Jorge.'

Given her atrocious eyesight, I'm hardly surprised at this reported exchange.

'Why didn't he bring us the mail himself instead of making you walk all the way up here?'

She gives a scratchy little cough starting her explanation with *pues*, a handy Mallorcan expression, meaning 'well'. '*Pues*, he was thinking about it, but I told him that Josep never bothered and always left your mail at the post office. He liked that idea. Anyway, I needed the walk so I offered to take it today.'

I sigh. That will no doubt have put the kibosh on any future postal deliveries to the house.

'Jorge says he's from Argentina.'

'Really?' I prompt, in hopeful anticipation of further revelations about our new postman. Absurdly, I find myself wondering whether he's any good at catching sheep. Margalida doesn't respond because, as is habitual these days, she has glided effortlessly to another plane. Her eyes, caught in a new, angelic dimension, are still and glassy and her breathing slow and ponderous. I wait a few moments and then give a polite cough. Rudely transported back to the present, she begins fiddling with the crumpled hankie on her lap and with small, quivering fingers reaches for the gilt crucifix that hangs about her neck. 'I think the rain will come from the east.'

She rises slowly, steadying herself on her stick and for a brief moment peers round the kitchen and *entrada*. In some confusion, she fumbles about in her pocket and, unearthing some heavy-framed spectacles, settles them on the bridge of her petite nose and scans the room once more. Then she frowns and turns to face me.

'*Dios mios!* What's happened in here?'

Supporting her right arm, I guide her gently to the front door and try to sound nonchalant. 'A stray sheep came in and ran amok.'

'If you fenced them in, this wouldn't happen.'

'But we don't have any. It isn't our sheep.'

She sniffs and grips the front door frame. 'Then it must belong to young Rafael. His sheep and hens are always running wild. I shall have a word.'

I'm not sure if this is the way forward. Rafael, owner of the town's main cake shop, gets impatient with Margalida, whom he regards as a rather bothersome grandmother. He now occupies the family *finca* in which he was born and has therefore known Margalida and her extended family since he was a child. They are usually on cordial terms, but occasionally the sparks fly when historical inter-family squabbles are resurrected.

'Don't worry, Margalida, I'll go and talk to Rafael.'

She hunches her shoulders. 'Better to get the senyor to speak with him.'

Old macho habits die hard in Spain. To Margalida's generation, it wouldn't be appropriate for a woman of my age group, and a foreigner to boot, to question a male neighbour about his tearaway sheep. This is a job for the man of the house.

'*No problema*,' I hear myself say, using that all-weather refrain beloved of Mallorcans. I walk with Margalida across the gravelly courtyard, feeling the hot sun on my neck. As we reach the makeshift wooden gate, she pauses to release my arm.

'I can walk back by myself. You go and tidy up before the *Senyor* gets home.'

No way José, but I'm not going to share such a bolshie sentiment with my elderly neighbour. She places her small and delicate hand on mine. Like the dried petal of a poppy, the skin is pale and papery. At nearly ninety years old, Margalida is as close to a Mallorcan grandmother as I could find, and treats me as a wayward granddaughter, indulging me one minute and chiding me the next. She is still feisty and resolute, and aside from the odd lapse of memory, is as sharp as a tack. She can recall life on the island during the Spanish Civil War with searing clarity and, unlike me, has an uncanny ability to remember useful details such as the dates of the annual fiestas and the telephone numbers of the local plumber and electrician.

'This will look splendid when it's all finished,' says Margalida, wafting her stick in the air as if it were a magic wand. If only it were. I look at the gravel in our courtyard, a reminder that we still haven't had it paved and that it will be some time before we accrue the funds to do so.

'There's still a lot more to do,' I mutter.

'Yes, there always is. It never ends.' Margalida eyes me critically. 'Of course, it doesn't help that you're always running back to London.'

'Come on, I'm there less than once a month now. We need the money.'

'What for?'

'To live, Margalida.'

She purses her lips, pats my hand and sets off along the track, leaning heavily on her stick whose polished amber surface glints like a shiny penny.

For a few moments I scan the front of the house and the courtyard, my eyes resting on the wild sea of jasmine surrounding the porch and the dark green canopy of ivy covering the loggia. In just a few years its tentacles have spread across much of the *finca*'s facade and the supporting wall of the porch, reaching as far as the old stone *pou*, our much prized well, which it has all but stifled. To the left of the porch a short path leads to the pond where a band of rowdy frogs are led in daily song by a corpulent toad whom we have christened Johnny. Water trickles from a wide brimmed ledge high above and small geckos dart up the damp and mossy walls seeking dark and shady nooks. Across the bristly lawn, and beyond the crooked old olive tree, a profusion of roses, blushing pink, cling to the wall of a small stone shed, heads lowered modestly under the scrutiny of the sun. The rhythmic chanting of cicadas can be heard from the trees.

The garden is a far cry from how it once was. I remember the tangles of rusted wire and broken wood from long abandoned rabbit hutches, and the decrepit chicken coop whose volatile inmates had either all escaped or passed on. Where the pond is today, a crude, cement *cisterna* towered over sun-scorched weeds, full of putrid water and scum the colour of bile.

My mind takes me back to the day we impetuously made an offer on this *finca* while on holiday. A chance meeting with a zealous local estate agent at the villa we were renting set off a chain of events which in time found us relinquishing our former hectic London lifestyle for a more simple existence in rural Mallorca. The *finca* had been a complete wreck and so for five years we journeyed back and forth, gradually restoring it with the help of a local builder. When the house was just about habitable, we took the plunge and relocated to the island, although I continued to hop back and forth to London to run my Mayfair based PR company.

I am rudely interrupted from my reverie by the trilling mobile in my pocket. It's past lunchtime and it's a London number so that must mean trouble. I mean, who other than Rachel, my super efficient managing director, or worse still, a client, would call during siesta hour unless it was something urgent? And indeed, it is she.

'What's up?'

'I've got great news.' There's a pause. 'You remember that pitch document we did for Miller Magic Interiors in New York?'

'That was ages ago. Didn't Bryan recommend us?'

Bryan Patterson, president of The Aphrodite Corporation in New York, is a mover and shaker in the fragrance business, and one of our clients.

'That's right. He and the owner, Daniella Popescu-Miller, are great mates.'

'What of it?'

'Well, Daniella's assistant has just called to offer us their PR account in the UK.'

'You're kidding? Without even seeing us?'

'Actually, Daniella is coming to London next month and wants to meet up. You have to be there.'

'Why?'

'Because she's insisted.'

'I don't like the sound of that. You know I'm a magnet for nutters.'

'Come on, she's a close friend of Bryan's – and he's normal.'

'He sleeps with a rabbit.'

'Leave poor Tootsie out of this. I can think of worse crimes,' says Rachel.

I give a snort. 'Anything else I should know about her?'

'There is something. She's married to a Hollywood actor.'

I dredge up some mild, voyeuristic enthusiasm. 'Oh, and who's that?'

The name tumbles out in a flurry. Not one that would immediately jog the old memory bank, but the genuine article none the less.

Rachel's tone is brisk. 'It makes sense for you to work on our client portfolio in New York. You've already got Bryan and Greedy George.'

George Myers is a long-standing, insatiably acquisitive and demanding client of mine, known endearingly in the business as Greedy George. It just so happened that no sooner had I moved to Mallorca, than George decided to expand his brand, Havana Leather, in the States. He urged me to sell up my PR company and become his new head of communications, commuting between New York, London and Mallorca. On the surface, the idea of working long hours in order to earn a substantial salary appealed greatly – until I thought about it. After all, the very reason we'd moved to Mallorca was to escape the grind. There was still the old chestnut of having to earn a living so I handed over the reins of my PR company to Rachel, agreeing, in the short term, to continue working with her on our more challenging clients. Greedy George was one of them. My game plan, in time, was to develop some modest business enterprise of my own on the island.

Rachel rattles on like an unstoppable highway express. 'By the way, it looks as if Greedy George is in London at the same time as Daniella so we can kill two birds. We also need to hook up with H Hotels when you're over.'

H Hotels. What kind of a name is that? Manuel Ramirez, its founder, is a Panamanian multi-millionaire who has recently signed us up to handle his publicity. Rachel conveniently got me to negotiate with him on account of my vaguely acceptable spoken Spanish.

'Let's hope he doesn't bring his gun to the meeting.'

'What gun?' she exclaims.

'The gold Kalashnikov I told you about.'

'Oh God, how could I forget? The one he keeps above his desk in Panama City?'

'The same.'

'What did he say again?'

'I asked him if the gun was real and he said...' I imitate Manuel's heavy, deadpan, Hispanic accent, ' "I hope you won't have to find out".'

She giggles. 'I take it back, you *are* a magnet for nutters. Anyway, how's the marathon training going?'

'The ligament's still playing up, but it should be OK soon.'

'I hope so for your sake because Greedy George must have pulled serious strings to get you that place.'

'So he keeps reminding me.'

'It shows he's got a heart,' says Rachel.

'Or that he's got a hidden agenda.'

'Whatever his motives, you'd better get cracking because loads of clients and press contacts are lining up to sponsor you. Injuries aren't an option.'

Inko, our part-Siamese feline with a kinky, deformed tail, saunters from the front garden to the shade of the porch and eyes me steadily. She wants her dinner and begins pawing at my legs, imploring me to finish the call.

I bid farewell to Rachel and am just returning to the stairs when I hear the sound of tyres scrunching gravel and the hum of an engine. The boys must be back. A car door slams and fast feet patter up the steps of the porch. Ollie throws open the front door, skidding breathlessly into the *entrada* clutching a football before scanning the scattered debris around him. I play the irritating mother card and pounce on him for a hug. Now that he's reached the grand old age of nine he has little time for unbridled affection. He releases himself hurriedly and points at the splinters of glass. 'What happened?'

'A sheep came in.'

Wordlessly he shakes his head, and saunters off into the garden. Alan appears, somewhat dazed, in the doorway. He's burdened down with a bag of fertiliser and what looks suspiciously like a sapling in a large pot. His addiction to nurseries knows no bounds. He dumps everything on the floor and stares about him.

'Before you ask, a ewe broke into the house.'

The Scotsman furrows his brow. 'Not the same wretched sheep?'

'No, it was a white one this time.'

He upends the overturned chair, replaces its cushion and looks thoughtful. 'You know, it must be one of Rafael's. How they're getting over the meshed wire or the gate beats me.'

We plod out to the back patio and garden. There's not a whisper or a baa-ing of a sheep.

'It went down into the orchard. Let's go and check.'

Our orchard of about forty lemon and orange trees sits cheek by jowl with a wild piece of terrain of the same proportions owned by a Mallorcan family. According to Rafael, the wife inherited this parcel of land from her parents a decade or so before and left it to its own devices. Over the years it has developed a biosphere of its own. It's a lost world of fauna and flora which Ollie and his friends relish exploring. They plunge into its dark recesses, pouncing upon harmless *garrigues,* the local field snakes, and rats rummaging about the swell of twisted brambles and long grass. A small stream trickles at its far end flanked by squat, spiky palm trees and dense, impenetrable scrub. It's likely that at one time it was sold off by a previous occupier of our *finca*, so that the pasture we now own is its forsaken twin. We would buy this strip of potential paradise and return it to its former glory, but so far, the asking price is too steep.

Alan braves the darkness within, believing that our unwelcome visitor is lurking deep in the undergrowth. He soon emerges with shirt covered in burs and hair askew.

'No sign of the creature!'

With stick in hand, he strides boldly among the lemon trees at the bottom of the orchard while Ollie and I, joined by a curious Inko, watch from the terrace above. There's not a trace of ewe number two. I'm beginning to think I imagined the whole episode, but then Ollie suddenly grips my arm.

'Look! It's over there.'

I spot a woolly head only a few feet from the Scotsman. We begin yelling and pointing. He follows our gaze, but fails to see the culprit as she lies low behind a thick clump of long grass. As in the best pantomimes, we both jump up and down as the sheep sidles out and creeps behind another tree.

'Where is it now?' bellows Alan, centre stage.

'It's behind you!' we cry in tandem.

The sheep bobs its head out a fraction and then takes cover. Alan spins round a second too late. Eventually, the panto villain is exposed, and the chase is on. Darting around the orchard in hot pursuit, the Scotsman tries in vain to head her off but she outwits him and makes an inelegant loop back around the trees. Ollie and I prance about like amateur matadors with flimsy sticks, trying to block her path back to the *finca*. Exhausted, Alan finally manages to steer her up into the front courtyard and to the exit, whereupon she hurtles down the track towards Rafael's house. We rush over to the wooden gate and pull it shut. None of us wants any further sheep encounters tonight.

We return to the house and clear up the mess. Lovingly Alan takes the young sapling he's just purchased down to the orchard ready for planting in the morning. After fussing around the vegetable plot, he walks heavily up the stone stairs and potters about the patio and garden examining his plants and puffing on an enormous *puro*, one of his putrid cigars. Some time later he appears in the kitchen, pulls two glasses from a cupboard and uncorks a bottle of red wine.

'I don't know about you, but I need a drink.'

'You bet,' I reply. 'Now, what might you like for supper?'

'Lamb chops?' he proffers, with a waggish smile.

I'm off on one of my runs and passing Rafael's house when I hear a strangled cry from his kitchen.

'Hijo de puta! You want to bite me, eh?'

I turn to see my neighbour stride out onto the porch sucking his thumb. Trailing behind him is a cream Labrador pup, wagging its tail and yapping playfully at Rafael's side.

'What a beauty. Is he yours?'

Rafael's previous canine companion, Franco, a rather ebullient boxer, was sent packing when he began chasing chickens and then took to killing and eating them. The local animal sanctuary found him a new owner in Germany with whom I imagine he's having a great time eating *wurst* and learning the word for 'Catch!' in German. I miss Franco.

'*Si*, I buy new dog, but already he bite me. I must train him.'

'He's only a baby.'

He shakes his head. 'You English are always so bad with animals. You spoil them too much.'

Animal welfare is not a subject close to most Mallorcans' hearts. I've learned that it's best to side step the issue in order to maintain good neighbourly relations.

'So you start training for New York marathon. You take me next time?'

Rafael is a talented runner, having breezed through three full marathons and surpassing my best time by at least an hour in each one.

'Not a bad idea. You can carry my respirator.'

Once again I'm on the self-inflicted agony trail. Having completed the London marathon twice for charity, I have masochistically agreed to undertake a third for a small Sri Lankan orphanage of tsunami victims. It was Greedy George's idea that I should run in the New York marathon and seemingly overnight he managed to secure me a much prized place. Given his loathing for charitable causes, I'm not sure how or why he did it. What I do know is that I've got at least seven months to train, so things could be worse. Rafael comes over and punches me on the arm.

'I see from my bathroom window Senyor Alan knocking at my door last night, but I was in the shower. He want something?'

Ah. I feel a sheep moment coming on.

'He was going to ask about your sheep. We've had two running around our land in the last week.'

Rafael juts out his chin and rubs it vigorously with his right hand.

'Sheep? But I get rid of my sheep. Now I just have lambs.'

'Oh dear. I'm afraid we sent one ewe down the track yesterday thinking it was yours. Heaven knows what happened to the first one.'

He fixes me with a long stare. 'But where are they now?'

'Don't ask me. Perhaps they're with your lambs?'

'No. My lambs go. They stay in my friend's field for a month while I clear the orchard. Were they branded?'

That's a good point. Did either of us actually examine this latest ewe's hide to see if it had any identifying marks? Of course not.

'We didn't look.'

'*Per favor*! Now we don't know who they belong to. Mind you, no one around here has sheep.'

Aside from Rafael, I can't think of a near neighbour with sheep either.

He gives me a slow grin. 'You sure you saw sheep? *Segur?*'

'Oh, very funny. Look, I'm feeling a bit guilty about the one we sent off. Poor thing might be lost.'

'More likely some lucky *tio* will have both of them on his grill by now.'

I can't bear the thought of some passer-by or opportunistic neighbour snaffling them for his barbecue. Rafael throws his head back and laughs, whisks the Labrador up into his arms and returns to the kitchen. I stick my head round the door.

'Hey, what's the dog's name?'

'Llamp.'

'Yamp?'

'Is Mallorcan word for lightning. You pronounce it *yamp* but you spell it l-l-a-m-p.'

And why not? It's always good local sport to fox the hapless foreigner with the vagaries of the Catalan language and if the double *ll*, pronounced *y* in Catalan, seems tricky, the *x* presents an even greater challenge. Take for example the word *xarxa*, meaning net, which curiously should be pronounced charka.

I leave him with his excitable puppy and jog down the path. The days of putting off lessons in Mallorcan are coming to an end. Catalina, my close Mallorcan friend, has persuaded me to enroll on a free language course, courtesy of our town council, after the summer. In the meantime I shall continue to muddle along as best I can.

Out on the main road, I head off running up a steep track which eventually takes me onto the pine-clad slopes of the Tramuntana mountains. It's cool and musty and the soft powdery soil is gentle underfoot. At this time of the year, I keep an eye out for processionary caterpillars, the toxic little beasties that form huge candy floss nests at the top of the pine trees. When hatched, they march robotically in fast phalanxes down the tree trunks in search of new territory to destroy. Just to brush past one of these hairy fiends can cause skin irritations so grave that the victim can be incapacitated for weeks. Given that I'm already nursing a recurring leg injury I decide to avoid further handicaps and skirt round the trees.

An hour later as I puff my way back onto the winding lane leading to our track, the rain begins. It's April, so what should I expect? The first few drops are quite refreshing until the sky, like a gigantic, upturned bath, unleashes torrents of water and the drains cough and choke, spewing up thick chocolatey water. Painfully, I sprint through the cold spume bubbling up from the gutters and spilling onto the road, and reach the house just before I'm soaked to the core. Ollie is reading in the kitchen and munching on roasted sunflower seeds. With infinite patience, like a dexterous monkey, he cracks open each one with his teeth, chews the kernel within before systematically discarding the shell in a bowl.

'You're wet.'

'Well observed.' I begin removing my soggy trainers, noting with irritation the old and familiar nagging pain in my right thigh. I ignore it.

He observes me for a second. 'Do you know where you'd find the Bay of Pigs?'

'Pigland?'

He rolls his eyes. 'South-west Cuba.'

Cracking open another shell, he flicks over a page of his book and studies the content. 'I'll give you an easy one. Where do you find Siamese fighting fish?'

'Siam.'

'That's just being silly. Thailand.'

'OK, who wrote *The Clouds*?'

He furrows his brow. 'I've no idea.'

'Aristophanes,' I say triumphantly. Studying Ancient Greek literature had to benefit me some day.

He yawns and stretches his thin, wiry arms. 'Bang goes my football practice tomorrow.'

'It might clear up,' I say uncertainly.

He studies the rain mocking him on the other side of the window pane and with undisguised impatience slumps off to his bedroom while I wearily climb the staircase en route for my shower. As anticipated, Margalida's ominous prediction has come true.

The Scotsman, clad in a tatty and faded green Barbour jacket, tweed cap and wellies, blusters into the kitchen holding a bucket. It's the second day of torrential rain and the gullies are overflowing as well as the *marjades,* our garden terraces. Water is creeping into the cellar and seeping stealthily into Alan's *abajo*, his cherished den in the field in which his *puro* smoking can go unobserved. From the day we bought our age-old ruin, we were warned by locals that life in *el camp*, the countryside, could have its drawbacks. In the last three years since refurbishing the house and living permanently in our mountain valley, we have experienced some horrendous storms and flooding which have at times left us without electricity, water and heating for several days. We have learned the hard way, equipping the *finca* with sandbags, paraffin lamps, candles and the odd bottle of brandy for when it all becomes too much.

'It can't go on much longer,' moans Alan. 'I've used up all the sandbags so if it rises any more we'll be in trouble.'

'At least we've got electricity.'

'Can we have supper at Es Turo?' Ollie asks.

Now that's a warming thought. When the weather's dreary there's nothing more cheering than dinner up at our mountain village restaurant. I can picture a carafe of robust red wine and plates piled high with vegetable *croquetes* and *be rostit*, roast lamb.

'Why not? It's Saturday night, let's live dangerously.'

We pull on jackets and wellies, and make a dash for the car, driving carefully along our dark, water-logged track.

In the wind and lashing rain, I strain to see out of my window as we slowly pass Rafael's *finca*. It seems hardly possible, but I could almost swear that there in the heart of his orchard two blurry spectres are gambolling amongst the trees. I blink and look again. Nothing. Just a sea of swaying branches and, high above, a ghost of a moon.

TWO

WAR AND PEACE

A sliver of light penetrates a crack in the wooden shutter as the dawn chorus strikes up. It's a raggedy crew led by Rafael's histrionic cockerel whose mournful cry pierces the air, prompting a low clucking and crooning from his feathery female backing group. Rather like the crescendo of a grand musical opus, shrill little sounds peck the air, followed by melodious tweeting and louder trills, extravagant cawing, and the deep-throated quacking – yes they really do quack – of the frogs in our pond. The final drum call is the deep braying of the farmer's *burro*, his donkey, combined with the persistent buzz of a quartet of passing hornets and the feverish deep barking of the village dogs. Like a conductor, I am sensitive to every sound and puzzled that today the cat's choir has failed to take its cue. Inko, together with our German neighbour's trio, Fury, Fritz and Tiger, always strike up at the end of the symphony, a brief discordant requiem for empty stomachs. Where are the furry felines?

I lie in bed for a few more moments until I can barely hear myself think with the cacophony beyond the pane. The

Scotsman is deep in slumber, his head partly enveloped by a pillow. Carefully, I release the door handle, and tiptoe down the stairs. All is dark and still. As I open the huge creaking shutters that mask the French doors and windows of the *entrada*, tart lemon light suffuses the room, causing me to wince under the glare.

Slipping out onto the porch barefooted in my old white T-shirt, I survey the shadowy Tramuntanas. Suspended in a hazy, powder-blue sky, coppery mists of pine pollen await a soft and urgent breeze to lure them far away to a new and fertile valley. To the east and west, long plumes of smoke rise up into the still air, the last of the early morning bonfires permitted before the summer ban begins. A car starts up on the track and Rafael's booming voice can be heard echoing across the valley. A woman is engaging in cheerful, Spanish repartee with him. This is Isabella, Rafael's new girlfriend from Barcelona, who has been single-handedly responsible for the recent spruce appearance of his *finca*. The outside walls have been re-pointed, the window frames coated a rich olive-green hue, and a small garden created beyond the porch where once a dull concrete yard yawned onto the *horta*, the orchard. A fence is being erected around the corral to stop the flighty hens and skittish rabbits from escaping, and a dog kennel has been installed in the pen now housing canine newcomer, Llamp. In six months she has turned this bachelor pad into a home and I can only imagine her next task being to tame the wild ways of her boyfriend, an interesting challenge. Rafael's departure for work has reminded me to waken the boys. The school run beckons, a traffic snarled slog in to Palma, Mallorca's capital.

Ollie is already up and sleepily throwing on his school uniform while Inko remains sprawled on his bed. Even in such blissful repose, one lazy eye monitors his every move so that when Ollie steps towards the door, she leaps to the floor, racing ahead of him to the kitchen.

'Greedy old Inko,' he says softly, picking up her food dish and carefully filling it with her favourite, foul-smelling, fishy breakfast. He potters around the cupboards, preparing his habitual breakfast of fat black olives, olive oil and salt on home-made bread and a glass of water. What else could one expect a boy named Oliver to eat? Half an hour later and Alan has set off to Ollie's international school. I run upstairs to my office and fire off some emails before Catalina arrives. The sun is now up, and below my window young frogs bask on lily pads and large rocks jutting from the pond's surface. Occasionally there's a small plop as one dives into the murky depths to cool off or nibble at some unfortunate insect. They're singing at the tops of their voices and I'm sorely tempted to join in, but whenever I've tried, they blank me. Entry to this machismo boy band is by invitation only. A car skids into the courtyard and brakes abruptly. I skip downstairs to find Catalina, my guardian angel of household chores, bustling into the house.

'What you doing, you lazy woman? In the office?'

This is a normal Catalina refrain, always delivered with a radiant smile. Unlike many of her contemporaries in the valley, Catalina speaks fluent English, having spent some years as an au pair in both England and the States. She breezes into the kitchen and fills the kettle, noisily banging cupboard doors, and examining the gaping mouth and dark empty interior of the washing machine like a disappointed dentist.

'No washing?'

'Oh, it's in the laundry bin. I haven't had a minute.'

She clicks her teeth and stomps up the stairs, reappearing with a mountain of crumpled clothes which she brutally sifts through. Shovelling all the whites into the machine, she slams its door shut, starts the programme and begins her assault on the ironing. I slap a cup of black tea in front of her and sit down to munch some toast. This is our twice weekly ritual.

'When you go back to London?'

'Soon, I'm afraid.'

'It won't go on forever.'

I fleetingly consider the business idea I've been nurturing. Should it ever see the light of day, I would no longer need to make regular trips back to London.

Catalina holds the iron aloft. 'Don't forget *Moros i Cristiàs* next week.'

'How could I? It's all Ollie talks about.'

The Moors and Christians event is part of *Sa Fira I Es Firó,* a four day fiesta which includes *sa fira*, a livestock market, and *es firó*, a mock fight. It commemorates the famed battle which raged between the *moros*, marauding Moorish pirates, and the *cristiàs*, the Sóller locals, on 11 May 1561. The *cristiàs*, who successfully beat off their attackers, are assured victory annually. It's a one day, non-politically-correct marathon and a lethal assault on the ear drums.

'Is Stefan a Moor this year?'

'Stefan is always a Moor. Is more fun.'

Catalina's brother, Stefan, the builder who renovated our ruin of a *finca*, always throws himself wholeheartedly into the local fiestas or *festes* as they are known locally. His sister is just as enthusiastic. She eyes me through a puff of steam. 'By the way, Stefan wants to know when to put up the front gate?'

'Is it ready?'

She shrugs her shoulders and folds another shirt. *'Mes o manco.'*

More or less. Well, that sounds hopeful. The local blacksmith is making us a simple black iron gate to replace the old wooden effort we currently have propped up at the front entrance. We may not be able to fund walls all round the property yet, but the courtyard is a priority, as is the installation of a decent gate to prevent phantom sheep from popping up all over the place.

'He can come whenever he wants.'

The phone rings. It's Alan asking me to collect our mail from the post office. I trace a note of anxiety in his voice as if he's expecting something important. What can that be, I wonder? Apparently he won't be back until the afternoon because he and Pep, his partner in crime, have decided to meet for lunch in Palma. That doesn't bode well. The only reason these two meet away from our local town is so that they can hatch hair-brained business schemes away from prying eyes. In fairness, when the Scotsman learns what sort of venture I am contemplating, he'll be quite entitled to incarcerate himself in his *abajo* with a large *puro* and a bottle of Lagavulin.

Catalina offers to drive me in to the town to collect the mail but I tell her I'd prefer to go on foot. This is the season when the heavy and intoxicating fragrance of jasmine hangs in the air and rich clusters of lavender fill the hedgerows. Lemons, as common a sight as oranges in our valley, fatten and turn golden with the spring rains and wild baby asparagus shoots up along the banks. It's a good time to walk.

On reaching Sóller *plaça*, the main square, I head off to the post office only to find a mountain of mail and a rather cumbersome box with a New York stamp awaiting me. Somehow I manage to squeeze it all in to a large carrier bag proffered by one of the staff, and walk slowly up the main street. Remembering that my photocopier's out of ink, I pop into HiBit, the local computer shop which is owned by Antonia, a fast-talking *Mallorquina* with fluent English, and her American husband, Albert, a computer boffin. From the moment we arrived in the valley, this duo guided us through the technical and bureaucratic labyrinth necessary to get us connected to the Internet at our old *finca*. Several times during severe storms, our entire computer system crashed, and it was always thanks to Albert that we found ourselves up and running again, albeit some weeks later. Behind the counter with ear to the phone, Antonia beckons to me. I set my bag down and wait patiently for her to finish the call. After much *si-si*-ing, she props the receiver back on its perch.

'Hey,' she says, 'Exciting news! We have a new postman.'

'He's from Argentina.'

She looks astonished. 'Really? How do you know?'

'My neighbour, Margalida, told me. I haven't even clapped eyes on him yet.'

She grabs a half-finished cigarette from an ash tray in front of her and inhales deeply. 'He's a bit of a Don Juan – long hair, good muscles. I could tell he wasn't from around here.'

There's a groan from the office at the back of the shop and in a trice, Albert's tall and robust frame appears in the doorway.

'She's not on about the postman again?'

'It's a hot topic, Albert.' I give him a wink.

'I guess,' he drawls, 'Just that I've heard it about ten times already.'

Antonia wafts her cigarette at him. 'Don't exaggerate.'

'What is it about this guy?' Albert quizzes me. 'Even your chum, Juana, came by yesterday waxing lyrical about him.'

That's intriguing. I could never imagine Pep's inscrutable wife betraying a soft spot for anyone publicly. I buy a new ink cartridge and head for the door. 'Are you joining in the battle this year?'

'No way! It's too crazy. I'll be watching from the side, but Albert and the boys will take part,' Antonia gestures at her husband.

Albert holds up his hands in protest. 'Not this boy. I'll be safely in a bar discussing Argentinean barbers with the new postman.'

By the time I reach Cafè Paris for my habitual espresso, it's nigh on midday. The square is awash with German hikers in sturdy boots, and groups of cyclists clad in gaudy Lycra all-in-ones. They sprawl lazily on wicker chairs in the sunshine, sipping freshly squeezed orange juice and studying route maps. Waiters weave in and out of the tables, refilling glasses and occasionally stopping to share a joke with a passing local. In the raised bandstand opposite the lofty, ornate church, toddlers on tricycles career around the flagstones while their young mothers huddle around the old fountain chatting and smoking. There's the familiar *toot toot* and creaking of the vintage Sóller *tramvia* as it rumbles along the iron rails that carve an uneven, meandering path through the centre of the square to the station. I wait till the wheezing veteran with its wood-panelled carriages slowly passes by, and skip over the road to Café Paris. Within its cool, marbled interior I spy the usual suspects scattered at various small, round tables. A few heads bob out from behind *Ultima Hora* or *Diario de Mallorca* newspapers as I enter, clocking that I too am a regular. José, the young owner, greets me with a wave from behind the bar and plonks a small cup of steaming coffee and a bottle of mineral water down on my table. I wonder what would happen if I changed my order one day, just for the hell of it.

Across the room, I receive a furtive smile from Gaspar, the paper delivery man. He's looking rather hot and bothered and is in deep discussion with Senyor Bisbal, a tall and distinguished Mallorcan in his late seventies who has recently taken to greeting me. Rumour has it that he is one of the wealthiest and shrewdest businessmen in the valley, and I wouldn't doubt it. If there's one thing I've learned since living here, it's that well-heeled Mallorcans abhor outward signs of wealth and showiness of any kind. They would rather spend their money on acquiring land or property, or failing that, squirreling it away for a rainy day. The hallmarks of serious Mallorcan wealth in the rural areas include:

1. Scruffy, and at times dishevelled, personal appearance
2. Grubby, battered and dented jalopy, preferably lacking wing mirrors
3. Spindly, quivering Mallorcan *ca rater* hunting dog in tow

4. Faithful elderly retainer close at hand
5. Undying loyalty to a couple of simple restaurants serving wholesome local fare
6. Assiduous checking of bar and restaurant bills and leaving of small tips
7. Expensive Havana *puros* smoked by the men folk
8. Enormous property and land portfolio
9. A stake in several local businesses
10. Purchase of expensive *fincas* for all the offspring

Senyor Bisbal fits the bill perfectly. Rising from his chair, he makes his way over to my table, his fretful hound following at a discreet distance. With sleeves rolled back to the elbow and shabby old trousers buckled with a worn and archaic leather belt, he gives a slight bow and asks me if everything is in order. I tell him it is. Then, in elegantly phrased Spanish, he informs me that he has paid for my coffee. I remonstrate, but he holds up his hand, declaring that it is his pleasure. *Que fer?* What do you do? Give in gracefully, that's what.

It's late evening. Alan and I sit reading on the patio, the last dregs of a ruby Rioja playing at the bottom of our glasses. A candle glows between us, attracting a small white halo of midges that hover tirelessly above the saffron flame. I lean forward and blow into their midst, marvelling at how the tiny white forms disperse like the seeds of a dandelion clock, spiralling upwards into velvety infinity. As night casts a charcoal mantle over the valley, the tawny Tramuntanas, like pyrites, retain a golden afterglow cast by the dying sun. The relentless rasping of the frogs permeates the night, louder than the shrill cry of the ghost-like screech owls overhead, and more rhythmic than the clicking cicadas rustling in the trees. A dog's howl punctures the still air, and is soon echoed by a chorus of invisible hounds across the ebony fields of the valley. Alan drains his glass and with exasperation looks about him.

'I'll have to get out the didgeridoo.'

'Not yet,' I say, closing my book and yawning. 'They'll be quiet soon.'

He gets up, and with the candle, wanders over to one of the vine-clad pillars to study a plump gecko. Caught in the sudden glare it recoils with heart pumping, its tiny legs and arms splayed out against the stone like a captured fugitive in an American cop drama. I have an urge to shout out, 'Freeze!' A second later it vanishes without a trace into the night.

Alan turns to me. 'Did you manage to get to the post office today?'

I call softly to Ollie who shuffles out of the candle-lit kitchen with book in hand.

'Have you by any chance seen a large bag of letters lying around?'

He nods dreamily and disappears into the house only to re-emerge a few minutes later with the post. Alan tips the bag onto the table and begins sifting slowly through the various envelopes. He hands me a large parcel.

'This one's for you. It's from New York.'

Ollie scrutinises the package. 'I'll have those stamps when you've finished with them.'

'OK, as long as you get ready for bed now.'

He sighs heavily. 'Can I read for a bit?'

'Ten minutes.'

I watch him scamper up the unlit stairs to his room. Inko appears from the gloom of the garden and like an undercover spy follows him at a distance, furtively hugging the shadows of the stairwell, to his room.

I begin ripping at the brown tape binding the parcel until the flaps are free and a sea of foam chips burst from the opening.

'This must be from Greedy George. He's probably sent some new leather products sample for me to see before we meet in London.'

Alan gives a small distracted grunt, scanning the other items until he alights on a neat rectangular package. He stands up to study the label in the light of the kitchen doorway before quickly shunting it to the back of the pile. A flicker of a smile plays on his lips as he whisks the bundle under his arm and heads for the kitchen.

'I'll go and sort all this lot out and leave you to examine George's delights.'

Alone under the vast shadow of the mountains I dip my hand in the box and draw out a large felt drawstring pouch. Pulling undone its strings, I shake out the contents and contemplate the strange assortment of objects that clatter onto the table. I select a bold, red leather collar studded with luminous white stones and what look like diamonds. Surely they can't be the real thing? It appears to be for a cat because it's certainly too small for a dog unless of some obscure pygmy breed. Beneath it, wrapped in rustling carmine-tinged silk is a miniature tartan waistcoat trimmed with tan leather. I unearth a more daring creation in soft black leather. It looks a bit like a tiny diving suit with a zippable front and arms and legs which are fastened along the seams with Velcro. Attached to it is a hood sporting two small cavities, I presume, for little ears. It slumps forward when I hold it aloft. On the soft leather back, all is revealed. Emblazoned in diamante letters are the words, CAT GIRL. George has created a miniature cat suit, but why is anybody's guess. Somewhat warily I unwrap the final item. Cocooned in dusky blue felt is a black leather cape of diminutive size. It has a velvet collar and on its back, spelt out in dazzling, turquoise gems are the words, 'BAT CAT!'

Holding the cape in my hands, I breathe in the rich pungent smell of new leather. Its texture is silky and smooth, unlike the hide of our resident toad, Johnny. I remember once daring myself to touch his gnarled skin and being amazed that it was as tough and dry as parchment. Inko pads across the patio and rubs her soft cream fur against my leg. I lift her onto my lap and with sly moves manage to fasten the cape around her neck. With a look of alarm, she leaps to the floor and swirls around, the cape billowing up behind her like a tempestuous sea. I pounce on her and undo the Velcro clasp, setting her free. With a filthy look in my direction she stalks off up the stairs, presumably to find solace in the company of my less treacherous son.

I delve into the box of white chips hoping to find some written clue that might help unravel the mystery of the bizarre items within. Triumphantly, as though plucking a prize from a lucky dip, I pull out a slim piece of paper. A jumble of spidery letters, written in ox-blood red ink runs across the page. The message is sparse:

Hi guv. New leather cat range. Dogs next. Aren't I fab? Let's discuss when we meet. George.

A warning bell sounds in my head. It wasn't that long ago that Greedy George dreamt up a range of leather lizard air fresheners which took London by storm, earning him the double accolade of design genius and eccentric oddball.

The dogs begin partying. Barks of all kinds fill the bowl of the valley, echoing around the hills and startling the feral cats that perch like sphinxes on the high terraces under the silvery moon. Alan strides from the kitchen into the shadowy garden with his brightly painted didgeridoo, a random purchase from Ibiza, and begins blowing deeply. It emits a low pulsating drone and before long, each and every bark melts into silence. The air is still and warm and for a while the valley holds its breath, a brief truce of peace.

It's Monday, the day of the *Moros i Cristiàs* battle re-enactment and a perfect excuse for us all to get as pickled as herrings. On this day alone, every adult in the valley is encouraged to storm the streets clutching swords, sabres and blunderbusses while masquerading as swarthy, turban-clad Moors or Christian peasants in breeches and sack cloth shirts. The emphasis is on community spirit and if dressing up, imbibing to excess and playing out mock battles is your game, so much the better.

Today, when Rafael's demented cockerel blasts us at five o'clock, I roll onto my stomach, pillow clasped to my head, fantasising about roast chicken. Unable to sleep, I shower, dress and slip downstairs to the kitchen. Inko is already scratching at the back door, her furry pot belly flattening against one of the glass panes. Greedy Inko indeed. I grab a trug and set off to pick lemons in the orchard, my morning ritual. The luxury of having a ready supply of lemons on our land has meant that we use them for all sorts of dishes and drinks throughout the day, a great excuse for picking them fresh off the trees every morning. The air is heavy with the rich, sweet fragrance of honeysuckle, and drops of dew spill from the petals of roses. With a pair of secateurs I set about clipping a lemon free of its branch, inhaling the delicious citrus aroma of its skin before tossing it into the trug. Yawning and rubbing my eyes, I yank branches and remove dead leaves as I move from tree to tree. At times I am showered by a flurry of ants and stop to shake them off my arms and hands. The amber sun rises higher behind the mountains and soon, soft light filters through the leaves. With a groaning trug, I stroll back to the house and find Ollie sitting crossed-legged on a kitchen chair, barely clothed and eating hummus with his fingers from a bowl.

'It's very early.'

He nods. 'I know, but I need to organise my costume for the battle.'

'It's not until tonight.'

He shrugs, making patterns in the purée with his fingers. 'Yes, but I won't have time after school and football.'

I put the kettle on and draw up a chair beside him.

He gives me a small frown. 'You look tired.'

'Well, I'm feeling pretty washed out after the weekend's madness.'

Ollie says nothing, but shakes his head disapprovingly.

The weekend's festivities have already left me bleary-eyed. On Saturday I strolled into the *plaça* with Catalina and her twin daughters, Sofia and Carolina, to watch the investiture of the Valentes Dones, at which two young girls are elected to represent the brave women of Sóller who, four centuries ago, helped fight off the invading Moors. Ollie balked at the idea of a girl-powered event so slipped off with Pep's son, Angel, for a game of football. We snapped up an unoccupied table outside Cafè Paris and spent the rest of the afternoon drinking iced coffees in the sunshine and watching the annual procession of *La Mare de Déu de la Victoria*, pass by. This slow, undulating line of local families and children wearing traditional costume snakes its way from Calle sa Lluna, the main shopping street, to the church in the square, and is always a jolly affair. Later, Alan and I spent a raucous evening with Mallorcan friends, and on Sunday the tempo got hotter as we slipped into Palma for a wild, celebratory dinner with newly weds until the early hours.

'What time does the battle start tonight in the *plaça*?'

'About eight o'clock.'

He gives a big sigh. 'If I didn't have to go to school I could see the Moors arriving in the port.'

Preceding the evening event, a series of explosive sea battles take place in the local port between the Moors and

41

the Christians. I intend to go for a quick run to the port this afternoon to witness the spectacle.

Ollie puts his empty bowl by the sink and stretches.

'I fed Inko,' he says. 'She was starving.'

'She was born starving.'

With difficulty he gathers up the rotund feline, a ball of beige and cream fur, and drapes her over his shoulder.

'We'll be in my room if you need us.'

And with that, he disappears up the stairs.

I am approaching the port, sun in my eyes, and wondering whether this was such a good decision. As I pound along the main esplanade, I am aware of blunderbusses and muskets booming from the beach. Groups of tipsy youths in costume loll around the bars and block the pavements, guns dangling by their sides. One of them topples onto the road, flagging me down with a vodka bottle. I grind to a halt and peer at him. It is one of the tilers who worked on our house and a friend of Catalina's brother. He offers me a slurp and for a mad moment I nearly take him up on his offer. Young women clad in headscarves and wearing long, black cotton dresses stand in clusters, laughing loudly and swigging on bottles of warm beer. Catalina is amongst them and hurtles towards me with a huge grin on her face.

'What are you doing running along here, you mad woman?' she screams.

I pat her arm as I run by. 'You know I like to live dangerously.'

The air is laced with the peppery tang of cordite and a veil of smoke like pale muslin hovers over the port. It's hot enough to singe skin and spectators are splashing bottles of mineral water over their heads to stave off the rays of the sun. The smell of brine wriggles through the hot musty air as I weave a path along the esplanade. Finally, I reach the car park and am about to head back when there is a massive explosion from the sea and several small boats burst into flames. I peer across the water just in time to see the defiant chin of a large black pirate vessel jutting out from behind steep cliffs in the distance. The ship hovers on the far rim of the bay, its frame resplendent in the glowing rays of the sun. Slowly and steadily it forges a menacing path towards Platja d'en Repic, the beach on the south side of the port. I stop to gulp some water and am aware of a woman calling hysterically in English from her open car window. I jog over to the vehicle as firecrackers snap and guns blaze. Inside, a pale-faced, elderly couple sit strapped in their seats, a tartan flask resting between them. Can they seriously be drinking tea in this heat? She's wearing a head scarf while her partner's diminutive frame is buried inside a beige quilted jacket.

'What's going on?' the woman shrieks at me. 'Is it some kind of riot? We've locked ourselves in the car, but it seems to be getting worse.'

'It's just a fiesta,' I yell as cheerfully as possible with rockets whizzing and whirring overhead. I crouch by her window as I wait for the ensuing BOOM and flash of white light as they explode.

She gapes at me in disbelief. 'Fiesta? It's more like Iraq! Our rep in Magaluf told us Sóller would make a nice day trip. I'll have words with her when we get back.'

I'm about to reply when there's a sudden whoosh and thunderous thud as a nearby blunderbuss unleashes its charge. We hold our ears and scrunch our eyes shut as the scorched air is filled with dust and grey acrid smoke.

'The road will be clear in about an hour. Why not just enjoy yourselves until then,' I hear myself shouting above the din.

'We're not leaving the car,' she quivers and hurriedly winds up the window.

As I beat a retreat I see, appearing out of the haze, the towering hull of the pirate ship approaching the beach. With a united war cry, swarthy, sabre-rattling Moors leap into the shallow water and up onto the sandy shore. Guns blaze and swords whip the air as they join battle with the awaiting Christians. I leave the scene, relieved that this lively pageant distracted me from the gnawing pain in my leg. As I reach our track the only sound to be heard is the distant braying of a donkey. Peace at last.

It is ten o'clock and the sky is ablaze with stars. Tightly packed in the leafy *plaça*, singing and swaying forms raise a cheer as El Capità Angelats, Captain of the Christians, wrestles victory from El Rei Moro, the King of the Moors. He stands aloft on the first floor verandah of the town hall and thrusting his sword in the air leads the town in song. Around the square, defeated Moors link arms with their vanquishers to sing the Mallorcan national song, 'La Balanguera'. Firecrackers thrown into the throng by mischievous boys sizzle and splutter, their bright flares briefly illuminating the dark earth.

We sit at a quiet cafe just off the *plaça* with our friends, Pep and Juana. Ollie and their son, Angel, have commandeered another small table and sit playing cards and sipping cola. The waiter bustles over and places glasses of cold cava in front of us. In characteristic mode, Pep is smoking a *puro* and wearing a wide-brimmed panama which obscures his grey wavy locks.

'Did you know,' he says, fixing his bright blue eyes on me, 'that "La Balanguera" only became the national anthem in 1996.'

'Who exactly is *la balanguera*?' I ask.

'Who indeed?' sighs Pep, inhaling deeply.

'It's just a bit of Mallorcan folklore,' says Juana.

Pep gives her a frown. With some impatience he taps his cigar against the table, grinding the ash under his foot. 'The words were written by Joan Alcover I Maspons, a friend of my grandfather. He had a tragic life.'

'Why?'

He slips me a smile. 'Probably because *la balanguera* decreed he should.'

'Oh well, at least he'll be remembered,' says Juana, taking a gulp of cava and fidgeting in her chair.

'Cold comfort,' Pep replies.

'Let's raise a toast to *la balanguera*, whoever she is,' Alan says.

We are clinking glasses when a confident young woman strides towards us. She smiles indulgently at Alan.

'Do you live here?'

'Thankfully, yes.'

'Great! I wonder if you'd mind doing a brief piece to camera? I'm filming with Channel Four. Be good to get a resident Brit's perspective on the fiesta.'

A gaunt man trails behind her in the gloom, gripping a large furry object to his chest, indicating that he's either a sound engineer or a rodent fetishist.

Alan rises from his seat.

'How much are you paying him?' quips Pep.

'Nothing, I'm afraid, but he'll be on TV.'

'Ha! Your brief moment of fame,' he cries, patting Alan on the back.

'I must see this,' says Juana, with a certain irony in her voice.

They walk off in the direction of the floodlit town hall, leaving Pep and me slouching lazily in our wicker chairs.

'I'm back to London soon.'

He yawns softly. 'So much for all your talk about starting a business over here.'

'I'm working on something.'

He takes a sip of cava. 'I'm listening.'

'It's a bit complicated.'

'The best things in life are.'

I call over the waiter and ask for some olives and crisps.

'I'll tell you when I'm ready.'

He shrugs. 'By the way, I've completed the deal on that holiday flat in the port. Now that it's mine, I can start renting it next month.'

'Congratulations.'

We clink glasses.

He taps my arm. 'Actually, I've asked Alan to manage the rentals. We discussed it over lunch the other day.'

'He hasn't mentioned it yet.'

Pep fans the air with his hand. 'It could be a lucrative little business for him. I'm too busy working on other things.'

'What markets will you go for?'

'Brits, Germans and Swedes, mostly.'

I'm not sure how Alan will cope with juggling bookings for a holiday flat, but he'll no doubt enjoy greeting clients, especially Swedish hen parties. I munch on the olives brought to the table by our waiter while the boys snaffle the plate of crisps for themselves. A few minutes later Alan and Juana return, talking animatedly.

'That producer thought Alan was a natural for TV. She's taken his details.' Juana sounds breathless.

Pep and I share a smirk.

'She was probably just being nice,' says the Scotsman modestly. 'Mind you, stranger things have happened.'

We drain our glasses and Pep settles the bill before we can remonstrate.

Pulling back his chair, he slots his old leather wallet back into his trouser pocket. 'Come on, let's leave before the stampede. Juana will prepare a light supper.'

'Who says?' she simmers.

'I can cook something,' I say quickly, desperate to avoid one of their bickering sessions.

'I'm only joking,' says Juana throwing Pep a cautionary glance. 'This time.' We set off as the *plaça* begins to clear and overhead a stray firework crackles and splutters, unleashing a thin plume of bright fuchsia smoke into the raven black sky.

Ollie is shaking me awake. I peer, bleary eyed, at my alarm clock. Thankfully, I haven't overslept. Light is streaming in from the window.

'What is it?'

'Jorge's here.'

'Who?'

'He says he's the new postman. He knocked at the front door.'

I belly flip out of bed, grab a bathrobe and hop over to the mirror. Late-night celebrations at Juana and Pep's house have taken their toll. Alan is laid out on the bed like a corpse, although his lungs still appear to have life. I tiptoe downstairs to the front door and there, like a heavenly seraph bathed in primrose light, is the Argentinean Adonis. He smiles shyly, his long mane of chestnut hair fastened loosely behind him, his eyes as blue and mesmeric as the Indian Ocean. I extend a hand.

'You're Jorge, the new postman?'

His eyes widen in surprise as he addresses me in formal Spanish. 'You know my name? News travels fast in this town.'

'It certainly does.'

'I'm sorry to arrive so early, but I wanted to introduce myself before going to the depot. Time won't permit me to deliver to your house every day, but I'll do my best.'

'Well, that's better than in the past.'

As he passes me the mail, I stealthily notice a small black tattoo of what looks like a letter 'R' on his bronzed wrist.

'You are British?'

Well, even by a long stretch of the imagination, he can hardly think me a native.

'That's right.'

He smiles apologetically. 'Ah, I speak German, Russian and French, but no English. I will have to learn.'

Why a quadra-lingual Argentinean deity is delivering post in the Sóller Valley, I'll never know.

'Perhaps you can give me lessons,' he says, with a beatific smile.

Like a shot.

'Maybe one day.'

He shakes my hand and, with a slight nod of his head, saunters off down the track, his tall, muscular frame undaunted by the heavy mailbag slung over his shoulder. Ollie hovers behind me.

'He's really cool. I told him one of my jokes.'

'That's nice.'

Ollie's blue eyes follow the fast-moving figure, now just a blurry silhouette devoured by the sun.

'I do hope we'll see him again.'

Indeed, let's hope we will.

THREE

RAINING CATS AND DOGS

Sunday 11 p.m., Mayfair

The taxi cuts a gash through two lanes of stationary vehicles waiting at the lights, and then turns into a dark, stubby little side street which leads directly onto a small square. A less enlightened or kindly passerby might consider it more of a parking bay flanked by a few grand terraces and an underground car park, but Audley *Square* it is. The rain continues to blubber inconsolably beyond my window as the car draws to a halt by the pavement, shivering involuntarily, perhaps with the chill. I stare beyond the blurred window at the tall redbrick building which now serves as my home from home when I'm back in London. A minute's sprint away is The Dorchester, rising like a decorous wedding cake, its lights twinkling in the leaden sky, and the posturing Hilton with its shiny windows and black beetle limos outside. For all its charm, my club could do with a generous lick of paint and modernising and so, like a dowdy cousin, hangs back from its more glitzy relatives along Park Lane. Its quaint and cosy aspect attracts scores of female members brought up on a diet of Mallory Towers, whose most cherished childhood memories include winceyette pyjamas, pillow fights, and a time when lemon sherbet was presented in small twists of white paper – I am one of those girls. The rain is bucketing down and I briefly contemplate how wet I'm going to get dashing to the front door without an umbrella, and with a truculent case in tow. Very, that's how. The driver grins at me in the mirror.

'Forgotten your brolly?'

'Well, it is May.'

'Makes no difference, love.'

He's right about that. The weather in Britain is impossible to predict any more so why don't I remember to pack an umbrella? Because I'm a dolt. Simple as that. I thrust the taxi receipt in my pocket and wheel my case out onto the wet pavement. In a blink I'm at the front door, but still manage to get soaked. The night porter, Noel, lets me in and tuts loudly.

'No coat?'

'Well, it is May.'

'What?' he exclaims.

Oh, let's not go there again, I sigh to myself. After signing in, I spend the next few minutes warming my toes by the hearth in the lobby. There's no fire in the grate but, bizarrely, it feels comforting just sitting in front of it. Noel is from Sri Lanka, and together we are trying to help raise funds for an orphanage in Colombo. In fact, it's entirely his fault that I shall be running the New York marathon. I bid him goodnight and squeeze into the tiny lift which might usefully double as a metal coffin. In my room, with its floral eiderdown, flannelette sheets and feather pillows, I am whisked back to childhood holidays in Wales staying in my grandfather's cottage in a remote village.

A year ago when Alan and I had taken the decision to sell our flat in Pimlico, we knew that I would still need a pied-à-terre for my work trips back to London. Friends helpfully offered rooms but, not wanting to become the proverbial bad penny, I decided to hunt out an inexpensive refuge of my own. By sheer luck I discovered my club, an extraordinary oasis from the ravages of London life, and home to an irresistible cocktail of colourful, eccentric and quixotic members. The deciding factor for joining was the dark and musty oak-panelled library with its faux bookcase behind which lay a secret chamber. For that alone I would have signed up. True, the bathrooms were mostly shared, at times the water ran cold, and in the bedrooms the drawers and windows jammed, but for all that it represented one of London's hidden jewels, a national treasure to be lovingly preserved.

I slowly unpack my case and with effort get ready for bed. Before setting the alarm I take a cursory glance at my loyal and tatty old leather diary. Since moving to Mallorca, I have stubbornly resisted embracing the new age of electronic gadgets and that includes fruit-branded diaries. My gun-toting client, Manuel Ramirez of H Hotels, has warned me about the perils of such toys. Apparently, last month while washing his socks in the bath of a plush Parisian hotel, his BlackBerry® fell from his jacket pocket into the bath water and that was the end of it. Of course, had he used the hotel's laundry service, the BlackBerry® might have remained intact and his socks in better condition, but that's neither here nor there.

I turn the page and groan. In the morning I have an early breakfast meeting with the owner of Miller Magic Interiors in New York. Anyone with the name Daniella Popescu-Miller, spells trouble. And then at six-thirty, joy of joys, I'm due to see my old adversary, Greedy George, to discuss the delights of cat suits and dog collars. It's nearly midnight and I'm too exhausted to read the blur of other appointments, so I switch out the light. In my mind's eye I can see Alan and Ollie asleep in their beds. The cats will be prowling in the orchard in search of mice and rats, and my beloved frogs will be crooning in the pond.

Monday 7.15 a.m., the club, Audley Square

Someone's knocking on the bedroom door. I squint at my watch in the gloom. The overhanging light bulb has blown and I'm dressing by the sickly light of the bedside lamp. The chintzy curtains are drawn back, but it might as well still be night. Rain pounds the window and the sun continues to slumber beneath a soft quilt of slate cloud. Having risen at six o'clock, I managed to run around the quagmire of Hyde Park for the best part of an hour before returning, sodden, to the club for a quick shower. Now I'm attempting to dress and slap on some make-up before my first meeting of the day.

'Coo-eee!!'

I open the door.

Bernadette is gawping at me from the other side. 'What kept you?' she asks with her Irish lilt.

'Ah, Bernadette! I'm in a bit of a hurry. Is everything OK?'

This bustling, singing, duster-wielding ball of Irish fun, who relishes tuna sandwiches before the sun is up and whose auburn hair is always immaculately set come rain or shine, is the club's esteemed housekeeper. She is cherished by the members and feared by those who attempt clandestine midnight feasts. She can sniff a chocolate wrapper ten feet away and her ability to detect biscuit crumbs in the bed is uncanny. It doesn't matter whether you're a baroness, an honourable, a lady, an MP or a commoner: as far as Bernadette is concerned everyone's guilty until proven innocent. We are all at her mercy and the promise of some much coveted shortcake biscuits left on the tea tray in our rooms is enough to have us playing to her tune.

'Always in a rush you are,' she scoffs. 'God, look at you. Like a whippet, poor creature, no flesh on you. Nice to see you back. Did you notice the shortcake I put on your tray last night?'

'You're an angel.'

'Go on, get dressed, before you upset the other old ladies.'

I stand by the door, wet hair clinging to my face as Bernadette bustles down the corridor rowdily singing an Irish ballad as she goes.

8 a.m., Piccadilly

Standing on Piccadilly, I survey the vast grey frontage of The Wolseley on the opposite side of the street. Drizzling rain blurs this snapshot of Venetian styled elegance, as I peep out from the rim of my dripping umbrella. Strictly speaking, I can't claim ownership, given that it's on loan from my club. In front of me, long, metallic tentacles of traffic extend slowly east and west, their progress impeded by the rain and sluggish traffic lights. I weave between cars and hop onto the pavement, entering the chic, grand cafe through one of the arched portals. It's eight in the morning and already a dull hubbub of noise rises like smoke to the very top of the domed ceiling. At the front desk a woman whips the wet umbrella from my hand and leads me into the main restaurant and through the maze of occupied tables. At a discreet corner table, tucked away beneath one of the marble pillars, sits Rachel. She's already scribbling furiously in a voluminous notepad, her honey brown hair scooped up into an efficient French pleat. She gives me a winning smile.

'Excellent. You're early.' She leans forward and pecks me on the cheek then orders herself another cappuccino and a Darjeeling tea for me.

'I like the suit.'

She brushes the fine wool sleeve of her jacket. 'You know my penchant for red. It gives me confidence.'

'You don't need it. Tall people never do.'

'I'm not so sure.' She slams her notebook shut and leans towards me confidentially. 'Now, did you have a chance to read up on Daniella?'

'Yep, I googled her. She's definitely one for the nutter file.'

Her clear blue eyes lock onto me. 'I don't care if she's a psychopath as long as we win the account. She's got a $100 million dollar turnover and is the toast of New York.'

'Did she tell you that?'

'No,' she says impatiently. 'I've only spoken with her personal assistant, Mary Anne Bright. She says Daniella is a phenomenon.'

'That's what's worrying me. She'll have an ego to match.'

'Here, look at her catalogue. It just arrived yesterday. The products are amazing. She's got two stores in Manhattan selling her accessories and the interior design business is run from Trump Tower.'

I flick through the thick, glossy pages of alabaster candelabras, scented candles and silver and porcelain ornaments. In fairness, it's quite tasteful, if a little predictable. Rachel gives a hiss.

'Damn. She's already here.'

Our breakfast appointment is effortlessly skimming the black and white marble floor in killer kittens.

Rachel sounds breathless. 'I recognise her from the biog snaps. Listen, let me handle negotiations, while you schmooze her.'

It's too late to respond because Rachel has leapt to her feet with hand thrust forward. I rise to face the phenomenon for myself. Oozing Coco Chanel and draped from head to foot in mink, the goddess of design extends a perfectly manicured, bony hand. On the middle finger sits a colossal diamond and on the wrist a gold charm bracelet of small diamond trinkets which glint under the light of the chandelier. Her face is masked by owl-like Gucci shades which hover above towering cheek bones and glossy lips pumped to perfection. Her hair, a rainbow of gold, cinnamon and amber tones, is coiffed into a lacquered spire vaguely reminiscent of Mr Whippy ice cream. A waiter stands spellbound, unsure whether this fusion of Cruella De Vil and Narnia's Snow Queen is the living thing.

She lowers her glasses and beckons to him with a nail as sharp as a razor shell. 'Can we order? My time is limited.'

Tremulously, he hands her the menu.

'May I take your coat?' his voice is faint.

She strokes the silky brown fur of the lapel. 'I don't think so, do you?'

Rachel avoids my eyes and enthusiastically grips Daniella's hand.

'It's wonderful to meet you at last, Miss Popescu-Miller.'

She removes her glasses altogether, revealing a pair of hypnotic jade irises. 'Oh please, darling, call me Dannie.'

After enthusiastic introductions we take our seats. Dannie casts her mink onto an abandoned chair where it flops, defeated, in a heap. She gives a cursory glance at the menu handed to her by our waiter.

'Just some granola, summer fruits and an Evian for me,' she drawls.

Rachel and I order brioche and toast. She winces. 'Watch the wheat, girls. So destructive to the digestive system.'

An ungainly woman in a pale-blue trouser suit is waving from the entrance. Who's this? Dannie gives a terse nod.

'Here's my assistant, Mary Anne. Her surname's Bright, which is kind of ironic.'

We titter politely.

'Sorry I'm late,' puffs the unfortunate Mary Anne. 'Have you ordered me something?'

'Well, let me see,' says Dannie, theatrically studying the menu again. 'There don't appear to be any troughs of mayonnaise on here.'

'Oh, she's always such a meanie,' screeches her assistant in paroxysms of hollow laughter, whipping the menu from Dannie's bejewelled hands. 'I'm a bit of a food addict, you see.'

The waiter approaches her.

'Ah, now these Cumberland sausage sandwiches, are they good?'

'They're very tasty, madam – made in Cumberland in England.'

'How nice. Well, I'll have a small one of those and a latte. Oh, and maybe a chocolate brioche. Thank you so much.' She hands him the menu.

Dannie flashes her a menacing smile. 'Nothing else, dear heart?'

Rachel comes to the rescue. 'Given that you're short on time, Dannie, is there anything specific in our proposal you'd like clarified?'

She smiles seductively. 'It's perfect, girls. Mary Anne and I feel you have just the expertise we're after and my old friend Bryan Patterson says he loves working with you guys. That's all I needed to know.'

Although Bryan still uses our services to promote his fragrance emporium in the UK, his star is waning with the press since he switched his business to pyramid-selling.

'We have another client in New York now,' I hear myself saying. 'His name's George Myers. Do you know of him?'

She bites her lip for a second and then her eyes brighten. 'The English leather man who's just opened on Fifth?'

'The same.'

'My God, why didn't you say? I met him at the Forbes party only last week. He's a scream.'

I force a smile. 'He certainly is. I've worked with him for years.'

'Yes,' says Rachel, now on a roll, 'They're very close. In fact, you'll be visiting him in New York in a few months time, won't you?'

'Actually, not until November when I do the marathon.' I glare at her.

Dannie gives a little scrunch of her nose. 'How marvellous, darling. Are you running for charity?'

'An orphanage.'

'Oh we must sponsor you, mustn't we, Mary Anne? Just think what a fun time we'll all have when you come over.'

Indeed. I can hardly contain myself. The waiter returns and we commence our breakfast. While Rachel and I attack our brioche and toast with gusto, Dannie sits toying with her granola and fruit, only taking tiny spoonfuls in between hefty sips of mineral water.

'So girls, what do you really think of my products?'

'Very stylish,' says Rachel, her teacup poised mid-air.

'Your catalogue's really polished,' I add, 'although it would be great to see some actual products.'

Dannie drums the table with her fingers.

'We'll get a box of samples sent over to you. Anything else?'

'Your existing press material would be helpful,' says Rachel.

Dannie turns to her assistant. 'Can I leave all that with you?'

Mary Anne, cheeks bulging, nods enthusiastically but says nothing.

Another sip of water and Dannie drops the spoon back into her bowl, the contents barely touched, and dabs the sides of her mouth with her napkin.

Mary Anne continues to gobble her food hungrily and then sits back, replete, watching Rachel and I finish the last of our toast. Her mousy hair falls forward as she bends to see her watch.

'OK guys, shall we sign the contract tomorrow afternoon at the hotel so that we can get motoring on the PR programme?'

Rachel and I nod in agreement.

'How about four o'clock at The Berkeley?'

'Fine by us,' I hear myself say.

'Wonderful,' smiles Dannie. 'It's been a pleasure meeting you both.'

'Likewise,' Rachel chips in.

Breakfast is over. Dannie sweeps up the voluminous pelt and swings it over her shoulder so that its hem almost kisses the floor. Lumbering behind her like a clumsy bridesmaid, Mary Anne fretfully attempts to hoist it up as if it were a gossamer train. Rachel and I watch them depart. I narrow my eyes at her.

'Trust me. We're in for a rocky ride.'

12.15 p.m., Starbucks, Marylebone High Street

Ed, my hypochondriac friend with a penchant for Internet babes – girls he can date online – jazz and all things calorific, is meeting me for a quick lunch at Starbucks. This suits him perfectly because the Marylebone branch is situated just a few doors from the BBC building in which he works as a producer. Moving to an area renowned for its private medical practitioners has been, literally, a lifesaver for Ed. The fact is that the common cold, sore throats, coughs, wheezes and sneezes, bugs, bruises and burns, lesions and abrasions, rashes, infections and viruses of a contagious nature persistently plague Ed in a manner rarely experienced by the rest of humankind. In the course of one week, Ed can have experienced anything from suspected heart failure, beriberi, thrombosis, Lassa fever and hepatitis, to malaria, pneumonia and salmonella. One night he called in panic to report a stiffening of the joints and asked shakily whether rigor mortis could be setting in. I explained that one normally had to have died first but that he shouldn't rule it out. Rather like a disgruntled vampire, Ed pounds the streets of Marylebone in search of new blood; a physician who will take him seriously. Within the labyrinthine streets of Wigmore, Wimpole, Harley and Devonshire he has visited every mews, close, place, square and street – both upper and lower – and is on first-name terms with most of the resident medical fraternity. Despite numerous examinations, indulgent diagnoses and panaceas, his symptoms, puzzlingly, persist. Consequently, Ed feels justified in mistrusting medical evaluation, illustrating the point with an anecdote about a Swiss respiratory specialist who once branded him a hypochondriac.

'A what?' Ed had exclaimed in outrage.

'Do I have to spell it out, young man?'

'You most certainly do.'

'H-Y-P-O-C-H-O-N-D-R-I-A-C.'

Ed had left the surgery in a state of apoplexy and indignation, deciding from that day forth to equip himself with his own trusty medical emergency kit (known as MEK) wherever he went. It has never left his side since.

Reaching Starbucks some time before Ed and I are due to meet, I decide to have a leisurely espresso. It's still raining and clusters of grey thunder clouds, like aimless teenagers, hang sulkily above the London skyline. At the counter, the man ahead of me is gesticulating animatedly to a barista. She looks mystified, as do the rest of the counter staff.

'Anyone here speak Italian?' she asks no one in particular.

'*Español!*' the man says in a wounded voice.

Without thinking, I greet him warmly in Spanish. He looks relieved, saying that he wants to eat something freshly prepared, not pre-packed. I explain that it's not that kind of cafe. With some distaste he settles for a cellophane wrapped tuna sandwich and a coffee and follows me to my table.

'Can you help me?' he asks plaintively, settling his tray down and opening a map. I offer him a seat.

'I'm looking for Buckingham Palace.'

He takes off his wet jacket, revealing a T-shirt emblazoned with a Catalan logo.

'Where are you from?'

He shrugs. 'Mallorca. Have you been there?'

Have I been there? When I mention that I live in Sóller, he is palpitating with excitement.

'But you must know my mother?' he yelps, giving me detailed directions of how to reach her *finca*, a death rattle away from the town's cemetery. I nod uncertainly but promise to keep a beady eye out for her when next strolling around the graves. Jordi, for that is his name, tells me that he is having five days sightseeing in London, staying at a small hotel in Pimlico, before heading off for Paris. His travel agent in Alcúdia, on the north side of Mallorca, had fixed up the trip and aside from a few language hurdles he insists there have been no problems.

'What do you think of London?' I ask.

'It's wonderful,' he replies, 'but Mallorca is the most beautiful place in the world, as you will know.'

I find it endearing that Mallorcans on the move demonstrate such loyalty and fervour for their island. By contrast, ask a Briton holidaying in Mallorca for his thoughts on the UK, and a stream of invective will be unleashed on subjects ranging from the cost of living and crime to education and the weather.

Some time later, Ed crashes through the front doors, gripping his MEK in one hand and his dripping telescopic umbrella in the other. Then, with head tilted, he begins sniffing the air like a wary deer, scrutinising each table from behind large brown frames until his eyes rest on mine. He waves enthusiastically with his umbrella before depositing it in a small bin at the entrance. Jordi rises from his chair and kisses me on both cheeks.

'It's been good to meet a British *Mallorquina* in London. Thanks for your company. *Hasta luego.*'

He saunters off while Ed follows his departure with some curiosity. As soon as Jordi has left the cafe, Ed makes his way over to my table.

'Who on earth was that chap?'

'A Mallorcan I just met.'

'But you looked like bosom pals.'

'We are now. I'm going to meet his mother.'

'You never change.'

He shakes his head sorrowfully and offers to buy me a sandwich, returning some minutes later with a mound of food and chocolate cake.

'It's been so long, Scatters. I wish you came back more often. Don't you miss running the firm?'

'Nope. It suits me perfectly and Rachel loves being the boss.'

'That girl will be running the country one day,' he says grumpily.

'We live in hope.'

I ask him about his latest romantic disaster.

'Splitting up with Julia has been painful not least because she could get me any medication on the market,' he says mournfully. 'She gave me some beta blockers for my last birthday, which was thoughtful.'

It must have been a blow to lose Julia. A nurse doesn't fall into a hypochondriac's lap every day, not even a tipsy one.

'Can't you make it up with her?'

He chokes on a breadcrumb. 'Good God, no! Too late for that. She's got another bloke, a saxophonist from Muswell Hill.'

'You'll find someone else.'

He takes a deep breath. 'Actually, I've met a New Yorker called Charlene.'

'Met? Where?'

He frowns and says nothing.

'Oh, not another Internet babe?'

'This one is different. She's normal.'

'How do you know?'

He whips out a photo. 'Isn't she great?'

In fairness, she has a nice smile and a full set of teeth.

'Hmm. What does she do?'

'She works in the travel industry and can get me cheap flights to New York.'

'But you won't fly.'

'I visited you,' he huffs.

'Only because Julia gave you Valium and forced you on the plane.'

'Well, it's early days.'

He gulps at his coffee and looks lovingly at his chocolate cake.

'So, what's Alan up to?'

'Our friend Pep has just bought a holiday flat in the port which he's going to rent and has asked Alan to manage the bookings. No doubt it will end in tears.'

'Why Alan?' Ed anxiously stuffs a piece of cake in his mouth.

'He trusts him and besides, Pep says he's got other fish to fry. Actually, I'd rather not know about his other ventures. It's safer.'

Ed swallows hard. 'He's always sounded like a shady chap to me. Do watch Alan.'

I laugh. 'Pep's far less dodgy than Greedy George.'

'Any news on that front?'

'He's just over from the Big Apple so we're meeting up later. He's now designing leather wear for cats.'

His large eyes freeze. 'You are joking?'

'Sadly not.'

'I'm highly allergic to cats.'

'Lucky he's not employing you then.'

He guffaws. 'Odd you and I both having a connection in New York now.'

I groan. 'Actually, Rachel's about to take on another New York client. A loopy interior designer we met this morning.'

His face brightens. 'Just think, we could all meet up in Manhattan. Wouldn't that be a hoot?'

3 p.m., the office, Berkeley Street

Rachel is weaving a pen through her locks and leaning back in a black leather office chair, heels skimming the edge of the desk.

A half-eaten sandwich sits on a plate next to a long abandoned mug of tea. She greets me with a weary expression as I pop my head round the door.

'I might as well give up trying to have any lunch. The phones never stop.'

'You should get out of the office more.'

'Easier said than done.'

I pull out a chair and survey her as she grabs at the ringing phone like a snappy croc. 'Who? Tell them I'm in a meeting.'

I wait till she drops the phone back on its cradle and her legs to the floor. She sits upright.

'So, what's up?'

'I've just had an intriguing call.'

'Mmm?'

'Do you remember John Harris, the lawyer we met at that Asprey's party in Bond Street last year?'

'No.'

'He had red socks.'

Rachel fixes me with impatient eyes. 'I try to avoid men with red socks.'

'OK, well this chap just called to see whether we'd like to pitch for an amazing project.'

'Which is?'

'The definitive book of the Crown jewels. A prestigious tome that's taken more than forty years to research and write.'

'Blimey.'

'We'd have to do market research, and handle the media and launch party at the Tower of London. It would be incredible.'

A smile plays on her lips as she fiddles with a biro on the desk. 'Well, well, it seems that the old PR glint is back in your eye.'

'Not at all, I just love books.'

'Give me a break. You like to win, simple as that. It's just the old killer instinct coming back.'

I ignore her. 'It's being produced by The Stationery Office and will set the punter back a thousand quid.'

Alarm is stamped on her face. 'Are you deranged? Who the hell is going to cough up that sort of dosh for a book?'

'You'd be amazed. Anyway, this isn't just any book. It will be a one off.'

'So do we have to pitch?'

'Apparently. Mr Red Socks is coming back to me with a brief tomorrow.'

Rachel nods slowly. 'Let's just hope he delivers and you'll have your chance to be sent to the Tower.'

6.30 p.m., Soho Hotel, the West End

Greedy George and I have agreed to meet at the Soho Hotel, one of the new breed of chic boutique hotels sprouting up all over London. I enter the lobby and am momentarily distracted by a gigantic bronze cat guarding the entrance. At least George will feel at home. As I clip-clop across the oak floorboards I see him ensconced in an armchair by an elegant French fireplace, reading a magazine. He looks up and gives me a smirk.

'Not wearing your beach bum wear then?'

'Not today.'

He heaves himself off the chair and gives me a bear hug.

'Fancy a drink?'

'What do you think?'

We cross the lobby into the spacious restaurant at the side of which a vast pewter bar yawns across one wall. Running behind it, a long, wild mural in bright colours depicts some kind of frantic traffic scene. George squints at it.

'They erected that in memory of the multi-storey car park that used to be here.'

The barman smiles and nods. 'He's right, you know. So what can I get you?'

We order glasses of champagne and sit on one of the velvety sofas. George beams and gives me a hearty slap on the thigh.

'Well then, how's tricks?'

'Good, especially now I'm not back here so much.'

'Come on guv, you love the buzz. Imagine being stuck in Mallorca all the time. You'd be bored stiff.'

'Maybe.'

'As sure as *huevos* are *huevos*,' he says idiotically. 'Anyway, you're over that flying phobia nonsense, aren't you?'

'Just about.'

'Course you are. Now, more importantly, did you get my stuff in the post?'

'If you mean the cat fetishist range, then yes.'

'And?' He rubs his big paws together and eyes me keenly.

'To be frank, squeezing into the cat suit was a bit of a challenge, but the cape just about fitted.'

'Ha ha. Very funny, guv. Glad all that cava hasn't addled your brain.'

'So what's with the cats and how's New York?'

He takes a slurp of champagne. 'It's been surreal. You wouldn't believe some of the people I've met.'

'Met or upset?'

He gives me a shove. 'Both, now you come to mention it. There are a load of arseholes, but some good eggs too. Anyway, a few months back I banged into this hot chick at one of Bryan's cocktail do's and she asked me if I did bondage gear for dogs. Got me thinking.'

'I'm sure. How is Bryan?'

'Same old woofter. Tootsie, his rabbit, is still going strong. Daft bugger asked me to design it a leather jacket, can you believe?'

I sip my champagne and stretch back on the sofa, wondering how I've managed to keep sane all these years.

George is still chortling. 'That's when the pet gear idea came to me. I mean, everyone's soppy as hell about cats and dogs in Manhattan. I'm starting production next week.'

He rustles in a bag at his side. 'I've brought you some dog wear samples.'

'You're all heart.'

He spills the contents of the bag out onto the small square table and ferrets through it.

'Ah, here we go. This is the dog's bollocks. A croc collar inlaid with emeralds. I'll retail that at around three thousand dollars.'

'You're kidding?'

'Course not. This stuff will walk out the door.'

'I suppose you'll have a fashion preview for the press? Some little pooches and Persians mincing up a catwalk?'

He ignores the irony in my voice. 'Not a bad idea, guv. I like that.'

'So how soon would we be able to launch this pet wear range?'

'I'm aiming for November to catch pre-Christmas sales.'

'Perfect. That gives us bags of lead-in time.'

He orders more champagne and for the next few hours we set about a marketing strategy for his new range. The PR team he has hired in Manhattan are predictably 'awestruck' at his brilliance, but given that they're being paid $20,000 a month, they jolly well ought to be.

I scan my watch and realise that I have to leave. James and Sophie, some old friends of ours, have invited me to a dinner party at their home in Pimlico. Greedy George is off to the launch of a new jewellery store on Bond Street and promises to email me product information and images soon.

'The sky's the limit, guv,' he yells coarsely as he strides through the lobby, stopping to stroke the bronze cat on the way out. 'I'll be the cat's whiskers of Manhattan, just wait and see.'

And with that, he disappears into the night.

FOUR

THE BURROWERS

The sky is clear and the air as hot and fiery as dragon's breath. Boring through the kitchen window an intrusive sun rests its honeyed gaze on my fingers as I sit sifting flour into a large wooden bowl. It would be a misnomer to tag me domestic goddess, and yet with all the cocoa powder and energy I can muster on a day crackling with heat, I decide that the time has come to earn filial respect. This is no easy feat. Cake day beckons at Ollie's school, an occasion when mothers are encouraged to bake and deliver home-made morsels which are sold for a charitable cause. In London it might be acceptable to breeze along to Waitrose or M&S to snap up some pre-packed cup cakes without a thought, but here it's not so simple. There's an expectation, unspoken though it is, that real mothers bake their own. With some impatience I scan the pages of the tattered American cookery book splayed out on the oak table. I've decided to make chocolate muffins. What can be easier than that?

Some time later Catalina bursts into the *entrada* holding a massive package. She dumps it on the table and in automatic pilot mode, fills the kettle.

'Something smells good. Cooking Alan a birthday cake?'

'He's on a diet, remember.'

She pounces on the cake bowl and runs her finger round it. 'Life's too short for diets. Where is he anyway?'

On cue, Alan strides into the kitchen. 'Is the kettle on?'

'I'll make you a coffee as it's your birthday,' she gives him a wink. 'By the way, that's for you.'

Alan follows the jerk of her head and approaches the table. 'Can I open it?'

Catalina leans against the work surface and watches as he removes the outer packaging. Inside, the head of a bonsai tree pops up. A shawl of red foil and silver ribbon billows around its neck. Alan is entranced.

'Just a little something from Ramon and me.'

'I've never had a bonsai,' he declares, gently examining the gnarled bark of its miniature trunk. 'I can't thank you enough.'

I look at my watch and declare that the muffins should be cooked. In anticipation, Catalina and Alan hover like vultures around the oven door. I lift out the trays one by one, immediately realising that something has gone awry. The muffins have risen up from their cases like enormous, brown mushrooms. How did that happen? We all look at each other.

'Too much baking powder,' I lament.

'So what? I bet they'll taste just as good,' says Catalina, helping herself to one of the largest. She takes a bite and then fans her open mouth with her hand. 'It's delicious.'

Alan pulls one from the tray then juggles it in his hands. 'It's a bit hot.'

I shoo them away. 'I haven't topped them with icing yet.'

There's a loud tooting from the courtyard. Catalina, carrying a mug of tea, walks through the *entrada* to the front door. She shouts over to us.

'Alan, it's a man from UPS. He has a delivery.'

A tall, cumbersome figure stands by the front door, holding an enormous box in his arms. He wrestles it to the marble floor and then returns to his car to fetch another, smaller carton. Catalina is full of excitement.

'What can it be?'

The Scotsman looks on, mystified. 'I've no idea.'

I wipe my hands on a tea towel, secretly amused at their growing curiosity. The parcels, I was informed by UPS, would have to be stored over the weekend at the Madrid depot. Given the nature of the content I was concerned that some catastrophic incident might occur, but the manufacturers in the UK assured me that nothing could escape and that everything would arrive alive and intact. I'm relieved that UPS has finally made it to the valley. The man mops his moist brow with a hankie.

'Could you sign this delivery note?'

Alan scrawls his name on the sheet and the man takes his leave.

'I suppose you know what's in here?'

'Maybe,' I give a small shrug.

'Let's get some scissors!' cries Catalina.

'Wait a minute,' I say, sounding a deliberate note of caution. 'Please be careful with the smaller package. The contents are very delicate.'

Alan is puzzled. 'Delicate?'

The telephone rings.

'Wait a second,' I hiss and flit back into the kitchen. It's Manuel Ramirez from H Hotels. His timing is always immaculate.

'Hello, I am Manuel,' he announces with aplomb.

In Spanish it would be considered normal to pick up the telephone and say, 'Soy Manuel', but, of course, it sounds silly in English.

I greet him warmly.

'Is this line safe?' There's a twitchiness in his voice.

'Of course. Why?'

'You never know who is listening.'

In Panama City, Manuel rides around in a limo with bulletproof glass and his trusted PA will never reveal either his home address or personal telephone numbers. Last time we spoke he mentioned *en passant* that he'd ordered some super lightweight, bulletproof outer wear from an ingenious tailor in Colombia who, he told me, kitted out the presidents of every Latin American country. He's an intriguing chap.

Manuel's voice takes on a strange huskiness. 'Listen, I will be brief.'

Thank heavens for that. I potter into the *entrada* with the cordless phone to my ear. Catalina has already fetched some scissors from the kitchen drawer and is jabbing at the outer packaging of the smaller box. Alan is trying to make head or tail of the label. Without pausing for breath, Manuel babbles on, swinging between English and Spanish. H Hotels has signed up another hotel in Tribeca in New York, and two in Cuba, he tells me.

'Marvellous,' I say distractedly, clicking the fingers of my left hand to attract Catalina's attention. She's already managed to yank up one of the side flaps of the box.

Catalina frowns at me. *'Que?'* she mouths.

I frantically click my fingers again and point at the box with a warning grimace hoping this will stop her from delving any further inside.

Manuel stops dead. 'What was that? I think someone's tapping the line.'

'No, Manuel, I can assure you everything's fine. Carry on.'

Catalina ignores me altogether and with Alan's help begins pulling at the polythene inner wrapping.

'We will have a November launch for the Tribeca hotel,' Manuel is steely. 'And I expect you and Rachel to attend.'

'Of course, but is there any chance of it coinciding with the marathon? You remember I'm running in it?'

He suddenly breaks into hysterical, manic laughter. 'Of course, woman. I've timed everything to coincide. The hotel launch will take place the day after the marathon. As far as that's concerned, you will run in under four hours and I will give you a donation of two thousand dollars.'

'In *under* four hours?'

The Scotsman is thrusting his hand into the package. I jump up and down and shake my head, but he and Catalina are too engrossed.

'A second over and you fail me,' Manuel says darkly.

Perhaps that's when he'll pull the gold Kalashnikov from the wall and finish me off.

'That's very generous of you, Manuel, but it's a bit of a tall order.'

He is deadpan. 'I have made you my final offer. Tomorrow, I'll send you the hotel launch brief for your comments. Don't show anybody. Now I must go. *Adios.*'

The line hums. He's gone. The man's a completely paranoid lunatic and now he's my client. Thanks a lot, Rachel. I drop the telephone onto the sofa.

'*Ah!!!!!*'

It's too late. With fumbling, eager fingers, Alan has delved into the smaller cardboard box and with a sharp cry of surprise, pulled out his hand which in turn releases several wriggling worms. Catalina recoils in horror.

'I told you to wait. It's full of worms.'

The two of them stare at me in disbelief.

'I can see that!' snaps the Scotsman. 'I thought it was a box of bulbs.'

'There are two thousand worms in there. It's a wormery.'

Catalina pokes the soil inside the box. 'This is full of *cuques*? Two thousand of them?'

'Well, so they say, but I'm not going to start counting.'

Alan wipes his hands on his shorts, a troubled expression on his face.

'You could have warned us,' he mumbles.

'What is a wormery?' Catalina persists.

'I suppose you'd call it a *Cuques* Hotel in Catalan. It creates great compost.'

Although somewhat shaken, Alan opens the larger box to reveal sections of wood ready for construction into a wormery. Having coped with the initial sensory shock of touching an untold number of squirming little bodies in the dark soil, he is clearly delighted with his new toy. He gives me a wry grin.

'Don't you *ever* spring a surprise like that on me again!'

Remembering my towering, deformed muffins, I return to the kitchen and begin reviving the icing, which has become rigid. Adding some hot water from the kettle and some melted chocolate, I whip it up and hurriedly spread it over the muffins. The hot mixture dribbles down the sides of the cakes, but I pay no heed. With a flourish I take our various small packets of brightly coloured sugar and chocolate decorations and sprinkle them over the tops. Catalina is suddenly at my side, clucking.

'I never see a worm hotel before. My father won't believe his eyes.'

She studies the trays of muffins. 'You have so many.'

'Well, I've made some for Margalida too. She has a sweet tooth.'

Alan walks into the kitchen and winces at the gaudy home bakes.

'What on earth are those supposed to be?'

'Monster muffins. Didn't you know, they're the latest vogue in home bakes?'

The small huddle of men standing around the wooden wormery are deep in discussion. Catalina's father, Paco, dressed in old cords and checked shirt, squats at the side of its legs and pulls out the bottom tray on which some loose soil sits. Miquel, our young taciturn *siquier,* the town's irrigator, lifts off the lid and examines the squirming worms inside.

'They are British worms?' he asks suspiciously.

'Through and through,' replies Alan.

Miquel shrugs a little sulkily. 'So what happens if you need more? You get British or Mallorcan worms?'

Alan puffs out his bottom lip. 'Well, I suppose there's no harm in mixing them, is there?'

Paco's face displays a rascally smile. 'Apart from a few linguistic problems, they should be fine.'

Catalina and I have been standing quietly behind the men. I waggle a finger at her.

'Hello old chap, my name's George Worm.'

'Ah, *mi amic, som José Cuc!*' she replies in a squeaky voice, 'You like Mallorca?'

Miquel turns round and observes us coolly. 'You may joke, but it is sometimes bad to combine species. You don't know what might happen.'

Rafael, who has up until now been drinking a coke and slouching against the wall with Llamp playing at his feet, claps his hands together theatrically.

'Yes, you could create a monster breed, Alan, or maybe they end up fighting. We Mallorcans are very nationalistic, remember!'

'Don't say I didn't warn you,' Miquel growls.

He plods off across the patio, past the pool and down the steps to the field.

'Where's he going?' asks Rafael.

Alan looks glum. 'To check on our water level.'

This is a critical time of the year for gardeners. As June approaches, the free, gushing mountain water we receive through a series of sluice gates in the field dwindles, and our water tank, the old *safareig*, runs dry. During the summer months, the water is rationed and must be used sparingly. It's a worrying time for the Scotsman.

'So,' says Rafael. 'Explain to us again how this contraption works.'

Alan, who is finding the Spanish hard to keep up with, sighs. 'Can I explain in English and Catalina will translate?'

'*Vale*,' says Rafael.

Catalina views him sternly. 'OK, but you shouldn't have given up those lessons with Paula. You're forgetting your Spanish.'

He pulls a face. After a lengthy translated explanation, Rafael fiddles with the shelves of the wormery. 'So you put the kitchen rubbish in here and the worms eat it. Then some weeks later, by some magic, it turns into compost?'

'That's just about it.'

He and Paco look admiringly at it.

'No waste, no electricity and good compost. It's a fine investment,' Paco says.

'We should all get them up here,' adds Rafael.

Alan has a glint in his eye. 'Not a bad marketing idea.'

I give him a thump on the arm dreading that this might become another fanciful business idea for him and his chum, Pep to explore. 'Don't even think about it.'

For the past few days, our builder Stefan and two of his men have worked tirelessly on building a stone wall at the front of our house to which they have attached an electronic gate. Now it is finished, Ollie and his father spend an inordinate amount of time trying the newly installed entry button which is linked to an internal telephone on the kitchen wall. They seem to derive infinite pleasure in seeing the gate open and close of its own volition.

The telephone has been wailing all morning. A friend in the village of Fornalutx has been caring for a pair of abandoned male kittens and, with much lobbying from Ollie, we have agreed to give them a home. She calls to say that she will deposit them at the house this afternoon. Much as the Scotsman might prefer the presence of a dog around the house, he has a sneaking affection for Inko and has finally succumbed to the idea of two more felines joining the family. I barely finish the call when Catalina is on the line, making final arrangements for this evening. Together with her wonderful aunt, Maria, we are off on a midnight snail hunt. The hunting of *cargols* is a national sport and late May is the best time to find them lurking in the hedgerows and in the long grasses. I flit outside and begin telling Alan about the kittens and the timing of my snail excursion but the shrill sound of his mobile stops us in our tracks.

'Blasted phones!' he mutters, dropping his hoe and extracting the vibrating fiend from the pocket of his gardening shorts.

'Who?' I hear him cry irritably. He potters off towards the house.

I stroll over to the garden pond and peer into its murky depths. Tiny, gymnastic frogs dive from the stony wide-lipped fountain into the water, intimidated by my sudden appearance. There's an urgent croak and Johnny, my wisecracking American toad, appears from nowhere and watches. I give him a smile, but he continues with his impassive stare. Since moving here, Johnny and I have had many a profound chat. A cynic might say I'm mildly delusional and that Johnny is just a figment of my imagination, but to me he's very real. He helps me mull over things and gives me a wonderful excuse to slip out of my office and sprawl at the pond's edge taking in the music of the trickling water with the sunshine on my face. When I worked full-time in London, I always had colleagues to chat with but now when Ollie's at school and the Scotsman is out for the day, I have to make do with Johnny or the cats for conversation. I cock my head towards the house and turn to leave. There's a small cough.

'Not so fast!'

He's squatting on a lily pad, his low slung girth resting on its cool surface.

'Did I hear you right? You're getting more cats?'

I take a deep breath. 'Look, Johnny, I know Inko's been a pain at times, but she's not been near the pond for weeks.'

'Pah!' he shakes his head. 'That cat is a nightmare and so is the fat tabby next door. It's bad enough being stalked daily by a psychotic heron without this extra stress.'

He's right about the heron. For some months now our amphibians have been plagued by this arrogant and fearless creature that carries off unsuspecting fish and tiny frogs in the early hours of the morning. We have tried to keep vigil, without much success.

'Don't worry about the kittens. I'll keep any eye on them.'

He sniffs and gives me a sullen expression. 'When you came here you didn't give a rat's ass about cats. Now you're all over them. And what's with the worm hotel?'

'It creates great compost.'

'Next thing', he groans, 'you'll be opening a cat motel.'

I step back, startled. Can he read my thoughts?

'On my mother's lily pad, you *are!*' he splutters, eyeing me keenly. 'Jeez! You've finally lost the plot. Wake me up when you're back on medication.'

He plunges into the scum. I sigh heavily and walk back into the house. Alan is standing in the kitchen doorway with hands on hips.

'You won't believe who just rang.'

'Surprise me?'

'That nice girl we met from Channel Four. She said she's recommended me for a TV advert.'

'Well, I never.'

'I'll have to audition with a local production company called Focus Films.'

'What kind of advert?'

'It's for a bank. Apparently, I have to play golf.'

'Who knows,' I say. 'This could be the start of a new career.'

The sky, a bale of oyster silk, cups an exquisite pearl of a moon in its soft folds and envelopes the highest peaks of the Tramuntanas. Entwined in a wicker basket, our new arrivals, Minky and Orlando, sleep softly, their tiny grey paws twitching as they dream of darting mice and lizards and ponds abundant with baby frogs and fish. The kitchen door is open and a sudden gust of warm, aromatic air tickles the dog-eared corners of a pile of paper on the old oak dining table and flutters the velvety petals of a solitary white lily in a vase by the window. I glance at my watch. It's midnight. Catalina and her irrepressible aunt, Maria, should be here by now. Where are they?

There's the sound of hollow metal clanging as the front gate creaks opens and a battered, old white van slowly drives into the courtyard. Grabbing my torch and plastic carrier bag, I close the doors of the kitchen and *entrada* gently behind me. The Scotsman and Ollie have chosen their beds in preference to a night's culinary excursion on the snail trail. I jump into the backseat, wincing at the brightness of the interior light. A beaming Maria sits with arms folded in the front passenger seat while Catalina takes the wheel. I greet them both as Catalina loops round the courtyard and swerves out of the front gate.

'Is the electronic key working all right?'

She smiles at me in the mirror. 'It's perfect. So nice not to have to stop and open the wooden gate any more, no?'

We reach the end of the track and head off up into the mountains. The inky road unfurls like a smooth black snake, its skin glistening in the headlights of the car. We climb higher and soon ours is the only vehicle on the road. The predictable terrain of black, squat rocks and stubbly grasses soon changes and we find ourselves flanked on either side by austere and craggy mountains, and dark, impenetrable forestland. Gusts of warm air with the dry tang of rosemary rush through our open windows, rustling the plastic carrier bag at my side and caressing our hair. The road widens and Maria indicates that we should take a left turn. We follow a narrow, dusky track for a few miles until she instructs Catalina to park under a sturdy olive tree. Shards of ivory moonlight pierce through the leafy branches, but in the deep undergrowth beyond there is nothing but thick, treacly darkness. We are surrounded by woodland and, I sense, thousands of alert and bright-eyed diminutive lookouts with spindly limbs, wings and antennae. The ghostly silhouette of a screech owl, like a streak of white flame, scorches the sky and is gone. In the higher reaches of the valley, there's the muffled clanking of sheep bells and the soulful braying of a donkey. Armed with plastic carrier bags, we clamber out of the car onto the muddy track and switch on our torches. The soil is still very damp from a sudden and prolonged rainfall earlier in the evening.

'This is a good place for finding *cargols*,' announces Maria, whose snail dishes at her Fornalutx restaurant are renowned far beyond the confines of the valley. She is also queen of *seta* mushrooms, and in October is to be found combing the mountains at dawn for these much prized fungi to serve to her customers. We trudge into the forest and by the light of our torches begin our search. The wet leaves have made the ground slippery underfoot and we take care as we weave through the maze of trees. Maria stops abruptly to feel a handful of soil.

'The rain is a godsend. There should be plenty of snails here.'

I'm relieved that she's switched from Catalan to Castilian Spanish, which is so much easier for me to follow. Catalina has already alighted on a huddle of snails, their viscous antennae recoiling in the light of her torch. She picks them up one by one and pops them in her carrier bag.

'You like eating snails?' asks Maria, her compact form turning to face me.

I flinch at the question. In the past I have tolerated the odd plate of the delicate, *petit-gris* Gallic breed dressed in a sauce of garlic and shallot butter, but their more robust Mallorcan cousins have never quite appealed. They seem so much fatter and more voluptuous than the French variety and, dare I say it, look rather chewy.

'Only the French ones because they're so nice and small.'

She gives me a little frown. 'You're wrong. The snails from Burgundy are just as large as ours. You pick them during the winter months. The thin ones you speak of are from Provence.'

With a tremulous hand I whisk two snails with enormous protruding heads into my empty carrier bag and wipe the slimy residue on my jeans.

'Well, you can tell I'm no *cargols* expert, Maria. I promise to try your snails at the restaurant tomorrow.'

She puts an arm round my shoulder. 'Then you will taste a morsel of heaven.'

We roam the forests, the needles of light from our torches illuminating rats and bats, lizards and wide-eyed geckos. Insects tickle my legs and spiders' webs embrace my face as I duck the higher branches and try to concentrate on the booty's silvery, luminous trails under the trees. Time, an old peasant, ambles along unhurriedly while we forage around the long grasses, our carrier bags bursting with squirming little bodies that burrow forever deeper into the dark recesses of their brittle homes. At two o'clock we head back to the van, and dump our haul in the boot.

'So, tomorrow you sample fresh *cargols* with my niece,' says Maria, bobbing her head towards Catalina. There's a flicker of amusement in her small hazel eyes.

Catalina relishes the moment. 'Yes, tomorrow we'll see how much of a Mallorcan you really are.'

The car door slams and Ollie runs up the front steps of the porch clutching a small paper bag. I don't need to enquire about its contents as this is a weekly ritual. Every Saturday he will spend a few euros of his pocket money at Cavall Verd, a tiny Aladdin's cave of a shop in Sóller where the owner, Bel, sells the most magical marbles. They are not the clear cat's-eye marbles of my childhood but delicately painted creations in every conceivable size and hue which sit in a glass jar by the window, glistening in the lambent sunlight like iridescent bubbles.

'I've bought five new ones, bringing the total to two-hundred-fifty-eight,' Ollie announces loudly as he scuttles up the stairs to his room.

Alan marches into the kitchen with numerous shopping bags which he deposits in a heap at my feet. He plods back out onto the porch and begins heaving some large wooden planks against the stone wall. A few minutes later he reappears, running a hand through his tousled grey hair.

'That was hard work.'

I pour us both a glass of cool water from a bottle in the fridge.

'What exactly are you going to do with all that wood?'

'Ah. It was going to be a bit of a surprise.'

'Let me guess. You're going to make another wormery strictly for Mallorcan worms.'

'Don't be inane. I'm going to build a corral.'

'As in a corral for hens?'

'Exactly. Pep and I have decided to build our own. I recently sent off for a gem of a book all about how to make corrals.'

I recall the small package he was so keen to retrieve from the post bag a few weeks ago.

'It would have been nice to have been consulted.'

'Talking of which,' he says, 'I picked up a package for you today and couldn't help but notice the intriguing words on the front of it.'

He pulls the offending item from one of the bags heaped on the tiled floor and hands it to me. My eyes are drawn to the British stamps and my Spanish address written by hand in neat block letters, below which runs a line of black print. It reads:

FAB. Feline Advisory Bureau. Boarding Cattery Manual.

He studies my face.

'It's just a little business idea I've been mulling over.'

'A cattery?' he sinks into a chair at the table, a blank expression on his face.

'More a chic cat hotel.'

He gives a cynical grunt. 'Is this one of Greedy George's madcap ideas?'

'It's nothing to do with him.'

'That doesn't make it any less ridiculous.'

'Why are you being so negative?'

'Because we've already got our hands full, what with the chickens and...'

'That's the point,' I say, cutting him short. 'If we've got a wormery and a corral, would a cattery really make much difference?'

FIVE

HIDDEN TALENTS

With the golden village of Deià a blur of sun-scorched stone melting fast behind me, I course along the winding mountain road, distracted by the sparkling sapphire sea to my left and the yachts gliding on its glassy surface like tiny specks of white spume. It is June and yet the route is clear of the usual cyclists and kamikaze hikers spilling out of the forests onto the open road. I have all the windows lowered and the wind races inside, tousling my hair, flapping the newspaper lying beside me and churning up Alan's pyre of cigar ash and old cellophane *puro* wrappers hidden beneath the front seat. They rasp and flutter, eventually disappearing from the car window altogether, floating high up into the sky. This morning, as is habitual on a Saturday, I finished my Pilates class and headed off with my companions to Cafè Sa Font Fresca for an espresso and an *entrepà,* a crusty roll with Manchego cheese, accompanied by sweet tomatoes the size of tennis balls thickly sliced on the plate. Normally, I would loll in a chair catching up on local news for some time longer, but today my budding thespian is making his acting debut in a NatWest advert, so I must hasten home with all speed so that he can use the car.

I reach the end of my track and see that Margalida is shuffling around her small front garden and patio, leaning laboriously on her stick. I call out to her and she walks stiffly over to me.

'*Un moment.* I have something for you.'

I stealthily look at my wrist and realise that I'm not wearing my watch, a lazy habit of mine these days.

'*Vale,* but I must be quick. Alan needs the car.'

I jump out, leaving the engine running, and follow her to the patio where she has placed three delicate branches from a jacaranda tree on a stone bench

'These are for you. A thank you for the chocolate *magdalenas.*'

Having sampled my first batch of monster muffins and developed a penchant for them, Margalida is delighted when I bring her new supplies but insists that I am rewarded with fruit or flowers from her garden. I've given up remonstrating.

'These are beautiful. I love the jacaranda flower.'

She peers into my face for a few moments. 'It's my favourite flower because my husband…'

I wait, but the words dissolve into silence as her head droops, a little gasp catching in her throat. Gripping her scrawny arm, I guide her to the stone steps leading to the front door, but she falters at the bottom.

'I don't think I want to go inside just yet. I'll sit here for a while.'

She lowers herself onto a step and squints up at me. Her eyes have pooled with water.

'What are you wearing?'

'Just some old sports clothes.'

'I think you'd look nicer in a skirt.'

'Maybe, Margalida, but it wouldn't be very practical for my exercise class.'

She gives me a small smile. 'I suppose.'

I leave her sitting dreamily on the steps of her home, her face vulnerable and expectant like that of a young child.

Alan greets me in the courtyard. He's carrying a trug full of artichokes and peas.

'Last of the crop. I've just planted the tomatoes and aubergines.'

The thrill of planting and eating our own vegetables and awaiting the new crop never dwindles, although I miss my regular forays to the local market to see my friendly stallholder, Teresa. I observe the perspiration clinging to Alan's well-worn, blue linen shirt.

'I thought you'd be ready to set off. What's the time?'

He looks at his watch. 'Actually, I was an hour out. I don't have to leave just yet.'

'Well, I hope you'll have a shower before you go.'

He eyes me with some exasperation. 'Of course I will. I've got to change into golf gear anyway. They want us spruced up and ready to film on arrival.'

Despite the outwardly calm veneer, the Scotsman has been getting fretful about the impending shoot, fussing over his dusty golf clubs and unearthing a pair of archaic golfing shoes, a gift from his time as a director at Dunlop. For the next three days, along with three other willing victims, he will be spending his time on a Palma golf course, wheeling around a set of clubs and driving a golf buggy. The producer, who obviously has a sense of humour, has described them all as 'distant talent'. Still, he'll get paid a daily fee and might even have time for the odd round of golf.

Ollie greets me in the porch with a face like thunder.

'Have you been stealing my marbles?'

'Well I lost my own years ago, but I wouldn't dream of taking yours.'

'It's no laughing matter,' he says grimly. 'Five of my favourite marbles have gone from my jar.'

'Are you sure?'

'Of course I'm sure. I count them every night. Daddy claims he hasn't touched them either.'

'Maybe it's the ghost?'

Our resident ghost has apparently been a regular visitor to Ollie's bedroom since we moved here. Though Alan and I have never actually seen him, our son matter-of-factly tells us that he's an elderly man in a long black dress who wanders around his room and takes his leave through the external wall into the garden. We used to put all this down to Ollie's fertile imagination until Margalida informed us that back in the annals of history, at least a century ago, our house used to be the local presbytery. Apparently, in those days the priest would walk across the fields to the church from the front door that was at the time situated where Ollie's outer bedroom wall is today. That certainly gave us food for thought.

'The ghost? Why would an old man want my marbles?'

Ollie throws his arms up in the air dramatically and stomps off into the house.

Alan knits his eyebrows. 'Not guilty.'

I wrestle my unwieldy exercise mat out of the car and retrieve the ruffled newspaper, the *Majorca Daily Bulletin*, from the front seat. Alan takes it from me.

'What photo have they used in your column today?'

'Ken Livingstone.'

'Were you writing about him then?'

'Well, I had a bit of a rant about his discontinuing Routemaster buses in London.'

'Oh, not that old chestnut again?' He taps me on the head with the rolled-up paper and ambles into the house with it under his arm.

For a while now I have been writing what my sister describes as 'the weekly rant' for the island's English daily newspaper. It's a great way of letting off steam.

In the kitchen I find our new feline twins, Orlando and Minky, curled up in their basket. The knot of soft, grey fur purrs deeply, oblivious to life going on around it. Alan scans the pages of the *Bulletin* while I make myself an iced coffee.

'By the way, I posted off that application form.'

The Scotsman lowers the paper and observes me over the top of his tortoiseshell reading glasses.

'You're quite serious about all this, aren't you?'

'Of course.'

Having taken out a subscription with the wonderfully named FAB, I've decide to take my business idea a little further by enrolling on a tailor-made training course at a top Dorset cattery. A year ago we went on holiday for two weeks and packed Inko off to an island based cattery. The experience was a disaster. We returned to find our beloved cat a shadow of her former self, withdrawn, full of infections and with a weepy eye. I was so incensed that I vowed to open a small, elite cat hotel for islanders who loved their felines as much as we did. At the time, Alan assumed I was joking but the idea took hold and I began working on the framework for a business plan. I decided that the adjoining piece of orchard land would make an excellent plot for my cattery but then we didn't own it, and neither did we have the funds to buy it. Nothing has changed but now we've finished most of the costly building work on the house it might be time to revisit the matter.

'So, when do you start?' he says stiffly.

'Mid September.'

He takes his glasses off and rubs his eyes. 'I'm really not happy about it all. I mean, this course seems like a complete waste of money.'

'It's hardly expensive.'

'But what's the point of doing it? We don't have a place to build a damned cattery and we don't have money to invest in such a hair-brained scheme.'

'Oh and I suppose your whisky shop was such a brilliant idea?'

'That was just a passing fancy of Pep's and mine. We certainly didn't waste any money… '

Ollie reappears in the *entrada*. 'I think one of my sea monkeys is ill.'

He holds the small plastic sea tank aloft and points at a black speck the size of a pinhead.

'You see? He's just floating.'

'Maybe he's having a kip?' I proffer.

'Of course he's not. He seems anxious.'

How in heaven's name my son can determine the anxiety of a suspended black dot is beyond my imagination. The sea monkey fad, currently all the rage in the UK, was brought to us in the mountains by his godmother, Jane, from London, who supplied Ollie with a tank, instant life crystals and a packet of live sea monkey eggs. These creatures, a hybrid of the brine shrimp which never grows beyond the size of a vertically challenged ant, have now multiplied in the tank and keep Ollie busy for hours. He dumps the diminutive tank on the kitchen table in front of us in an attempt to gain our attention and, waking up the kittens, carries both in his arms up to his room.

'Maybe he can run your cattery?' Alan says dryly.

'I'm banking on it.'

He gets up and stretches. 'Look, I'd better get going. I can drop Ollie off at Nancy's on the way.'

The locally celebrated elderly American artist, Nancy Golding, has for the last year taken Ollie under her wing. She's the grandmother he never had and together they read, draw and swap stories and jokes.

I'm pouring fresh water into the tank of sea monkeys when Alan heads for the front door sporting casual golf attire. He wheels a set of clubs behind him, in the side pocket of which he has tried to secrete a title by Patrick Leigh Fermor.

'You're not going to have time to read,' I quip.

Ollie has packed his own rucksack of pencils, paper, books and games. He carries this bag everywhere with him, rather like his godfather, Ed, with the MEK. I'll worry when he starts popping in medicinal curatives. I wave them off and potter downstairs to the cool *botiga*, our cellar, which now serves as a guest room and my dugout when free of visitors. I like writing down there because the French doors open directly onto the orchard and the peace is almost tangible.

While I tap away at the keyboard I am suddenly aware of a sharp, tinkling sound coming from the *entrada*. For a moment I hold my breath, thinking that one of our phantom sheep has returned, but the noise continues with the same methodical *tink, tink*. It hasn't the whiff of a sheep about it. Very quietly I open the door and tiptoe barefooted up the cellar stairs. In the *entrada* Orlando, one of our new kittens, is standing by the open front door making a strange rasping noise. I wonder if he's choking, but he suddenly releases his jaw and a shiny marble bounces onto the stone floor. As soon as it's free, he chases it like a demon around the *entrada*, finally propelling it into the garden. He follows it into the sun but returns a second later, defeated. The marble has disappeared. Enterprisingly he creeps up the stairs to Ollie's bedroom, oblivious to me tracking his movements, and helps himself with a paw and jaw to another marble from the large jar on the dresser. The marble thief has been caught in the act! For some time I watch him happily repeating the exercise until I count that four marbles have been pilfered and lost. I decide enough is enough and remove the jar and hide it in Ollie's wardrobe. Orlando looks forlorn and, with a plaintive mewl, pads off to the front garden where I predict he'll sit drooling at the side of the fish pond until mealtime.

The light is fading as I reach Nancy Golding's modest apartment block on a cluttered side street a few minutes walk from the main *plaça*. Her name is brightly illuminated in oxtail brown italics above her bell and as I press it, I hear the familiar low growl of her Irish terrier, Rosie, from the open first-floor window. A moment later Nancy speaks huskily into the intercom.

'Come on up.'

There's a click and the heavy door opens a fraction, allowing me to turn the handle and enter the stark hallway. Rosie has been unleashed and, with tail wagging and tongue lolling, dashes down the steps towards me. I bend down to fondle her and in so doing spill the contents of my straw shoulder bag on the floor. I sit clearing up the mess. Nancy has walked falteringly from her apartment to the upper landing and leans over the banister looking down at me with a sublime smile on her face.

'Now that's the sort of thing I thought you only ever did at my age.'

I hoist myself off the floor and plod up the stairs to greet her. Inside the cluttered flat we enter her studio, a child's paradise full of boxes overflowing with brightly coloured pens, pencils and brushes and assorted canvasses daubed with rich paint, stacked precariously against cupboards and chairs. The walls are suffocated with random photos, newspaper clippings and handwritten scribblings and on the large, paint-smeared table on which she works, Post-its with indecipherable jottings litter the surface. Ollie sits quietly at the table painting, barely acknowledging my presence when I appear.

'Take a seat, dear,' she says in her easy drawl. 'I'll fix us both a drink.'

'Let me do it.'

'I may be decrepit, but even I'm good for opening a bottle.'

She gives a girlish laugh, revealing an immaculate set of white teeth. The sculptured face with its ivory skin and luxurious, thick black lashes reminds me of the flawless complexion of a Victorian doll.

She patters off into the kitchen returning with two glasses of white Rioja. Settling them on the table, she leans over and whispers to Ollie. He nods and wanders out of the studio, reappearing with a large glass of juice and some crisps. We sip at our wine, watching the gathering dusk beyond her window.

'So, how far have you got with the exhibition?'

She clasps her hands together, the heavy amber stone rings seeming incongruous on her long thin fingers.

'I'm about halfway finished. You can take a look if you like.'

She gets up slowly and shuffles over to a large stack of canvasses.

'Here, take a peek at these.'

I study each one carefully, alighting on a haunting work in shades of gold and purple, overlaid with slivers of silver and gold foil. It has a whiff of Klimt about it. Nancy bobs her head over my shoulder.

'I've called that *In the Land of the Mayans*. You like it?'

'Very much.'

'It'll be waiting for you at the gallery.'

I laugh. 'I'll have to start saving.'

As is customary when visiting Nancy, I wander around the studio, invading her private domain, reading postcards, scrutinising old photos and random poems. She never minds, often following behind and enlightening me, yet again, on the content of each one.

I met Nancy a year ago when she was exhibiting at a local gallery. Barely able to walk as a result of a recent operation, she sat regally in a corner clad in a striking fedora and chic black dress. At her neck a riot of jade played with the light and chunky amber stones swallowed up the fingers on both hands. Along with other guests and the town's mayor, I waited patiently to pay homage to the queen of art as she sipped delicately from a flute of cava and chatted in a bright and breezy manner with those nearest her. We have been firm friends ever since.

Nancy stifles a sneeze.

'Are you cold?'

'That's the darn thing. It can be blazing outside, but it's like a morgue inside.'

'I can bring round some blankets or a heater.'

'Bless you, but I'm all right,' she titters. 'I just pile on the jumpers if needs be. Besides, aren't we painters supposed to suffer for our art?'

Nancy was one of the exotic early pioneers who in the sixties swapped the fast lane for a frugal and yet more enriching existence in rural Mallorca, and never left. Despite severe arthritis, she hasn't the funds to move from her drab and drafty first floor apartment in the centre of Sóller. She bends down and, with a giggle, gives me a flyer for her next exhibition. As usual it is a humorous self portrait.

'I don't know why, but every time I draw a new one of these, the wrinkles keep getting deeper.'

Ollie comes over to look and strokes her hair. She smiles up at him and pats his hand.

'I'm hoping this exhibition will set me up for the winter, you know, pay the rent and keep me in hooch.'

Despite the wry humour, I worry about her living alone in this dank dwelling, especially in the winter, but it's cheap and central and the large studio is ideal for her painting. We finish our drinks.

'Don't worry about me. I've survived far worse than this and that's only half the story.'

Her tinkling laughter fills the room. Ollie and I say our goodbyes and make our way out onto the street. I open the car door and he jumps into the passenger seat clutching a photo of an otter, Nancy's favoured animal, and two of his own *oeuvres*. As I put my bag in the back seat, I suddenly hear her calling me. Nancy is leaning out of her window.

'Hey, tell my furry friends that I'll be down with some scraps later.'

She waves and closes the shutter.

I turn to the huddle of scrawny cats by the bins but their eyes are already trained on the shuttered window above. I hesitate for an instant, but then head off home, certain that Nancy's feline groupies will have listened to her every word.

I am in the basement working at the computer when Rachel calls.

'Good news!'

She's a clever psychologist, my MD. Whenever she has anything to impart that requires my wholehearted support she greets me with an item of good news first. It's a wonderful way of lulling me into a false sense of security.

'What's good?'

'Aside from The Glade Hotel pitch next month, The Stationery Office has come back to say they'd like to meet us about the Crown jewels book. They were impressed with our preliminary proposal.'

Inexplicably, I feel a huge surge of excitement. Before starting my own agency I worked for the *Guinness World Records* and lived and breathed the book. It isn't remotely the same sort of publication, but it's another one-off, a rather eccentric work of art created by academics, something of substance. This could be the final big, prestigious project, my glorious swansong from the world of luxury PR. However, I shan't be sharing these thoughts with Rachel just yet.

'Are you still there?'

'Sorry, Rachel. I was just thinking.'

'I've warned you about that.' She gives a hoarse laugh. 'Now, can you put together a presentation? I'd do it, but this is your baby.'

'Leave it with me.'

'Excellent. Well if we play our cards right, we could be winning two new clients next month. Wouldn't that be fab?'

It's late evening as we sit by the pool drinking *herbes*, the local Mallorcan herbal *digestif*. A fat ivory candle glimmers from the belly of a wrought-iron elephant sitting in the centre of the old Moroccan table. Here and there in the deep blue circular mosaic pattern, tiny slivers of coloured stone are missing, casualties perhaps of torrential rain during one of our inclement winters. Underneath the table my bare foot brushes the rough leather of a discarded sandal. Its owner is Pep who lies back in his chair, replete and patting his stomach.

'I've eaten too much.'

'What do you expect, eating two slices of lemon tart?' says Juana.

'As usual my wife is very sympathetic.'

Ignoring him, she tosses her head back and stares up at the sky. 'You can almost kiss the stars. It's so peaceful here.'

'Not for long.' Alan gives Pep a meaningful look.

'Why?' she asks.

'Well, once Pep and I have built our corrals, the cocks will be crowing.'

'Yes, and if your mad wife opens this cattery, you'll have loud caterwauling night and day.'

Over supper, Pep, like Alan, has already expressed his misgivings about my cattery concept and so I don't want to encourage further discussion now.

'Leave my cats alone. They'd be as good as gold.'

'Yes,' says Juana. 'At least they'd be contained. I'm not sure about having a corral with hens running about all over the place.'

Alan exhales smoke and props his *puro* against the ashtray in front of him. 'Oh come on, Juana. That's absurd! You want fresh eggs, don't you?'

'Yes, but not at the expense of sleep.'

'*Per favor!*' exclaims Pep. 'We're going with Ramon to buy the pullets next month and that's the end of it.'

Catalina's husband, Ramon, is a bit of a hen expert, having a corral of his own, and has promised to organise a boy's trip to the livestock market in Sineu once Alan and Pep have their corrals constructed.

'I'm surprised you'll have time for your hens with all this acting and looking after our holiday flat,' says Juana crisply.

'Well, I think that advert was a one-off. To be honest, all that hanging around on the golf course was a bit boring.'

'Maybe next time you can get a speaking role instead of driving a buggy around in the background,' I say.

Pep tries to stifle a laugh. 'Yes, near, rather than distant talent.'

Orlando does a sweep of the table, brushing up against the legs of Pep and Juana.

'You don't need to open a cattery. Look at all these flea-bitten cats you're already feeding for free,' goads Pep.

Alan picks up Orlando, whose thick, fluffy grey fur gives him more the appearance of a bear cub than a kitten. Wincing at the candlelight, his little paws paddle in the air until Alan sets him on the ground again.

'This one's a mischief. He's been stealing Ollie's marbles. We've had to hide them.'

'You see,' says Pep theatrically, 'They can't be trusted like dogs. You know, in some of the nearby villages, they lay down poison twice a year to get rid of the strays.'

I try not to rise to the bait.

Juana is embarrassed. 'It's horrible, but what do you do? They breed so quickly and no one takes responsibility.'

'You mean that we don't cut off their *collons*.'

Juana gives him a kick. 'Don't be so crude.'

'It's true,' Pep shrugs. 'We Mallorcans think it's cruel to turn our cats into eunuchs.'

'You think it's kinder to poison them instead?'

Pep sits up in his chair and squeezes my arm. 'Actually, no I don't. Not at all.'

Alan gives a small cough and re-lights his cigar. 'It's a full moon,' he murmurs.

'So,' I say, gulping down a bubble of irritation, 'when do your first holiday tenants arrive?'

'Mid July,' says Pep, perking up. 'I'm surprised Alan hasn't told you. It's a nice group of Swedish girls.'

'A hen party?'

He gives me a wicked grin. 'No, a birthday celebration, I believe. There'll be five of them. I'm sad I won't be here to help out.'

'Where are you going?'

Alan answers for him. 'Pep's on a business trip to Switzerland.'

'So he says,' Juana scoffs. 'I can't think why any bank would give him consultancy work. I never see any of the money, that's for sure.'

'That's because I leave it in Switzerland where you can't get your paws on it.'

Alan puts his arm round Juana's shoulders. 'He's a devil!'

'You're telling me?'

There's a shrill ringing from the house.

'Someone must be at the front gate. It's a bit late.'

Alan gets up and saunters into the kitchen, releasing the front gate's electronic catch. Moments later he cheerfully welcomes two hazy figures at the front door and ushers them through the *entrada* and into the garden. It is our nearest neighbours, Wolfgang and Helge, who live most of the year in Berlin, hopping back and forth to the island for short holidays. Ollie is always delighted when they arrive because Helge plays football with him while Wolfgang spends many an evening sitting on his terrace teaching him card games. Our dinners together are a chaotic and entertaining verbal mixture of German, English, Spanish and Russian.

'Where is my little Ollie?' cries Helge in Spanish, given that she speaks no English.

'In bed, I'm afraid.'

I usher her to a chair.

Pep gets up and pads, shoeless, into the kitchen and helps himself to some glasses from a kitchen cupboard. He returns and pours them both a drink. Alan hovers by the kitchen door, puffing on his cigar.

'So', says Wolfgang, with a solemn face as he settles into his chair next to Juana. 'What's with the Berlin Wall?'

We all look puzzled.

'You have built a new wall and gate,' says Helge softly.

Alan puts his hand on Wolfgang's shoulder. 'But it's only a low wall. While you've been away we've had a terrible problem with sheep… '

Wolfgang shakes his head, mirth crinkling his face. He turns and gives Alan a good-natured punch on the arm. 'You know, even after all this time, you British still don't know when a German is making a joke.'

SIX

THE PERFECT PITCH

Tuesday 7 a.m., Audley Square

I pull back the metallic doors of the lift and swing straight into Bernadette's arms. She staggers back, a look of surprise on her face. I notice that she's wearing a light raincoat, but there's no evidence of an umbrella.

'Sorry, I didn't see you there.'

'That's all right, my lovey. Look at you now in that nice suit! Where are you going today?'

'I'm doing a hotel pitch.'

'And what in heavens name is that when it's at home?'

For a crazy moment I imagine whisking Bernadette with her feather duster into a taxi and bringing her with me to Leatherhead. I could just picture her bustling into the doubtless staid and airless boardroom where we will be doing our pitch, and telling the directors exactly what she thought of their dreary concept for a country house hotel while munching on a pungent tuna sandwich.

'There's no such thing as a six star hotel, you bunch of wallies, and in Leatherhead? Are you off your heads?' she would cackle.

Bernadette is eyeing me curiously. I snap out of my reverie.

'A pitch? Well we have to go and sell ourselves to a potential new client and hope we win the account.'

She sniffs into her hankie. 'Is this in London?'

'Unfortunately not. We have to go to Leatherhead.'

'Nice bit of country air, though,' she sings. 'Do you the world of good. I must be off to clean the old ladies' rooms now. Ta-ra, darling!'

She pops into the lift I've just vacated while I drop my key with its round leather fob on the reception desk and head out into the windy street. An anaemic sun is peeping from behind a sheet of grey cloud as I jump into a taxi. South Audley Street is fairly deserted but I know that within half an hour it will be choked with traffic and clouds of exhaust fumes will fill the air. Lazily, I glimpse the dossier of notes Rachel prepared and left for me at reception the night before. Today we will be meeting the executive management team of The Glade, a new golf and country club which they claim in their brief will be a six star venue, attracting the likes of Tom Cruise, Tiger Woods, Michael Douglas and a whole list of golf-loving, celebrity A-listers. I re-read the client brief and snigger. Hollywood comes to Leatherhead. It's not that I have anything against the place but in truth this stretch of leafy suburbia is hardly a likely hang out for Hollywood divas. Someone at The Glade must have a good sense of humour. We have arrived at Waterloo Station. I fight my way across the concourse which is teeming with early commuters and head for the Leatherhead platform where I am supposed to meet Rachel and Sarah, one of our young account executives. In some bewilderment I listen to the deafening tannoy announcements, the brief snatches of loud conversations, music blaring from a cafe, the urgent tooting of a passing rubbish cart, and imagine by contrast the sounds of the Sóller Valley at this hour of the morning. I close my eyes and hear Rafael's cockerel, the plaintive meowing of the cats, the bird call and the sound of a distant tractor. Someone rudely shakes my arm.

'Well, hello. What on earth are you doing?'

Rachel is staring into my face and laughing. 'I told you to meet us on the platform, not by the flower stall. You're hopeless!'

'I was on my way.'

'Yes, well, let's get going. We can discuss the brief on the train and do a mini-rehearsal.'

She leads the way, the powerful, determined heels clip-clopping ahead of me and the long hair swinging like a pendulum behind her back. Standing pale-faced and anxious at the platform gate is Sarah. She's wearing a tailored black trouser suit which accentuates her slight frame, and is gripping a thin leather briefcase. She looks relieved to see us.

'I've got our tickets. We'd better get on.'

Rachel gives her a cheery smile. 'OK, all present and correct. Now, let's get down to work.'

10.15 a.m., The Glade, Leatherhead, Surrey

We are sitting in a makeshift boardroom within a grey, prefab workmen's hut plum in the middle of a drab and barren expanse of terrain which will one day house The Glade Golf and Country Club. For more than an hour an earnest group of men and women in suits have been pounding us with questions and the pitch isn't going well. Despite Rachel and Sarah's best efforts I have been unable to feign even the slightest enthusiasm and have an overpowering dislike of the man leading the questions, a beefy red Irishman named Frank O'Connor who will be The Glade's general manager. I listen to Rachel eloquently highlighting our spa credentials and excellent knowledge of the travel and health press, and have a terrible desire to yawn. Out of the corner of my eye I notice a mouse running the length of one wall, scurrying into a tiny crevice near the door. A moment later, it pops out and stands on its hind legs, eyes bulging and ears twitching as if listening in disbelief to the droning going on at the table. There's a cough. Frank O'Connor, like a squat toad in a shiny grey suit, is glaring at me.

'Sorry?'

He exhales impatiently. 'Why do you think celebrities will choose to stay at The Glade?'

Masochism? Inherent insanity?

'That's a good question,' I hear myself reply.

'I thought so, too,' he says with an ugly leer.

Under the table Rachel scrapes a heel against my leg and glowers at me.

'A good question,' she says airily, 'because it's obvious to us that the first class facilities of the club will be an absolute draw. We believe that there'll be nothing quite like The Glade anywhere in the world.'

At least we're agreed on that point.

Sarah gives a nervous little cough. 'And of course the proximity to Heathrow and Gatwick, not to mention having your own private helipad, will be a huge attraction.'

Frank O'Connor allows the slightest nod of the head but his expression remains sour. I sit sulkily twirling my pen and watching the expressionless faces of the other directors. How do people end up like this? Just years of sitting around cheap mahogany tables bleating the same old claptrap with only the odd mouse for diversion. Sarah sits erect, a neat folder of background sheets and information in front of her, politely chipping in when Rachel gives her the eye. Minutes pass.

'Well,' the bearded American sales director says, 'I think that just about wraps it up.'

'One last question,' says my burly nemesis. 'Before you came here today, did you bother to visit this site to see the building in progress?'

Rachel shifts uncomfortably in her seat and turns to me.

I find myself on my feet, smiling at him. 'Yes, indeed, Mr O'Connor.'

'No one here ever saw you,' he snaps.

'We came in disguise.'

There's a general flurry on the other side of the table.

'Disguise?' he snarls.

'Yes, I came as Groucho Marx and Rachel was wearing a beanie hat and a false nose.'

Suddenly the people in suits are giggling and nudging each other. Frank O'Connor doesn't appear to like my tone.

'Are you being funny?'

'Well, moderately, I hope.'

It's over. I can't quite remember how it all ends, but the Irishman lets out a roar of rage and strides from the room on a wave of hysterical laughter from his colleagues. In the corridor the sales director shakes my hand.

'He's an arrogant jerk so I can't really blame you for what you did. Shame though. It would have been fun to work with you guys.'

Rachel, icily professional and monosyllabic, ushers Sarah and me from the hut. We head back towards the station. She is wearing a stony expression and Sarah, puffing frantically on a Silk Cut, buries her face in her collar. A bright cafe catches my eye en route. I stop.

'Look, I'm sorry. I know what I did was completely immature and pathetic.'

Rachel and Sarah grind to a halt but say nothing.

'I ruined the pitch and I let you both down.'

'Yes, you did,' says Rachel sternly.

'I just decided we could never work for that… '

'He was a complete cretin,' Sarah blurts out, betraying a thin smile. 'And the club's going to be so naff.'

'Maybe, but what you did in there was unbelievable. I want to win new business. In all the time I've known you…' Rachel runs a weary hand over her face and begins to shake. At first I think she's crying, but no, she's laughing. Laughing hysterically. 'Groucho Marx? I mean, for crying out loud, what made you say that?'

'God knows. I just can't take this stuff too seriously any more. I promise I'll try. Look, let me buy you both a coffee and a bun.'

As I pull the cafe door towards me, Rachel stabs me in the back with her long tapered fingernail.

'I'll forgive you this time, but never pull a stunt like that again. If you do, Manuel Ramirez and his gold Kalashnikov will be the least of your problems.'

5.30 p.m., Regent Street
I'm in a rush. Daniella Popescu-Miller and Greedy George are both back from New York and I have arranged for us all to meet for a drink in Jermyn Street. Before I do that I need to buy a few things to take back to Mallorca. I've rifled Nike Town and stocked up on Dri-FIT running wear, but now must do battle with Hamleys for Ollie and, horror of horrors, buy Barbie Alice bands at the behest of Sabine Ricard, the mother of Véronique, a ballet-obsessed French child in Ollie's class. God willing, I may just make Hatchards to stock up on books before my meeting.

6.30 p.m., The Cavendish Hotel, Jermyn Street
I race up the stairs to the first-floor lounge where Greedy George is already ensconced in a huge beige armchair drinking a glass of champagne and munching on a bowl of nuts. *The Daily Telegraph* is stretched across his lap and on the glass coffee table lies an open copy of *Private Eye*.

'There you are,' he puffs, crackling the pages of the newspaper and dumping it in a heap at his side. 'When's Miss Romania turning up?'

'If you're referring to Dannie, she'll be here shortly. Anyway, how did you know she was Romanian?'

He emits a cackle. 'Popescu was a bit of a giveaway. Believe it or not, I had a Romanian mate at school called Popescu. He used to wear a garlic clove round his neck to ward off Count Dracula and he ate dog biscuits for lunch.'

The waitress brings me over a glass of champagne. I raise it in his direction.

'Good to see you anyway.'

'You too, guv. I haven't clapped eyes on you for weeks.'

'That's why I'm managing to remain sane.'

'Less of the sarcasm, Missus. Listen, what's the deal tonight?'

'I simply mentioned to Dannie that you'd be in London this week and she insisted on meeting you for a drink even though she wasn't due here until next weekend. She got Tetley to change her plane ticket.'

He juts his chin towards me. 'I'm flattered. Who's Tetley?'

I pop a peanut in my mouth. 'Her psychic tea leaf reader. She's called something strange, but I've nicknamed her Tetley for obvious reasons.'

He slaps his leg and wheezes with laughter. 'I love it! So does Tetley double up as her secretary too?'

I take a sip of champagne. 'No. Tetley merely informs Dannie's secretary which dates are propitious for her to travel on. Tetley also decides the airline, row and seat number for each business trip.'

He shakes his head in genuine wonder. 'It's unbelievable.'

'That's not all. If she can't get the exact row and seat on the plane, the trip's cancelled, so you're lucky to be seeing her at all.'

There's a kerfuffle at the top of the staircase and there in a tight, white silk suit is Dannie together with two hotel staff and what looks like a liveried chauffeur. She catches a glimpse of us and throws me a piercing smile.

'Here she comes,' I whisper.

Greedy George gives a deep cough and, straightening his suit, rises to greet her. The hotel staff and chauffeur evaporate in her wake as she glides towards us.

'Darling, how marvellous to see you again.'

She leans forward to air kiss me.

'Oh and George! I've been dying to have a proper chat ever since the Forbes bash.'

He seems slightly awestruck by the mirage before him. 'Let me get you a glass of champagne.'

She controls a little yelp. 'No! I'd prefer a vodka and mineral water. Thank you so much.'

The waitress hastens to Dannie's side. 'So it's a vodka and still mineral water, madam?'

'Yes, and I want a straw, and three green olives on a cocktail stake, I mean stick, placed vertically in the glass. OK?'

George manages to stifle a guffaw as he leans down and fiddles with his newspaper.

'So,' he says ridiculously. 'Ever met a vampire, Dannie?'

She exhibits a set of ice white teeth. 'Are you referring to my lineage, George?'

'Well, wasn't old Dracula supposed to hang out in Romania? Thought you might have run into one of his descendants at some stage.'

She gives a deep, mirthless chuckle. 'You're very perceptive. Actually I am a direct descendant of Vlad the Impaler, the Dracula of fiction. I was born in Sighisoara, his birth place.'

Greedy George narrows his eyes, uncertain whether he is being mercilessly ribbed, but her blank face shows little humour.

'Damn, and I forgot to pack my crucifix and garlic,' he gurgles.

Dannie smiles in her glacial way. I'm relieved to see the waitress hurrying back with her drink. Fascinated, I watch as Dannie fiddles constantly with the cocktail stick, but leaves the olives untouched.

'So, George, everyone's been talking about your new pet wear range. I hear *Vanity Fair* might be doing a spread.'

He gives her a smirk. 'Well, they get enough advertising out of me. I've suggested we kit out some A-lister dogs and cats, you know like Paris Hilton's flea on a lead, and photograph them with their owners.'

She listens politely, the enormous diamonds in her lobes glinting as they catch the light.

'Ingenious,' she simpers.

George blushes slightly and then launches into a spiel about his future aspirations for Havana Leather in the States. Dannie sits perfectly still, one well-honed bronzed leg draped over the other, her hands clasped in her lap.

'And how's Mallorca?' she says sweetly, suddenly turning to me. 'Michael says the North West is beautiful.'

'Michael who?' blurts out George.

'Douglas, of course.'

'Sure,' says George, crunching hard on some peanuts and not daring to look at me.

'You should visit sometime, Dannie. I think you'd like the village of Deià.'

'Where the British writer Robert Graves lived, right?'

George's eyes open wide. 'Played a lot of Trivial Pursuits as a kid, Dannie?'

'No, but I've read his works. Is it true he has a simple gravestone with the words: *Robert Graves. Poeta*?'

I'm slightly thrown by Dannie's knowledge of my home turf.

'Spot on.'

George is chortling. 'I know what they'd put on mine: *George Myers. Bastard.*'

I give him a kick but Dannie rolls her head back and laughs. 'That's very funny, George. You're such a tonic.'

Suddenly Dannie's mobile trills. She holds it to her ear, mouthing an apology to us.

'Obviously, I didn't make myself clear,' she breathes frostily. 'I want Suite 319 or we change hotels. Forget the little people and call the general manager.'

She scowls at a distant wall in the lounge, tapping a shiny Manolo heel against the table leg as she listens to her caller. 'Mary Anne, stop mewling and get it sorted. Call me when it's done.'

She slams the lid of the tiny mobile phone shut and tosses it into her butterscotch Gucci handbag.

'Everything all right?' quizzes George.

'Perfect,' she beams manically. 'I just have a few minor staff issues.'

'Sorry to hear that,' says George, glugging down the remains of his glass.

Dannie sucks up the last drops of vodka with her straw, leaving the speared olives naked and intact. With a quick flick of the wrist she scrutinises her watch face and begins to rise. Her eyes lock on to mine.

'You know staff should be handled like wayward dogs. It's simply a case of bringing them to heel.'

And with that she air kisses us, agrees the time I shall be meeting her in the morning, and glides down the stairs to her awaiting car.

Greedy George shakes his head and whistles. 'I hope for your sake, guv, that you haven't bitten off more than you can chew.'

9 p.m., Pimlico

The taxi driver deposits me outside the home of Sophie and James, a smart three-storey Edwardian house whose terracotta

107

window boxes overflow with narcissi and hyacinths. The narrow street is already dark save for the twinkling street lights. I skip up the small flight of stairs to the front door and ring the bell. A light shines in the hallway and there's a sound of laughter and clinking glasses. The door flies open and candles in the elegant hallway emit a honey warm glow. James, workaholic lawyer and King of Cordon Bleu, is wearing a white butcher's apron and wafting a glass of champagne in the air. He kisses me lightly on my left cheek.

'Darling, you're late.'

'Didn't you say eight o'clock?'

He proffers his watch. 'In England when we say eight it's customary not to arrive at nine. Keep your *mañanas* for Spain.'

I give him a hug. 'Sorry, I got held up in the office. Where's Sophie?'

'Entertaining the troops. Fraser's waxing lyrical about the NHS and Mike's in depression about his latest book review so it promises to be a fun night.'

He raises his eyebrows a notch and en route to the drawing room makes a detour to the stylish Shaker-inspired kitchen to pour me a glass of bubbly. I take a sip and enter the elegantly proportioned front room with its high ceiling and subtle coving. Rich, ruby red drapes fall luxuriously from brass rails above the windows and soft amber light radiates from crystal candelabras on either side of the roaring hearth. Sophie, brilliant barrister and 'hostess with the mostest', sees me first and scurries over to peck me on the cheek. I notice she's wearing a stylish black dress while I'm in attire more suitable for an Ibiza beach party given that my wardrobe is geared to the sun and has subsequently become far more casual and colourful. Grabbing my hand, she leads me over to the sofa where Mike Harding, novelist and journalist and perhaps the scruffiest man in London, sits broodingly in an old hacking jacket and frayed green chords. I discover that he is in heated discussion with Seth Golding, an obscenely rich investment banker, who at thirty-four, is already thinking of retirement. He is also dangerously handsome, a reasonable wit and finds those of us in the poor seats an endless source of mirth.

'So, what if the book bombs, Mikey?'

The hapless author flinches in displeasure at the chummy mutation of his name.

'Then we go and live in a foreign shack like marathon girl here.'

He jerks his head in my direction and gives Seth a sulky look.

Seth straightens his costly, woven silk tie and gets up to greet me. Mike follows suit, sneaking an envious glance at the banker's immaculate navy ensemble as he bends down to kiss my cheek.

'Mikey and I were just discussing his latest book,' Seth says in his Eton schoolboy crisp manner. 'It's been scorched by the reviews and I was just saying how very precarious it is being a writer. Better maybe to have a proper day job. You know, back on the payroll with *The Telegraph* or...'

'It was *The Guardian*, actually,' fumes Mike.

'Is it still in business?' quizzes Seth airily.

'Actually, it did a huge feature on Havana Leather this week,' I cut in.

'I suppose they've got to fill the pages somehow,' counters Seth, an evil glint in his eye. I give Mike a reassuring smile and say that I'd love to read his latest thriller. He dashes over to his rucksack by the door, retrieves a copy and shuffles back to us.

'Didn't offer me one,' huffs Seth theatrically.

'I didn't know bankers could read,' he mumbles petulantly as he opens the book and scribbles a message inside.

'So what's old Alan up to in Spanish Utopia?' Seth asks breezily, ignoring Mike and lighting up a slim cigar.

'He's been talent spotted for a banking advert and is about to start managing a friend's holiday flat.'

'It's all right for some,' Mike grunts. 'So what happened to his whisky shop idea?'

'Oh, died the death.'

'And the landscape gardening business?' he persists.

'On hold.'

Seth blows small circles of smoke above my head. 'Must be tough for him being out of the corporate world now.'

'On the contrary, he looks ten years younger.'

He frowns. 'So no regrets then about swanning off?'

Mike gives a bitter laugh. 'Why should they have? We're the poor sods left behind.'

Making my excuses, I take the signed paperback and wander over to Fraser, a weary, hard-working GP who is languishing in a brocade armchair. Patiently, he is explaining the cut backs in public health spending to Vanessa, Seth's thirty-something, well-heeled and glamorous wife. She is wearing a black Armani number, Ferragamo mules and has the physical profile of a wafer biscuit. Vanessa doesn't work and like most of her friends she is ALOSIK (always lunching or shopping in Knightsbridge). Sitting on a straight-backed fireside chair opposite him, with legs neatly crossed in front of her, she clasps a glass of water daintily in her right hand.

'We should just get rid of the NHS,' she opines loudly in a rich, cut-glass accent. 'It's a drain on the State and, quite frankly, redundant. Do you know anyone who doesn't have BUPA these days?'

Fraser looks at her in some confusion, hoping that she is being ironic.

'Darling,' she says, touching my arm. 'I love the turquoise top, so Mallorca chic. How are things in Spain?'

'So far, so good,' I say.

'But what about education?'

Vanessa and Seth have a two-year-old dumpling called William who is already down for Eton. I assure her that we have discovered a very good British school and that Ollie is well on the way to being tri-lingual.

'But what for, when everyone speaks English? I hope you've got him down for Eton.'

'Good God, no. Look what it did to Seth.'

Fraser laughs. 'Exactly.'

'Actually, we may move him into the Spanish system in a year or so.'

Her eyes widen in horror. 'Isn't that a little irresponsible?'

I savour the cool champagne. 'Not if he wants to become a flamenco dancer or a matador.'

'Don't be inane,' she snaps.

'They say it's the tri-lingual foreign kids who are cleaning up in the City now. Forget your old boy connections.' Fraser gives me a surreptitious wink.

'And what about health care?' she persists with mild irritation.

'My local Mallorcan doctor sees me immediately, charges me nothing and kisses my hand when I leave the surgery.'

She wrinkles her perfect, aquiline nose. 'How bizarre.'

'Does he need an assistant?' Fraser rejoins.

'Things that good in the NHS?'

'Pretty bleak. We're two doctors short and the surgery's at bursting point, but we just can't fill the vacancies.'

'That's because they're all leaving the profession in droves,' says Diana curtly. Until now she has been standing by the window talking intently to Sophie, but quietly comes over and sits down on the arm of Fraser's chair. She is wearing vintage Laura Ashley and has her shoulder-length greying hair scraped back behind a black velvet Alice band. She's a freelance radio journalist who never made it back on the BBC ladder after raising her three children. Now she divides her time between doing voice-overs, chauffeuring the kids to and from their exorbitantly expensive private school and massaging Mike's constantly battered ego. I decide that it can't be easy being married to Mike.

'Oh well,' says Vanessa with a horsey laugh, 'Maybe all our doctors are off to Mallorca where the grass is apparently greener.'

Diana gives her a grim smile at which point James bustles into the room, wiping his hands on a teacloth and lightening the atmosphere.

'Cheer up everybody,' he says with a smile, 'Dinner is served.'

Wednesday 10.30 a.m., Claridges

The doorman ushers us politely out onto the street. Rachel strides regally ahead of me along Brook Street while I manage to drop several files and sheets of notes on the pavement. A few indulgent passing swains stop to help me retrieve them. Rachel turns back and sees me grovelling in an ungainly fashion on the floor.

'What are you doing?'

'Throwing my toys about.'

She waits until I'm at her side. 'Have you got time for a coffee?'

'No. I'm meeting Dannie at eleven o'clock.'

We hover on the pavement.

'So, how do you think it went?'

'Difficult to say. I think it went marginally better than The Glade pitch.'

Rachel gives a grunt. 'Well, that's a surprise! Seriously, I think they liked us and you made it abundantly clear you wanted the job.'

I shrug. Having set my heart on winning the Crown jewels project, I would be bitterly disappointed if we were to fail, especially having put in so much spade work. I feel I need to redeem myself in Rachel's eyes after my bad behaviour at The

Glade. The only problem is that we'll be up against several other PR companies itching for the project. She shakes my arm.

'Chin up. We did our best and you were on top form. I've got a good feeling about it.'

'Really?'

'As far as I'm concerned we did a near perfect pitch and you can't do better than that.'

Her mobile trills and, whipping it out from her voluminous bag, she puts it to her ear and saunters off in the direction of Berkeley Street.

Wednesday 12.45 p.m., Vogue House, Hanover Square

Dannie stands by the open door of the spotless charcoal limo clutching a half-consumed bottle of Evian, her enormous shades glinting in the sun. At a discreet distance a chauffeur dawdles on the pavement.

'I think we pitched it perfectly, honey.' Her tone is mellow and husky. 'I mean those girls were riveted.'

My eyes stray to the revolving door of Vogue House, home to Condé Nast's glossy lifestyle publications. One of the editors we visited briefly on this whirlwind tour of *Tatler*, *Vogue* and *World of Interiors* is still watching us from the glass lobby, mesmerised by Dannie and her entourage. Mary Anne pats my hand.

'We can't thank you enough, sugar. They recognised a star in Dannie, and you helped them to see that.'

'Actually, I can't take any credit for…'

'No,' says Dannie dramatically, holding up a perfectly manicured hand. 'You have opened doors here beyond my dreams.'

I feel a stab of panic. I may have opened editorial doors but so far not one publication has shown the remotest interest in writing as much as a one-liner about Dannie or her products. Flanking Mary Anne is Dannie's make-up artist, Earl, an emaciated New Yorker with a peroxide quiff, and her hair stylist, Rocky, a muscle-bound Californian with bouffant blonde hair and a gold crucifix in both ears. There's no garlic in evidence. They both crowd me with ultra-white, toothy smiles.

'Great, well, I mustn't keep you all.'

'Remember we love you, Cupcake.'

'Thanks, Mary Anne. That's very kind,' I say absurdly.

We say our farewells and I am showered with air kisses. Politely, the chauffeur strolls over and when all are finally seated within, closes the limo doors. I stand alone on the pavement waving at the tinted glass windows as Dannie and her entourage soar off in the direction of Knightsbridge.

1.10 p.m., Le Caprice, Arlington Street

Panting for breath, I arrive at Le Caprice and hurl myself through the revolving doors. Manuel Ramirez is already sitting at a table, immaculately groomed and wearing a tailored linen suit. Jesus, the restaurant's Bolivian manager, glides towards me and whispers, 'I've fixed him a Bloody Mary. Don't worry, he's fine.'

I thank him and put on my cheeriest smile.

'You've beaten me to it, Manuel.'

He rises from his chair and, kissing me fiercely on both cheeks, clutches my right arm in a vice-like grip.

'Remember, life is not a race.'

'No, indeed,' I say, prising my arm free.

'Here, take a seat.'

He clicks his fingers and lets off a torrent of Spanish at a passing waiter who returns with a glass of champagne which he places in front of me. I'm longing for a glass of water, but must bide my time.

'Please, we must drink to health and success.'

I raise my glass and take a small sip.

'You know I feel as if I am back in Panama. Everyone speaks Spanish here.'

He scans the room for a few seconds and then leans towards me conspiratorially.

'Don't look now, but there is a strange man by the window watching us.'

'Manuel, I wouldn't be concerned. It's probably just a curious guest.'

Before he can stop me I flick my eyes over the assembled throng of diners and see a diarist contact in the corner who gives me a cheery wave. I smile back.

'It's Adam Helliker. He's a journalist.'

'You're sure?'

'Positive.'

He relaxes and we order lunch. An hour later we sit drinking coffees, having agreed launch plans for the next three H Hotels in the States and Cuba.

'By the way,' he says casually, 'travel agents are promoting our hotels brilliantly after that sales document we developed for them. Their clients are, how you say, lapping it up.'

'Fantastic. I'd love to see it.'

His face drops. 'Why?'

'Well, it's obviously been a great selling tool. Might be helpful for us in promoting H Hotels to the UK press.'

He gives a dark chuckle and waggles a finger at me. 'Maybe you want this document so you can help our rivals, *si*?'

It takes a second for his words to sink in. 'What?'

'Don't look innocent. You are clever. Maybe you want to sell the document to other hotel groups so they know our secrets.'

I almost want to laugh, but he has a wild look in his eye.

'Manuel, I'd make a lousy Mata Hari. Have you forgotten that I'm actually working for you?'

He settles the bill and runs a large tanned hand over his perspiring brow. 'Everyone has a price.'

'Look, forget it,' I say with some frustration. 'I was just trying to help.'

He softens and touches my arm. 'Maybe I believe you, but there are enemies everywhere. Think of all the hoteliers who would kill to get their hands on this document. It is the secret weapon of H Hotels.'

I fleetingly wonder whether he OD'd on James Bond as a child. The man needs a good shrink.

'You too must be on your guard,' he says in a hushed tone. 'Let's go.'

He leads me briskly out of the restaurant and into the bright street.

'Trust will come. Be patient.'

He gives me a suffocating bear hug and, dashing across the road, his eyes darting in all directions, disappears into a passing cab.

4 p.m., Mayfair.

Rachel is still wiping her eyes. 'I don't think I've laughed so much in years.'

'Yes, well next time *you* go to lunch with him.'

She struts across to her desk and shuffles some papers together.

'I'm sorry, but Manuel loves you. I mean, you make him laugh. Paranoiacs find you reassuring.'

Sarah pops her head round the door. 'Your cab's here.'

'Thanks, Sarah.'

'Oh come on, don't look so morose.'

'I don't know, Rachel. I'm not sure I can do this PR thing anymore. It's all so pointless and ephemeral.'

Like a strict headmistress, she raps a knuckle on her desk.

'Listen, it's a job. It pays the rent. I don't like you being wet like this. It doesn't suit you.'

She's right. I'm damned lucky to have a job with so much freedom and it does pay the bills.

'OK, point taken.'

'You're just fretting about the Crown jewels pitch. We have to accept there will be competition. As you always say, if it's meant, it's meant.'

'You're right. Anyway, we'll know soon enough.'

The managing director of The Stationery Office has promised to let us know if our company is successful in a few weeks' time. Fingers crossed.

'By the way, Frankie Symonds rang earlier. She thinks *The Telegraph* might do a piece on Dannie. Can you call her?'

My ears prick up. Frankie is one of my oldest journalist chums and has been tirelessly trying to get a feature placed about Dannie. I owe her big time if this *Telegraph* article comes off.

'Thank God for Frankie! I'll call her from the taxi.'

Rachel pushes her long hair behind her ears and shoves a file under my arm. 'Take a look at all this on the plane, will you? Some potential clients I'm unsure about.'

'I was contemplating a vodka and tonic and a quiet read.'

'Too bad. Listen, don't worry about Manuel. He's just a bit insecure. You'll sort him out. Besides, just think of the big fee.'

At this precise moment I'd quite happily throw Manuel's fee to the wind. Rachel gives me a peck on the cheek.

'Have a safe flight and don't speak to any strangers on the plane.'

9.30 p.m., Palma airport

The warm air engulfs us as we speed away in a taxi from the airport in the direction of Sóller. I am sitting next to Victoria Duvall, erstwhile Hollywood film director and one of my long-time fellow commuters, and now a good friend. By happy coincidence we live a mere fifteen minutes' drive from each other and found ourselves on the same flight back to Mallorca.

'You seemed pretty chilled on the flight. Are you over your flying phobia?' Victoria asks.

'It comes and goes. A vodka helps if I'm feeling nervous.'

She sinks back into her seat. 'It'll be good to get home.'

'Mmm. I miss my boys and the frogs.'

We stare out at the darkened sky, both of us in our own sweet reverie. I can smell grass and rosemary, sage and bitter lemons, but it's a sensory mirage. We are still on the Cintura motorway, a good forty minutes from Sóller. Soon my eyes close and I drift off into a timeless zone, miles away from stress, lunatic clients and the rigours of London.

SEVEN

RULING THE ROOST

Under a penetrating blue sky the ancient town of Sineu rises before us, clinging doggedly to a small hill like a grizzled limpet on a rock. We are flanked on either side by orchards abundant with olive trees and flat, pastoral land that rolls monotonously like green baize to the foot of the crouching Serres de Llevant mountain range in the east and the Tramuntanas in the west. Choked with dust, the road stretches like a parched tongue across the Central Pla, the agricultural heartland of the island, willing itself to reach the cool, salty kiss of the coast beyond.

In the back of the car, Ollie, Ramon and I play cards and swig from small battered bottles of warm mineral water, our damp clothes sticking to our skin. In the front, Alan and Pep puff on *puros*, exhaling smoke into the stifling, still air beyond their open windows while a wild Arabic song bursts from the CD player. Pep jiggles about and slaps his thigh as he attempts to warble along with the music.

'Where on earth did you get this CD?' bellows Alan.

'From Sineu market. As you will see, they sell everything, not just animals.'

'Are we there yet?' says Ollie with fatigue.

Ramon tickles him and points out of his window at the swell of people swarming around the streets.

'We're here,' he shouts in Mallorcan. 'Now we'll find us some chickens.'

Jutting his head forward he begins making mad rooster cries and soon Ollie joins in, crowing and flapping his arms about. As we slow down, passers-by turn to look at our car and I can't blame them. It's resembling a mobile asylum and the din is dreadful.

'Can you lot be quiet,' I yell above the hysterical Arabic voice.

'What?' cries Pep.

'Turn the music down!'

He bobs his head round the seat. 'Senyora can I remind you that this was supposed to be a *machos* trip? You are, what do you say in English, a *passatger clandestí*?'

'I can hardly be a stowaway in my own car.'

Ramon claps me on the back, laughing. '*Si, estàs un passatger clandesti!*'

Alan turns down the music and follows a lean, cobbled road up past the main *plaça* where crowds of shoppers are picking over goods in the sprawling market. After a fraught fifteen minutes, we find a parking place in a sun-dappled street, a stone's throw from the market place.

'That was really lucky,' clucks Pep as we head off towards the livestock pens in the *plaça*. Above the square, the enormous church with its sombre stone facade glowers down at the bustling scene below while its haughty bell tower shoots up into the sky, a defiant rural landmark on the hazy horizon.

'You know this market was created in 1306 by King Jaume II?'

'Oh no, not another of your history lessons,' I moan.

'You live here, so I give you no choice.'

He puts his arm round my shoulder and pulls me towards a massive cage containing a none too chirpy young bull.

'Can we do an exchange?' he says in Mallorcan to the elderly vendor, pointing towards me. The farmer grins and nods vigorously. Other crusty accomplices sitting on a nearby wall join in the joke while I give them a watery smile.

'Right,' says Ramon, rubbing his hands together. 'The man I buy my chickens from is over there. Come.'

We traipse behind him, battling our way through the throng of shoppers browsing the tightly packed stalls. On all sides, fruit and vegetables are piled high on cartons, their skins baking in the sun. Bizarrely, in amongst the food are tables loaded with terracotta crockery, junk, CDs, clothes, handcrafts and even tractor and machinery parts. Ollie gravitates towards a stall selling lethally sharp kitchen knives and instruments of torture which Ramon assures me are for everyday use on a farm. Hanging from rusty metal hooks, red, meaty sausages and salted *jamones* swing above the heads of a queue of busty matrons waiting patiently for cheese and cold meats. Huge rounds of Manchego cheese and terracotta vats of green and black olives and pickles swimming in brine crowd the counter. I peer through the forest of heads to catch a whiff of the aromatic fare, but am whisked back by Pep.

'Chickens first, food later,' he growls.

Ollie and Alan have reached the far side of the square where rows of old metal cages house exotically feathered songbirds, parrots and finches. Ollie walks solemnly up and down, peering inside the crowded cages and talking sympathetically to the diminutive prisoners. Their song is melancholy, and I feel a sudden sadness at their captivity. It seems so wrong that on this beautiful day they should be sweltering in ugly enclosures, forbidden the freedom to spread their wings and soar up into the sky. Sitting on the floor beside a low wire pen full of tawny chicks is Ramon's contact, a ruddy faced, cheery fellow chewing on a chorizo sausage. He gets up slowly and shakes our hands one by one before smiling down at Ollie and ruffling his hair. He listens attentively to Ramon and Pep as they talk rapidly in Mallorcan and, nodding his head, beckons us over to where he has a van. As soon as the back door creaks open, a tremendous clucking and rustling of feathers can be heard. Stacked in metal cages, hens and cockerels peer out from between the bars, their heads making miniscule staccato movements as they survey the faces clustering before them.

'Are you sure you want cockerels?' asks Ramon.

'Well, we might as well try breeding,' says Pep.

'*Molt bé*. So we need to select a few cockerels and some *gallines joves*.'

'What are *gallines joves*? Young birds?' Alan asks Pep as he scrutinises the different types of fowl in the cages.

'It's what you call a pullet. This man says he has a batch of April chicks which could start laying in about another four weeks.'

'In August?' Ollie looks hopeful.

'Maybe, if you're lucky,' says Ramon.

Ramon and his chum disappear into the van and begin examining various birds. After some time they emerge, having agreed the selection. Alan and Pep are already in deep discussion about the merits of corn and oat feeds and how to protect their corrals from rats.

'He suggests six pullets for each of you and one cockerel. He's offering a good price and says he can drop them off later today.'

'Hang on, Ramon. We've only just got the corrals up. I wonder if we need more time to organise the runs?' says Alan.

Pep gives a snort. 'It's now or never, *mon amic*. We can sort out the details tomorrow.'

Ollie is ecstatic. 'Come on,' he grabs Alan's shirt sleeve. 'I can look after them tonight.'

I decide not to get involved in this discussion. Pep and Alan have spent some weeks building corrals around the hen huts in their respective orchards and I am none too sure that they are secure enough to withstand assaults from local predators despite the reinforced wire surrounding the enclosures. I haven't seen them purchasing grain either, so our new arrivals may well go hungry.

'Have we got food for them?' Ollie pipes up.

Alan frowns. 'No, we haven't.'

'Easily remedied,' says Pep. 'There's a man selling all sorts of grain over there by the sheep pen.'

We pay for the pullets and cockerels and pop back into the van to view our purchases. The scrawny little grey faces stare plaintively up at us as they utter weak little *cheep cheeps*. One of the cockerels throws me a mean scowl.

'He's cool,' says Ollie. 'I'm going to call him Salvador.'

The vendor finds this very funny and he gives a hoot of laughter. Rooting about in the back of the van he unearths a box full of assorted feathers and offers them to Ollie.

'Have the peacock one too. It'll bring you luck.'

Overcome with delight, Ollie gathers them up and thanking the man gratefully accepts his additional gift of a small plastic carrier bag for his spoils.

We set off through the *plaça* to one of Ramon's favourite cafes where an outside table has just been vacated.

'A little coffee and repose and then we continue shopping,' says Pep, flopping into a chair.

A waitress approaches the table and, recognising Ramon, gives him a smile and nod of the head.

'Where's Catalina today?'

Ramon shrugs. 'Looking after the *niñas* at home.'

She slaps his shoulder and tuts. 'You men have all the luck. So what would you like?'

'*Ensaïmadas* and coffees all round,' he replies with a complicit smile.

'And chocolate milk for me,' Ollie blurts out before she takes her leave.

Ramon is pleased with our purchases. 'Did you know that some pullets can lay more than three hundred eggs each year?'

'What?' Pep's eyes bulge. 'But surely that's exceptional?'

Ramon shrugs. 'It depends on the feed and the quality of the pullets, but it's possible.'

'Do all the eggs become chicks?' asks Ollie.

'Only if they're fertilised and then they take about twenty-one days to hatch.'

'I hope we have lots of chicks.'

'The object is to have lots of eggs, Ollie,' Pep tuts.

Ramon raps on the table. 'Buying the hens is the easy part. Now I need to teach you how to rear them.'

The waitress arrives with a tray of steaming hot coffees, Mallorcan *ensaïmada* pastries and a chocolate milkshake for Ollie. We tuck in with gusto.

'*Vale,*' says Ramon, when he has our attention. 'Get out your notebooks because your first lesson in poultry care is about to begin.'

Booming voices greet me as I stagger into Cafè Paris following an early morning run. I've managed more than an hour on my feet but the pain in my right leg has been worsening all the time. Stubbornly, I've refused to seek medical advice but now I'm beginning to think self-imposed martyrdom isn't necessarily the way forward. It is Saturday and Alan and Ollie have agreed to join me for a leisurely breakfast. Through the haze of cigar smoke I head for a vacant table at the far end of the room and scan my watch. We agreed to meet at ten o'clock so they should be here any minute. José gives me a nod while continuing to talk animatedly to an elderly man seated at the bar. I notice the old chap is drinking a glass of red wine which isn't an unusual sight at this time of the morning. A woman at a nearby table suddenly rises to her feet, hands on hips, and shouts something at José. Several regulars begin joining in, calling out to one another in fast flowing local dialect. Senyor Bisbal walks in and is barely seated before he too is sounding off. He gives me a courteous little wave while he's mid flow.

I find myself smiling, remembering the first time I entered this rowdy cafe in some awe believing that a fierce argument had broken out between the local patrons. In time I learned that this was normal morning banter up here in the mountains and that shouting loudly and thumping your glass down on the table was part and parcel of a lively discussion about anything from the price of petrol to the dates of the next fiesta. José shrugs his shoulders and begins laughing. Others join in. My Catalan isn't good enough to catch the joke but I'm working on it. Give me time. José comes over with a double espresso and a croissant and sets them down in front of me.

'Where are the men folk?' he asks.

'Probably still in bed.'

He clicks his teeth and raises his eyebrows as Alan and Ollie walk briskly into the cafe.

'The usual? Americano? Chocolate?'

They nod enthusiastically.

'How was the run?' Ollie asks, pulling off his jumper and sprawling in a chair next to me.

'Pretty good.'

'What about the leg problem?' quizzes Alan.

'Nothing amputation won't cure.'

He taps my arm. 'We picked up the post. There's a letter for you from Sri Lanka.'

He pulls a crumpled grey envelope from his trouser pocket. The dog-eared stamps run in a colourful row along the top.

'Can I have those?' Ollie asks.

He waits until I've drawn the flimsy sheet of paper from within and then pounces on the empty envelope. While I'm reading the letter José brings over a plate of croissants and hot drinks. Alan and Ollie dive for the plate like a pair of gannets.

'Who's it from?' Ollie asks impatiently, wiping crumbs from his lips.

I fold the sheet and place it in front of me.

'Well, it's from Teresa, the nun who runs the Sri Lankan orphanage. She says she and the children are very grateful that I'm running the marathon for them and that they are looking forward to our visit.'

'Eh?' says Alan, mid mouthful. 'We're not going to Sri Lanka, are we?'

'Of course not, but she says that Noel at my club says we shall be.'

'There must be some mistake,' he says casually.

'Let's go!' says Ollie excitedly. 'They've got monkeys and one of the most poisonous snakes in the world.'

'Oh, what joy!' says Alan.

'Actually, I read an article about Sri Lanka's tea plantations and a wonderful elephant orphanage up in the hills,' I add.

Alan slaps his coffee cup down in some exasperation. 'Look, we're not going so don't start…'

'I love elephants,' says Ollie.

'Don't we all, but that doesn't mean jumping on a plane to visit them,' retorts his father.

'I think I'll give Noel a call tonight and find out what's going on,' I say.

Ollie slurps the last of his hot chocolate and licks his lips. 'When I get home I'll dig out my book on venomous snakes,' he says, and then with a shrug.

'Just in case.'

It's late on Monday evening when I finally get round to calling Noel in London. I know he'll be doing the night shift at my club so wait until I'm sure he'll be on duty. The phone purrs and then Noel's soft voice fills the void. He seems delighted to hear from me.

'Is everything well with you?'

'Fine, Noel, but I've just had a letter from the Colombo orphanage…'

'As I expected,' he says cheerfully. 'Sister Teresa said she would be in touch directly. I hope you don't mind my having given her your details.'

'Not at all, but she seems to think I'll be visiting her in Sri Lanka.'

'Ah, yes, that would be best.'

There's a pause while I try to think of a fitting response. I look at the moon for inspiration but it stares blankly back at me through my office window. There's a chill in the air and I pull my dressing gown closely around me.

'Noel, why would I go to Sri Lanka when I can just send them a cheque?'

He gives a little giggle, probably at my naivety.

'It's not that easy. Many things get lost in the post and it really would be the only safe way of ensuring the money reaches the orphanage.'

'I see.'

'Your son would like it. My country is beautiful and we have a wonderful elephant orphanage…'

'Yes, I know all that. It's just a big commitment.'

'Why not make it your next holiday? Easter time is lovely. Think of the good you would do.' Noel's enthusiasm is dangerously catching.

'It would certainly be nice to meet the children and nuns in person.'

'Exactly.'

'Apart from the money, I suppose we could bring out toys and books.'

'Precisely,' says Noel, ever the gracious salesman.

Five minutes later I hang up the phone. Alan walks into the office with Inko in his arms.

'She's just killed a rat.'

'Oh dear.'

'That's what cats do. They kill vermin. Good old Inko, I say.'

I find rats rather repellent but still can't bear it when our cats play catch ball with them. I lighten the tone.

'I've just spoken to Noel.'

'Ah, good,' says the Scotsman. 'You sorted out the misunderstanding?'

'Absolutely. We *are* going to Sri Lanka.'

He narrows his eyes. 'You are joking?'

'No. Apparently we have little choice if we want the money to reach the orphanage safely. Noel suggests next Easter.'

'Does he indeed?'

'We've got bags of time to sort everything out.'

The door opens a fraction and Ollie stumbles half asleep into the room.

'I had a nightmare.'

'Poor old chap,' says Alan dropping Inko to the floor and whisking him up for a hug instead.

A devious thought hits me. 'I'll tell you something that'll cheer you up, Ollie. Your father's agreed that we can go to Sri Lanka next Easter.'

His eyes widen and with gusto he gives Alan a chummy punch on the arm.

'Really? You're the best!'

Alan exhales deeply. 'Now why didn't I see that coming?'

With a shake of the head he plods out of the room, one arm slung over Ollie's shoulder and with Inko, ever the faithful shadow, at his heels.

I am at the counter of Can Matarino, my favourite butcher's in the town. Like many of the shopkeepers in Sóller, the three Graces standing before me bearing hatchets and bloody knives spend considerable time patiently trying to make head or tail of my embryonic Catalan. Ordering cuts of meat in Castilian Spanish can be tricky enough, but in Catalan, it's a meaty minefield. Chicken, *pollo* becomes *pollastre*, cutlet, *chuleta,* transforms into *costella,* and a drumstick, *muslo,* is the more challenging *cuixa.* If that isn't confusing enough, Mallorcans put their own special twist on Catalan words which do not appear in any dictionary so for example, lamb, *be* in Catalan, becomes *xot* in Mallorcan. The wonderful thing about Can Matarino is that it exists at all. In London our local butcher wearily packed up his stripy apron and hung up his meat cleaver, unable to cope with the soaring shop rent. In his place came a huge, shiny supermarket with cellophane wrapped meat and vegetables suffocating in tightly packaged polystyrene. By contrast, regulars at Can Matarino can handpick bones and off-cuts for making stock or even to feed their dogs, and choose the organic fresh lamb, pork or beef that they wish to be minced. Handmade sausages, chicken *croquetes* and stuffed pork rolls are house specialities and there isn't the flash of a clingwrap package in sight.

Antonia, one of the feisty women, hands me a bag of meat.

'The sooner you start those Catalan lessons the better,' she says with mock sobriety.

'Then we'll teach you our own Mallorcan version,' adds Catalina, one of her accomplices, wiping her hands on her gore-smeared white apron.

Across the street at the grocer's, Colmado Sa Lluna, Xavier is mopping his brow.

'It's a scorcher today.'

His girlfriend, Teresa, is now working with him in the shop and nervously studies him as he finely carves a hulk of *Serrano* ham on the slicing machine.

'There's nothing to it. Come on, you try.'

She takes my order and, with an anxious expression, begins slicing some chorizo. The meat disintegrates into minute slivers.

'*Non!* Here, hold it like this.'

She stands back and shakes her head. 'This is going to take forever.'

He looks at me. 'What do you think of my new apprentice?'

'She's a natural.'

Teresa jerks her finger at her grinning boyfriend. 'Can you imagine having to take lessons from him?'

'No, it's bad enough having him correct my Catalan all the time.'

'Talking of which, why are we chatting in Castiliano?'

'Can't I have a break?'

He hunches his shoulders. 'Just today. By the way, Ramon tells me you've bought some chickens. That'll keep Alan busy.'

'He's out there every day with Ollie, fussing around the corral.'

'Watch the genets and rats. They've carried off some of my hens.'

I can cope with the concept of running into a spotted, furry genet in the corral, after all, these cat-like creatures with their bushy tails are rather beautiful, but I'm not sure about a rat. While eating supper al fresco the night before, we watched as a rat scuttled across the garden in front of us, its long grey tail slithering over the cobbles, and began scampering up the facade of the house, a feat I never imagined possible. When I quizzed Rafael on the matter, he shrugged dismissively, telling me that it was quite normal for a rat to climb a wall but that it would rarely enter a house even with the windows or doors opened. I remain unconvinced.

I collect my goods and amble up Calle Sa Lluna which is predictably awash with locals and summer holidaymakers. For Sa Mostra, the international folk dancing fiesta, has officially begun, turning Sóller's *plaça* into a veritable paradise for *Come Dancing* fans. Musical and dancing groups travel from as far away as Easter Island and Berundi to perform to appreciative audiences across Mallorca, using Sóller as their base. I pop into Art I Mans, the local art and picture framing shop, to buy Ollie some new pencils. The owners greet me like a long-lost friend, keen to direct me to those which they know are Ollie's favourites. Clutching the small paper bag of purchases, I arrive in the busy *plaça* just as dancers from Asturias in brightly coloured folk costumes start cavorting around the bandstand. Crowds whistle and clap while local children get to their feet and mimic the dance moves on the pavements to rapturous applause. I am entranced by the grace and confidence with which these small boys and girls follow the movements of the dancers. Somewhat distractedly, with eyes straining to keep pace with the dancers, I pass by the bandstand and in the process collide with Tolo, our deputy bank manager. He kisses me on both cheeks and exclaims incredulously that he has just seen Alan in the gym. This sweat shop for the masochistic is run by Jaume, a popular and incredibly sporty Mallorcan whose cycling prowess has won him many trophies. When I first plucked up courage to duck through the heavy metal chains hanging in front of the entrance, I expected to alight upon a group of sultry macho hulks with names like Rocky, but I had a surprise. The majority of the patrons were quiet, middle-aged and dressed in unpretentious sportswear.

'Alan's doing another TV advert and is becoming rather self-conscious about his expanding waist line.'

'Ah, now I understand,' says Tolo wryly. 'He wants to look his best on TV.'

'That, or it's a late middle-age crisis.'

Tolo gives a smirk and heads off towards Banca March while I hurriedly make my way to the baker's. My film director chum, Victoria Duvall, and her husband, Robert, who also used to be in the entertainment business, are coming for lunch and I need to get busy in the kitchen. Like us, they enjoy long, relaxing lunches with good food and wine and plenty of banter. Today I shall make a special effort with my dessert because I know Robert has a penchant for home-made puddings. A return visit to their ancient *finca*, an idyllic eyrie high up on a hill on the outskirts of nearby Fornalutx village, is always a culinary treat and a particular favourite with Ollie because of Victoria's star turn, a talkative and entertaining parrot named Phoebe. Their forthcoming visit is particularly welcome because as seasoned sailors with a beautiful yacht in the Port of Sóller, we need to tap them for some sea-faring survival tips. Foolishly, Alan and I have been cajoled by our friends Pep and Juana into joining them for a week's sailing course in Palma the coming week. I vaguely recall agreeing to this absurd venture during a jolly dinner at their *finca* when far too many glasses of good Rioja had been consumed. Now, as the date draws nearer, both of us are scrabbling for excuses not to go but having paid our deposit feel we must bite the bullet. An entire week spent on the high seas sounds rather daunting so I hope Victoria and Robert will pass on some handy tips such as how to find our sea legs or when in peril, the nearest coast guard.

EIGHT

LEARNING THE ROPES

Day One
The dreaded day has arrived and here we are at the Palma school of sailing, otherwise known as L'Escola de Vela. With its breathtaking panoramic view of Palma Bay, the school is hugely popular with aspiring Popeyes and during the summer months attracts children of all ages whose eager parents enrol them on courses while they slope off to enjoy uninterrupted peace at home. We are not so lucky, having foolishly signed up for this sailing course along with Ollie and Angel, the son of Juana and Pep. The two boys are full of enthusiasm and impatiently kick a ball around the sailing club car park as we all begin unpacking bags and belongings from the boot. When we last met, Juana and Pep suggested we take it in turns to make lunch each day so, having been allotted first duty, we arrive laden with a cooler box, food hamper, towels, swimwear and other life saving paraphernalia. At least we get to go home every evening so we don't need to bring pyjamas and toothbrushes.

133

Pep and Juana are full of good cheer. They're old hands at sailing and, although they don't own a yacht of their own, will do anything to hijack one belonging to somebody else. Much as I enjoy a little gentle sailing, I have never learned the ropes, preferring others to do all the leaping about, hoisting of flapping sails and kamikaze climbing of masts while I look out wistfully to sea, basking in the motion of the frisky waves.

Some years ago a British newspaper editor and I were invited to Indonesia to report on the construction of the world's tallest tower of bread, and who could refuse? It was enormous fun, until by misfortune we found ourselves in the midst of a maelstrom on the Java Sea in a private yacht provided by our wealthy host. As colossal waves reared like savage stallions around us, we slithered helplessly along the deck gasping for breath and drenched in spume. Praying we wouldn't be thrown into the mouth of a passing shark, we clung to fixed ropes and poles while our barefooted crew of two stood at the helm squawking hysterically in local dialect and crying every time they passed another fresh shipwreck. It was miserable hours later that our boat lurched into the port of Jakarta on a moaning wind, its engine having spluttered its last some time before. I remember crawling biliously from the deck and kissing the parched earth, vowing never to sail again while my companion downed a triple brandy at a nearby bar. I try to blank out the memory.

Pep nudges me. 'Hey, wake up, dreamer! We'd better all head to the main building or we'll be late.'

I scan my watch. It's nine o'clock and a sadistic sun is already glaring down at us. The boys skip ahead, their pace quickening when they see a large group of youths gathered on the marina. Angel begins waving at a tall boy in the throng and is delighted to see him return the gesture.

'That's Lucio! Come on, Ollie, let's get going.'

'Wait a minute, you two,' says Alan. 'We'd better introduce ourselves to the tutor.'

Pep fans the air. 'Leave them. It's OK. Angel has done this course many times. He'll look after Ollie.'

Much to my son's embarrassment I call after him, 'Wear a life jacket! Don't do anything silly.'

He turns round. 'I'm not a baby. Honestly, mother!'

And he's gone. I feel a panic rising. Why in heaven's name did we agree to do this? Alan is putting on his best Boy Scout smile to accompany his ancient olive green shorts. 'Ah, a bit of bracing brine in the air. Nothing like it!'

Juana slowly catches up with us. I notice she is carrying a trendy little rucksack while I lumber on with a wicker basket over my shoulder and a cooler bag in my arms.

We reach the doorway of the club, a dull white building set on three levels from which endless smiling youths emerge, their skin bronzed and lean, their faces animated. I notice that the club's frontage, with its rows of neat square windows facing the soft blue sea, is festooned with jolly nautical and international flags that flap in the breeze.

'There seem to be very few adults about,' I say.

'Well, apparently they don't get many takers for the advanced courses,' Juana replies.

'Advanced? I hope that's a joke.'

I'm beginning to wonder if I should make a bolt for it back to the car.

'Don't worry,' says Pep. 'Advanced just means we all have a reasonable knowledge of sailing.'

'But Alan and I don't have a clue! We should be in the absolute beginners' class,' I puff.

'Don't be ridiculous!' he says. 'If you've sailed once, you never forget the ropes. It's like learning to ride a bike...'

'Have you ever seen me on a bike?' I say.

'It's not a pretty sight,' interjects Alan. 'She's the exception to the rule.'

Pep waves his hands in the air impatiently and then takes out a cigar from his pocket.

'Listen, you'll take to it like, how you say in English, ducks to water.'

He lights up and lets out a plume of smoke while the two of us regard him suspiciously.

Juana slaps me on the arm. 'Pep's right. This is going to feel more like a holiday than a sailing course.'

At which moment an athletic man in blue shorts and a Ralph Lauren baseball cap approaches us and asks whether we are the two couples embarking on the advanced course. Pep nods enthusiastically and makes polite introductions. The man narrows his eyes and, looking each of us up and down, announces that he, Javier, will be our instructor.

'Only one other has enrolled for this week's course,' he says abruptly, studying a typed sheet of paper. 'She is flying in from Madrid and was instructed, like all of you, to meet me here.'

'*Pues*, it's only ten past nine. We can wait a little while.'

Javier shakes his head irritably. 'No. I believe in punctuality.'

Without further ado he strides onto the marina and we follow hurriedly in his wake.

'You have a basic knowledge already, right?' he barks, leaping onto a small yacht, his nimble fingers fiddling with some ropes.

'*Si, si,*' says Pep casually. 'Our friends might need a little help, and of course they are English so… '

He stops in his tracks. 'I don't speak English so what do you prefer, Catalan or Castilian Spanish?'

'Castilian,' I almost yelp. It's bad enough having to endure five days at sea with a self-satisfied crew for company without having to endure instructions in Catalan as well. Besides, Alan doesn't comprehend a word, so it would be a miserable voyage for him. We embark rapidly, and are about to set off when there's a cry in the distance and a pouting creature with tanned legs that seem to unwind endlessly from her chin, pants up to the boat. She throws back her head, golden curls spilling onto her back.

'Am I late?' she gasps in Spanish. 'I am Gloria. I just flew in from Madrid this morning.'

'Come on board.' Pep smacks his lips together unable to prize his eyes from her hour glass frame and chocolate brown eyes. He offers her a hand and she leaps up onto the deck. Javier gives her a curt nod.

'Put your belongings below deck please.'

Gloria swings her shapely legs down the wooden steps, all smiles.

'*Vale*, let's get going. Can you untie the fenders?'

Javier indicates the plastic protectors hanging from the side of the boat. I look gormlessly at Pep.

'*Per favor*, you must have untied fenders before?'

'What?'

'Let me do it,' he huffs.

'Can I help?' asks Alan cheerfully.

The noise of the small engine drowns him out and suddenly we are jet propelled out of the mooring and Javier is steering our vessel into the open sea. Juana is settled at the bow of the boat looking sublime as she dangles a leg over the side.

'It's so beautiful,' she murmurs. 'Like a painting.'

Alan and I totter up the side deck, sharing concerned glances.

'Sit on a bench,' Javier calls above the wind. 'I will come and explain everything in a minute.'

We thump down onto the wooden seat, bathed in sweat.

'I'm boiling.'

Alan gives me a sympathetic smile. 'Hopefully there'll be a nice breeze once we get out to sea.'

I look over at Gloria, the nubile goddess and, to my irritation, see that she is adeptly untying the fender knots with Pep. She flashes me a perfect set of gleaming teeth and then throws off her T-shirt and shorts to reveal a pair of enormous, bronzed, bouncing orbs in a tiny bra top and a miniscule bikini bottom.

Pep chokes frantically on his *puro* and has to sink down onto the deck with the shock. Grumpily, I get up and position myself at the bow near Juana.

'There's some *Madrileña* rock chick on the boat with us.'

'Oh? I thought it was just us.' She looks vaguely around her and shrugs.

'It will give Alan and Pep something to ogle. Why worry?'

The sea is choppy, but the motion is vaguely relaxing and soon I settle into it, ignoring the coquetterie going on at the other end of the boat. We head southwards across the waves, Pep now steering, until we finally arrive at a small bay which Javier tells us is Cala Vinyes.

'As it's the first day, we can relax a little,' he says indulgently, anchoring the boat some way off from the shore. 'Fancy a swim?'

We fidget a little and it is only when he affixes a small metal ladder to the stern of the boat, that we take him at his word.

'I don't need that!' scoffs Gloria, gliding off the side of the boat like a mermaid.

I clamber down the ladder followed by Juana and gasp at the coolness of the waves. Alan and Pep follow, their eyes trained on the voluptuous Gloria who appears to be doing cartwheels in the water.

'How old do you think she is?' asks Pep.

'Young enough to be your granddaughter, I'd have guessed,' I say sniffily.

He pokes his tongue out at me and sets off in her direction.

'Don't have a cardiac arrest,' I snipe at the Scotsman.

He grimaces. 'Look, the girl's all alone so we must be friendly.'

'He's all heart,' says Juana caustically as she slices through the water.

Half an hour later, Javier asks us to return to the boat. With effort we crawl up the flimsy ladder onto the deck, wiping the salty brine from our faces. Alan and Pep remain in the water and together attempt to ascend the ladder. SPLASH! Pep goes flying backwards and lands on Alan's head. With irritation, the Scotsman regains his poise, crosses in front of him and brusquely grabs the rail. CRASH! A wave hits him and he wobbles back into the brine. From the deck, Gloria watches the spectacle with delight while Juana and I sit tartly by the side of the boat, relishing their humiliation.

'Come on,' says Javier. 'Stop messing around!'

Like a pair of slippery eels, they slither about on the steps but neither can get a firm enough grasp as the waves knock them off their feet. Despite our *froideur*, Juana and I can no longer contain ourselves and along with Gloria, begin laughing. It's better than a pair of performing clowns at Billy Smart's circus.

'Oh, I feel so sorry for them,' says Gloria in broken English. 'When you are old, it is not easy.'

With some impatience, Javier waves a long metal pole at them, and like a pair of antiquated limpets, they grip onto it and clamber back on board, exhausted with the effort. Juana stands over them, a towel entwined round her midriff.

'By the way, I took some wonderful photos for posterity,' she says with an alligator smile.

Day Two

'You've done WHAT?' Javier screams at me above the moaning wind.

'I tried to hook the jib rope, but it came loose!'

JODER!' curses Pep, using a rather ripe Spanish expletive.

Alan rounds on him. 'Don't make a crisis out of a drama!'

The triangular sail, otherwise known as the jib, slumps hopelessly on the deck while the rope that should be attached to it spirals up the mast out of sight.

'This is not good,' says Javier. 'We're a kilometre from land and we need that sail up.'

'What did you two idiots do?' Pep grumbles.

In a moment of weakness, Javier had decided to give Alan and me the task of attaching the halyard rope to the jib sail. Somehow, when hoisting the sail, the hook we used to secure it came loose and the wretched rope flew off up the mast, leaving the sail on the deck.

'We'll have to turn back unless we can retrieve the rope,' Javier says crossly. 'The mainsail won't be enough.'

We crowd round the silver mast while the sun jeers at us from on high.

'Well,' says Gloria sweetly. 'I'll just have to go up and get it.'

'What?' cries Pep. 'In this wind it would be far too dangerous.'

'It's good practice,' she smiles. 'I'll have a go.'

'You're an angel!' he exclaims.

I nudge Juana. 'In that case, maybe her wings can jet propel her up there.'

We snigger together away from the men folk, who eye us critically.

With some relief Javier gets out a harness and soon Gloria, in her teeny bikini, is swinging in the air like an accomplished trapeze artist, hoisted up on ropes by her male admirers below. Higher and higher she goes, swaying in the wind until, with triumph, she grabs the rope and hook and descends quickly like an agile monkey. Javier whoops with joy.

'You're a brick,' beams a windswept Alan.

'What would we do without you, Gloria?' says Pep with a smug smile.

Juana gives him a cold stare. 'Yes, what would we do?'

Day Three
Javier is bobbing about in the choppy waves, trying to untwist the anchor rope. Alan and I watch anxiously from the deck.

'Tell your wife to reverse the rudder!'

'WHAT?' yells Pep as he leans over the side of the yacht, *puro* wedged between two fingers.

Juana grips the wheel, tension stamped on her face. 'What did he say?'

I shrug helplessly, not having caught Javier's rapid Spanish.

'I think he said something about turning the boat.'

Juana grimaces at me. 'Turn it, HOW?'

'God knows,' I trail off.

Juana shakes her head impatiently.

'Just keep it steady!' snaps Pep.

We are in open water off Cala Blava and in the wild, blustery wind are edging dangerously close to a vast old brigantine anchored close by. It is beautifully restored and its huge, billowing white sails, like bulging lungs, rise and fall in the wind. Javier climbs up the ladder and, dripping wet, shouts instructions to Juana at the other end of the boat. She in turn fires the engine and in what seems like a moment of madness, heads straight for the side of the brigantine.

'STOP!' we scream out in unison.

Javier is sashaying towards us along the deck, his dark hair ruffled and glistening with sea water.

'What are you doing?' he shrieks. 'I told you to put it in reverse!'

'I'm trying,' whimpers Juana.

The crew of the other boat peers anxiously over the side, the captain looking furious.

'Have you gone mad?' roars Pep at his wife.

'Oh, shut up! You do it if you're so clever!'

Juana desperately changes tack and, by a whisker, the boat slides past its towering neighbour just as Javier bounds up to her. There's a united sigh of relief.

'I thought that was it,' mumbles Gloria.

'You weren't the only one,' growls Pep.

'Some holiday this is turning out to be,' I mutter to the Scotsman.

He has opened a can of beer and takes a long draught. 'Never a dull moment, eh?'

'You could say that again,' I say, grabbing the can from him and taking a long swig.

Javier's eyes are still blazing as he brusquely shoves Juana aside.

'Let me have that!' he snaps, covetously grasping the wheel. 'Advanced sailors, indeed? You lot still have a great deal to learn.'

Day Four

The wind is but a dying man's whisper as we steer a course into the bay of Magaluf. To our side an enormous catamaran teeming with tourists barges its way from the shore out into the calm sea. Standing on the deck, a man in a white ensemble is hollering from a microphone and disco music thumps so loudly that the vessel appears to be both vibrating and gyrating to the beat.

'It's a disco boat,' says Pep.

'You don't say,' I reply.

He sighs impatiently and walks along the deck towards the bow. In the distance hordes of tourists swallow up the golden beach, and yachts bob up and down all around us.

'We'll have lunch here and hope the wind picks up later, OK?'

I give Javier a nod and carry on practising my infernal rope knots. I have conquered the bowline, a sort of hangman's knot, and, with help from Gloria, can just about perform the clove hitch, which is handy for hitching fenders to outer rails. Juana, Gloria and Alan lie sprawled on wooden benches basking in the sunshine while Pep clambers up onto the side of the boat, face to the wind. Just as the engine dies and Javier is securing the anchor, there is a loud cry followed by a tremendous splash. All of us rise in a flash and spring to the sides of the boat. There, coughing and spluttering in the water is Pep, a look of utter bewilderment on his face.

'What are you doing down there?' barks Juana.

'What do you think, you stupid woman? I fell in!'

Javier throws him a life ring and with the trusty long pole manages to direct Pep to the stern of the boat where with a ladder and much tugging we get him back on board.

'That'll teach you to show off,' I say.

'Yes, at your age you must be careful,' Gloria chimes in, a mischievous grin playing on her lips.

Alan offers him a can of beer from the cooler box.

'Here, this'll cheer you up.'

Moodily, Pep takes it from him and with eyes downcast, stomps off with a towel to the galley below.

Day Five

The waves are lashing the side of the boat and I feel as though the entire vessel is going to capsize as we lurch over onto the starboard side. The sky wears an ugly grey scowl and the wind is whipping the sails which dance about as if possessed. I grip onto a shroud, one of the sturdy wires that support the mast, and pray that we will get back to shore alive. The wind rattles the cloth of the mainsail so violently that Javier sways unsteadily up the deck and issues sharp instructions on all sides. Pep wrestles with the wayward wheel as Gloria leaps about adeptly unravelling sails and securing knots. We are all soaked to the skin as water cascades over the deck. I feel my teeth chattering and a cold fear courses through me.

'Don't move!' barks Javier. 'The sea is getting very wild and now we have a flotilla of racing boats approaching.'

I turn my head and see not far off behind us a line of fast moving yachts, their sails to the wind.

'They're competing in the Copa del Rey. We're going to have to tack.'

Why fate has decreed that competitors for the King Carlos Cup should wind up in our stretch of water at this very instant, I cannot say. Here we are in the enormous fist of the Bay of Palma and yet like dodgem cars we seem to be careering towards one another.

'All of you, sit over here, port side. We're going to swing round.'

Using our weight to ballast the boat, Javier manoeuvres the vessel and we change direction. We are heading into the wind, and the noise of the flapping sails and hissing sea drowns out the voices of my companions. Alan gives me a reassuring smile, but when he averts his gaze I see genuine fear in his eyes. Where the hell are the life jackets, that's what I want to know? Stowed away uselessly down in the galley, I suppose.

'Javier's going to gybe,' shouts Pep, as he huddles low on the deck and takes a seat on the bench beside me.

'He's what-ing?'

'Gybing. Don't you remember anything? We're going to turn the stern through the wind. Watch out for the boom.'

The one thing Alan and I have gleaned on this voyage is that when the mainsail's pole, the boom, swings horizontally across the boat, we must duck our heads to avoid decapitation. Like a pair of useless rag dolls, we sit watching the hyperactivity going on around us, our knuckles white from hanging on to ropes. At times, the yacht lists so close to the waves that I feel as if my hair must surely be touching them. Someone is shouting.

'The boom! Watch the boom!'

Instinctively we crouch down and the boom cuts through the air like a scythe. Suddenly the boat makes a wild turn and then levels off. Javier, his shirt clinging to his skin, staggers up the side deck and soon, to my relief, I see a shoreline come into view.

'Thank God!' I yell at Pep, pointing to the land.

He grimaces. 'Don't relax yet. The sea is crazy and if one of us fell in now, we'd be sure to drown.'

I'm unnerved to see he isn't smiling. We pound through the waves, one minute falling forward, another leaning back so far I am sure we will all be shaken over the edge into the mouth of the sea. Miserably, I wish I had never agreed to do this course, to have put my life in what I perceive to be unnecessary danger. I think of what would happen to Ollie if the worst happened, if we never made it back.

Pep is suddenly shaking my shoulder. 'Cheer up, it's not that bad. Believe it on not, I've been in far worse scrapes than this.'

'Really?'

'Hundreds of times! That's the thrill of it all and think how lucky we are to be right in the midst of the Copa del Rey?'

'Actually Pep, I'd rather be watching from a hospitality tent on dry land with a glass of cava in my mitt.'

'Me too,' says Alan, licking the brine from his lips.

It is thirty minutes later that the waves abate and, spent, our small battered yacht limps into the marina.

'God, I need a drink,' sighs Alan, visibly shaken.

Javier is laughing. 'That was fun, wasn't it?'

'I think that's the end of my sailing days,' I whimper.

'Nonsense!' he yells robustly.

We moor the boat and make sure everything is ship shape before we head for the bar. Sitting on high stools by the counter, licking ice creams, are Angel and Ollie. They whisper to each other and giggle, probably amused at our dishevelled appearances. I have never been so pleased to see my son. Shakily, I take a beer in my hand and salute the rest of the crew. Gloria curls a golden arm round my neck.

'You and Alan were such good sports. We have all sailed before, but for you it must have been tough.'

'*Una pesadilla!*' A nightmare, I say.

Javier gives me a hearty pat on the back. 'Come on, you enjoyed it really. A little adrenalin is good for the soul.'

Juana and Pep raise their glasses.

'At least we're still speaking,' says Pep.

'Just,' I reply, giving him a good kick on the shin.

'Before I forget,' says Javier. 'I have a little memento for all of you.'

From a leather folder, he draws out five certificates.

'This marks the beginning of your sea-faring career.'

Grabbing a waiter, he gets out his camera and holding our certificates aloft, we huddle together and say Manchego to the lens. Customers at other tables start clapping and Pep, ever the showman, gives a little bow. I look out incredulously at the tranquil scene before me, the shiny yachts rising and falling gently in the marina, and the bronze disc of the sun suddenly bursting forth from behind a cloud.

'Do you think we'd make good deckhands one day?' Alan asks.

I look doubtfully at him. All I do know is that this deckhand doesn't want to see another boat for as long as she lives.

It's Friday night. Rachel is on the blower, sounding breathless and keen to talk to me.

'Did you get my phone message earlier?'

'Rachel, I've only just resurfaced from a near-death experience on the open sea.'

'Ah! The sailing course. You survived?'

'Barely.'

'I knew you'd enjoy it! I love sailing. Nothing like a bit of adrenalin to make you feel alive.'

'So, what was the message?'

She gives a jubilant sigh. 'Great news!'

Oh, here we go. 'Which is?'

'Are you ready?'

'Oh, come on.'

'We've done it!'

'Done what?'

She can hardly suppress her delight. 'We've won the Crown jewels pitch.'

NINE

DEVILISH PURSUITS

Dwarfing the small *plaça*, the grand old parish church of Fornalutx waits patiently, as it has done countless times over the years, until the moment when it can announce kick off. Then, with a tremendous booming, its old clock begins to chime, and local children gather together with their parents in the *plaça* in preparation for the annual village procession. Falling into line, every child clutches a table-tennis bat on which a red bell pepper is attached with glue. Inside the belly of each one is an illuminated candle which flickers and radiates an amber glow in the gathering dusk. Despite the late hour, the air is hot and dry, for it is still August and the sun, like an irritable insomniac, hardly sleeps. To applause from those drinking at bars by the square, the procession slowly begins, winding its way from the church down the hill and along the cobbled streets of the village. As an adopted son of Fornalutx, Ollie has been invited, so together with Catalina and her twins we set off, holding our peppers aloft and attempting to join in with the singing as we march. *'San Bartoméu, estira te'l lleu, estira-te 'l tu…'*

I give Catalina a nudge. 'Whatever does that mean?'

'It's an old song making fun of San Bartoméu, telling him, how do you say, to draw out his own bile?'

'Charming,' mutters the Scotsman.

Catalina flaps a fan in front of her perspiring face. 'So, you have the Swedish women arriving at Pep's flat tomorrow?'

'I'll be there bright and early to greet them. I've put a welcome pack with a bottle of cava in the fridge, so they should be happy.'

'Ramon thinks you're very lucky.'

'Depends what they all look like,' he replies.

We begin the steep ascent up through the narrow, cobbled streets towards Es Turo restaurant. Here, at one of the highest points in the valley, the Tramuntanas appear huge and menacing, their black and grizzled forms circling the village in a suffocating embrace. At Es Turo, tiny lights are strung around its terrace and mystified diners greet our arrival with puzzlement and delight. Xisca, the proprietor, whose own offspring are in the procession, comes out on the porch in a white overall and, like a Pied Piper, easily lures the children into the bar area with the promise of *caramels*. The children crowd inside, swooping on the huge tray of brightly coloured sweets and for some minutes the singing stops. Gradually, parents shoo them outside and we continue up the hill to Canantuna, the restaurant owned by Maria, Catalina's aunt. She steps briskly into the street, wiping her hands on her apron, and dishes out more goodies. Catalina's girls and Ollie pile their spoils up on their bats, arguing with one another about who has the largest stash. At the top of the hill we stop to catch our breath. Before us, the tiny village rises up in a rocky mound, its honey stone-terraced dwellings pale under the moon. Unseen in the darkness is the labyrinth of thin, meandering alley ways and twisting paths that run like veins through the heart of the village and up high into the hills. As we turn to make our descent, the delicious aroma of grilled peppers fills the air as the fluttering candles begin singeing their vegetable cages. My stomach rumbles and Catalina observes her watch by the light of her pepper.

'Our dinner's already in the oven. When we get home, you can catch up with Ramon about your chickens. I told him about the genet.'

George the genet, as I have christened him, has spent the last few nights stealthily circling our corral and once nearly managed to burrow under the netting. By sheer luck, Salvador, our cockerel, made such a din that Alan woke up and rushed down into the field in the nick of time.

'He looks so sweet,' I say to Catalina.

'You won't think so when he finishes off all your hens.'

The procession reaches the square and, bidding goodnight to the assembled throng, we head off to Catalina's house for roast chicken.

It is past midnight as we wearily turn up our track towards the house. Suddenly, in the glare of the car's headlights I see the frozen form of a large rat. It is standing upright, its eyes wide, its whiskers translucent in the glare. Alan sees it too late and careers towards it.

'Don't hurt it!' I hear myself yell.

There's a tiny thud, almost indiscernible as the car hits its mark. I round on him in fury.

'Why did you kill it?'

He is irritable. 'For heaven's sake! I couldn't brake in time.'

'But I can tell you don't really care and now it's gone.'

'Sorry, had you wanted me to invite it in for a nightcap?'

'It wasn't doing us any harm. Just think of its family.'

Alan gives a brittle laugh. 'Its family? What is wrong with you? It's vermin and that's that.'

I hold my tongue, unnerved to feel tears pricking my eyes. I feel like an accomplice to a murder. We turn into the courtyard. Splayed out on the back seat, breathing deeply, Ollie continues to slumber. His thin, tanned arms and legs are flung across the seat and on his face there's the trace of a wry smile.

'Let me get this straight,' says Ed dramatically.

I potter out into the garden with the cordless phone to my ear. He is wheezing into the receiver.

'You're thinking of opening a cattery?'

'Yes.'

'You're being serious? I mean, this isn't one of your sadistic little jokes?'

I stifle a snort of impatience. 'I'm totally serious. Where does sadism come into it?'

He gives a heavy sigh. 'The whole idea is preposterous. Have you forgotten about my cat allergy?'

'I wasn't planning on inviting you to the opening.'

'Well, this is complete madness and this training course in Dorset sounds positively dreadful.'

Orlando and Minky watch me from under the olive tree. As usual they lie together in a heap, their paws and tails intermingled.

'What do you think, boys?'

Ed is confused. 'Hello? Who are you talking to?'

'Our new cats. They both say it's a fabulous idea, as long as they don't have to mix with the inmates.'

'You're exasperating. Trust me, next month the reality will set in when you go on this course.'

'Let's wait and see, Ed. Anyway, why are you coughing so much?'

'It's some terrible summer flu, possibly avian. I'm off work today. So how is the corral?'

'We have a wicked genet called George casing the joint, but other than that the hens seem perky. We're still waiting for them to lay an egg though.'

'This whole livestock obsession is absurd, especially with an avian epidemic gathering momentum.' He gives a distraught cough. 'And how is your leg?'

The leg issue is becoming rather concerning. Having reached a stage of near agony a month ago, I decided to pop by to see Joan Reynes, our local physiotherapist, who told me that to be fit enough to run in the New York marathon I would need to follow his advice to the letter. This meant a period of several weeks' rest, followed by a programme of sports massages and cold compresses.

'It's on the mend. Just another week or so and I can start training again.'

He is mumbling like a disgruntled wizard.

'Why do you have to put so much pressure on yourself? Besides, running is terribly bad for the heart.'

'Don't be ridiculous.'

I try to manoeuvre the conversation. 'By the way, how's Charlene?'

'She's a breath of fresh air. I've agreed to visit her in November.'

'What about the plane journey?'

'Valium cures most ills.'

There's a tooting at the front gate. 'Ed, I have to go. Email me.'

I amble into the kitchen, dump the phone back on its cradle, and push the gate entry button. It's Alan. Moments later he plods into the kitchen.

'Sorry, I forgot the gate key. Well, those Swedish girls were hard work.'

'Oh?'

'All of them were dark-haired and plump and told me the flat wasn't what they'd expected. Then, when I tried the tap, the accursed water wasn't working.'

'What did you do?'

'I've had to call Pere. He's over there now.'

Pere the plumber, one of the studs of the valley, should cheer the Swedes up.

'What on earth do you think Pep was playing at?' he grumbles.

'To be fair, it's not necessarily his fault. Maybe there's a problem in the whole block. Can't you call him?'

'He's in Switzerland. I'm not spending a fortune on my mobile.'

He dumps some fertiliser on the table. 'By the way, my worms have been a bit sluggish of late. I hope the heat's not getting to them.'

We wander outside and examine the wormery. Alan lifts the lid and pokes about with a stick under the vegetable peelings. There's a slight squirming in the debris, but to our dismay we see many inert bodies.

'Oh dear.'

'It's worse than I thought,' says the Scotsman glumly.

'Can't you call the manufacturer?'

'I'll have to.' He holds a dead worm in his hand. 'Poor old chap.'

He fiddles around with the compost drawer at the bottom of the wormery.

'Maybe Miquel was right,' I say.

'About what?'

'Mixing Mallorcan and British worms.'

'Don't be daft.'

As soon as I say it, his face clouds over.

'I hope not.'

'Cheer up. Let's go and see Ollie. He's with his beloved hens.'

We walk down into the field, the sun burning our backs. I stop for a moment, distracted by the abundance of tomato and aubergine plants on Alan's vegetable patch. He fusses around the leaves and pulls up some weeds.

'This heat is a killer. I'm losing so many tomato vines. They need constant watering.'

'I'll help water.'

He shakes his head sadly. 'You can't. The cistern's almost empty and the water channel has completely dried up.'

'Well, I suppose we'll just have to make do.'

Ollie is inside the corral, talking with Minny and Della, his favourite hens, while Salvador struts about with a disdainful expression, pecking at grain and occasionally nipping at the ankles of his harem. Sitting under the shade of a lemon tree, Daisy and Poppy, our youngest pullets, seem to be in deep, animated discussion.

'Did you open the front gate?' asks Ollie. 'Llamp's just been in the field. He was trying to get into the corral.'

Alan frowns. 'He must have sneaked in when I drove through. I'll have to tell Rafael to keep him in his run. What else can go wrong today?'

A streak of fur suddenly darts across the courtyard, a large bronzed object hanging limply from its mouth. It's Llamp heading for the closing gate with what looks like… He squeezes through just before it shuts.

'What on earth did he have in his mouth?' Ollie asks.

I think nostalgically of the fragrant roast chicken I took from the oven minutes earlier and left to cool on a plate by the kitchen table.

'There's no easy way to tell you this, boys. That little devil has just run off with our lunch.'

I awaken from a nightmare bathed in sweat and sit bolt upright in bed. The frogs are croaking hysterically from the pond, and the cicadas are hissing in the trees, but there's a rather more unsettling sound coming from the field. I leap from the bed and peer out of the window. The garden is bathed in muddy darkness, the milky pool water reflecting weird and sinister shadows under the light of the moon. I hold my breath and listen. Silence. Then I hear it again, a loud fearful clucking and fanning of feathers. I rush from the room barefooted down the staircase and out of the back door, grabbing a torch on the way. My heart is beating fast as I descend the cool stone steps to the orchard and head for the corral. The ground is strewn with clumps of brittle, sharp weeds and I wince with pain as tiny, sharp stones cut into my bare feet. Our pullets are frantically careering about in the yard, clucking and screeching in panic. Something has made them flee the hen house. Terrified, I shine my torch in the midst of the flapping throng and enter the corral. An insistent rustling in the long grass by the wooden hut catches my attention and I stumble towards it with trembling hand and torch outstretched. In my haste I trip over a plastic feeding bowl and nearly keel over, dropping the torch to the ground. It shines out eerily from a patch of long yellowing grass, so with trembling hand I pick it up and head for the hut, directing the beam of light on to the grass. I give a start. A lean, grey twitching face looks defiantly up at me, and then with a slither of its long tail, plunges into the darkness. Lying in a pool of blood is the lifeless form of a pullet. I sink to my knees, the torch at my side and lift her up. By the markings I can see that it is Daisy. The feathers are still warm, the eyes open, but the soft throat has been savagely torn apart. I stroke her beak, and wipe away tears as her friend Poppy tentatively bobs forward, seemingly confused at the spectacle before her. Around me, curious hens ruffle their wings and twitter.

Lights suddenly illuminate the dark walls, and Alan's familiar form comes jogging down into the field.

'What's happened?' he pants as he enters the corral.

Seeing the dead bird in my arms, he crouches down beside me and puts an arm around my shoulder.

'I was too late.'

'Did you see what killed her?'

'A rat.'

He shakes his head and sighs. 'Come on. Let's have a cup of tea. There's nothing we can do for her now.'

Having secured the hens, we shut the wooden gate behind us and make our way to the kitchen. Alan looks down at my bare feet.

'You went in there without shoes on?'

I nod.

He squeezes my arm. 'Well, all I can say is thank goodness the rat didn't get you too.'

Sabine Ricard sits at the oak table sipping her coffee and staring critically around the kitchen and *entrada*. Her long russet hair is pushed behind her ears and a pair of red rectangular Prada glasses rest on her nose.

'I cannot believe that you still haven't finished this house,' she exclaims in rich Gallic tones.

Alan and I exchange glances.

'I mean, you still have hardly any furniture. Where do you sit at night?'

'On our hands.'

She turns to me. 'No, don't joke. I mean when Michel and I bought our villa in Santa Ponsa, we made it perfect within a year.'

'Yes, but our *finca* wasn't even habitable,' says Alan heatedly.

'Look, I know Sóller is nice, but it's too rural. You really should live in a more civilised zone like us.'

'All depends how you interpret civilised,' I reply.

'At least we don't have killer rats by our pool,' she huffs. 'You could have been savaged. My grandmother in Brittany said that cornered rats can go for the throat.'

'Well, it didn't this time,' I sigh, thinking gloomily of the lifeless Daisy.

'Well, each to their own, I suppose. I'd rather live in a gated estate where we have proper security.'

'I don't think a few security guards would worry the Mallorcan rat population.' Alan scoffs.

'I can assure you that our estate is rat free,' Sabine bristles.

Alan stifles a snort.

She gets up and stretches her back. 'The views are nice here, but you haven't even started the outhouses. When will they be finished?'

'When we win the *loteria*,' I say.

She's not listening. 'What you need is a good architect and interior designer. I can recommend somebody. He's French of course.'

'Actually, what we need are funds,' says Alan.

I wonder why we put up with such abuse from Sabine, but the truth is that she's a lonely woman whose philandering husband, Michel, spends most of the week in Paris supposedly on business while she cares for their precocious daughter, Veronique, back home. This ballet-loving child is one of Ollie's class mates and his sworn enemy. Sadly, none of the children seem to like Veronique and parents run a mile when they see Sabine coming. I suppose that's why she persists in phoning us and popping by, even though we live miles away from her sanitised patch of the island. Given that she doesn't work or appear to have friends, I imagine she's bored witless and finds us a source of bucolic entertainment. If we were more courageous, we'd have dropped her like a hot stone long ago, but I pity her and so absurdly we keep up the charade.

'So, can I have your chocolate monster muffin recipe? Veronique is desperate for it.' Sabine views me intently.

I give a guffaw. 'Don't be silly!'

'No really, Veronique told me that Ollie sold all his cakes at the school charity sale while her strawberry cheesecake was left untouched.'

'That's because most kids prefer chocolate.'

She eagerly gets out a pen and minuscule notepad from her handbag.

'Sabine, I'm afraid my recipe is just a hotchpotch. I make it up as I go along.'

She pouts at me. 'You don't want to share it?'

'I simply can't trust that it'll work.'

'No problem,' she says in a wounded voice hurling the pen and pad back into her bag. 'Veronique will be upset of course, but that's life. It is full of disappointments.'

I refuse to be drawn by her amateur dramatics and begin clearing away the coffee cups. She stands in the kitchen doorway and stares across at the mountain range facing her.

'I would hate to live here,' she says with passion. 'Every day would feel like waking up to loneliness. All you can hear are animals and birds. It would feel as though I was the last person left in the world.'

'Is that so bad?' asks Alan.

'Yes, it's a horrible thought.'

She scoops up her car keys from the table and scans her watch.

'I'm afraid I must leave you. I have to collect Veronique from ballet. It was nice to pop by.'

She clops out to the courtyard in her elegant mules and jumps into the silver Mercedes. We wave her off at the gate. Her visits always leave me feeling drained.

'I think hell really will freeze over before we ever make it to Sabine in sanitised Surrey-on-Sea,' says Alan.

Ollie appears in the courtyard. 'You finally got rid of her.'

'Don't be mean. She's a sad woman.'

He pulls a face at me. 'Anyway, something great has happened.'

'What?' we say in unison.

'The hens have finally laid some eggs.'

I am overcome with joy. 'But they had such a terrible shock.'

'At last, a ray of light,' the Scotsman sighs.

'And something else.' He cups his mouth and looks down, giggling naughtily.

'What?' I say tremulously.

'I found Sabine's handbag on the front seat and hid an egg inside it. She'll get a shock all right.'

'Oh, Ollie. How could you?' I gasp.

'That was very naughty indeed,' scolds Alan in rather contrived tones. 'I'm shocked that you'd do such a terrible thing.'

Ollie feigns contrition as his father strides back into the house, his shoulders heaving up and down with laughter.

It's a hot and sticky evening in August. The *plaça* is teeming with demons and masked ghouls in black capes while up on a wide stage in front of the town hall a home-grown rock group bashes out a wild rhythm amidst rising pink and green smoke. This is the Nit de Foc, otherwise known as the Night of Fire, when hundreds of locals voluntarily hop and jump around the square as devils shower them with burning sparks and throw fire crackers at their feet. At midnight there is a spectacular firework display and everyone goes home nursing scorched legs and toes. Handily, the local firemen, known as *bombers*, turn up and hose down anyone who gets too singed during the proceedings. For the less valiant, the occasion offers a wonderful opportunity to meet up with friends and enjoy a sadistic sideshow completely free of charge. A large group of us are sitting outside Cafè Paris , drinking wine and discussing everything from politics to catteries. Llorenç the woodman, comes over to Alan and commiserates over his worms.

'Maybe you just need to put the wormery in a shady spot with lots of ventilation.'

'Well, a nursery in Santa Maria has offered me a stock of local worms so I'm going to start again,' Alan replies.

'To be honest, I think the English worms couldn't cope with the sun,' says Paco. 'Get some good macho Mallorcans and it'll be fine.'

Albert from HiBit gives a wry smile. 'How about some laid-back American worms? If they're from California, the heat won't get to them.'

Paco laughs aloud and nudges him. 'Miami worms might be even better because they'll probably speak some *Español.*'

Albert throws Alan a sympathetic look. 'Well, I think Paco's right. Get yourself some trusty Mallorcan worms.'

'I'll do that,' nods the Scotsman stoically.

Paco strains his head to see what's going on in the *plaça,* finally standing up to get a better look. 'What's wrong with my daughter? She does this crazy thing every year.'

Aside from bull running up in Fornalutx annually, Catalina also likes to hop around the firecrackers at the Nit de Foc.

'She's just a daredevil,' I laugh, straining to see her in the dark crowd.

'Well, it's her life,' he shrugs. 'Anyway, what have you done about your hens?'

'Alan's secured the run. We think the gate might not have been closed properly.'

'These things happen. The important thing is to learn from it,' he taps his cigarette on the ashtray. His wife leans across and touches my hand.

'Catalina's told us about your cattery idea, but where would you put it?'

This is a moot point. If we could afford to buy the land next to our orchard it really would make an ideal spot.

'Ideally, I'd put it in the orchard.'

'Are you sure? Think of the corral, and what about planning permission?'

She's right. There are a lot of issues to think about aside from Alan's bad humour and the cost. After all, is a cattery what I really want or am I just clinging to a possible escape route from London PR drudgery? To complicate matters I'm having fun planning the Crown jewels event and am not even finding the demands of Dannie too onerous. Maybe the heat's getting to me, but coordinating PR for George's absurd dog fashion show in the Big Apple has been, as the New Yorkers would say, a real blast.

Fireworks pop and crackle overhead and plumes of silver, turquoise and green sparks shower from the sky. Catalina emerges from the *plaça,* her clothes soaking wet.

'The *bombers* cooled me off. Hey, Ramon, get me a *cava,* will you?'

She sprawls down on a chair next to me and taps my leg.

'What's wrong?'

'Nothing. I'm just thinking.'

'Don't think, dance!'

She gets up and grabs my arm. 'Come on.'

'Where are we going?'

'To dance with the devils.'

Before I can object, I find myself whisked across the square into a maelstrom of gyrating, whooping locals and prancing demons while a cackling fireman unleashes a hoseful of freezing water which gushes over my head and right down to the soles of my shoes and to the very tips of my dancing toes.

TEN

GOING THE WHOLE HOG

The valley is dipped in golden light as I head from the Port of Sóller back along the blazing asphalt road towards the town. Trailing me on his pop-pop *moto* is Gaspar, the paper delivery man who has finished his round and appears to have nothing better to do than shadow me as I run, calling out *bravo* and tooting his horn at intervals. I feel guilty about Gaspar. Ever since our first faltering conversation a few years back he has begged me to take him running, but given his immense girth and slow breathing this would, of course, be a disaster. The sudden demise of the popular paper delivery man would not, I fear, endear me to my neighbours. So my compromise is to let Gaspar tootle along on his bike at my side whenever it takes his fancy and somehow this seems to make him feel happy, as if he is actually running the course himself. When I reach the steep hill that curves up from the port towards Fornalutx, Gaspar toots and waves, carrying on towards the town. I watch him disappear in a veil of acrid smoke, his plump buttocks, like a couple of beef joints, hanging over the side of the ancient *moto* and providing useful ballast as he sways along the road. With only two months to go I am desperate to keep up my training schedule. Between clients, well-wishers and friends I have accumulated nearly two thousand pounds in promised sponsorship money and have no intention of giving up now, injury or no injury. The road to Fornalutx is clear as I fill my lungs ready for the ascent. Some minutes later, perspiring heavily in the intense heat, I turn off to the right and find a tractor advancing slowly in front of me. On the narrow lane which barely allows the passing of a single car, I know it will be difficult to pass so I trot behind in some frustration until finally the tractor grinds to a halt, its engine still shuddering. An elderly man leans from the driving seat and beckons me over.

'*Perdoname*, I only just saw you. *Venga!*' he calls in Mallorcan. 'We don't mind waiting.'

I smile up at him and squeeze past the vehicle, wondering why he said *we*, when he appears to be alone. Maybe he's got an invisible friend. Glimpsing back to offer a wave, I do a double take. Sitting on the seat next to the friendly farmer is a fat hog, one of the special Mallorcan black breed. He looks haughtily down at me and then shakes his head as if indicating that I should run along. The man sees me gawping in confusion and pats his pet as if somehow to reassure me. I keep up the pace, reminding myself that some things are never quite as they seem in our valley. Glimpsing my stopwatch, I see that I have managed an hour and thirty minutes on the road, and only the tiniest gnawing pain persists in my right thigh. Surely it must be almost healed?

Margalida is standing outside her chalet watering plants. Her fat tabby cat watches me suspiciously as I approach.

'I wish you'd stop all this running. At your age it can't be good.'

'You used to say how young I looked.'

'That's because I'm half blind but then you foolishly decided to tell me your age.'

I swig at my plastic water bottle and throw some of the lukewarm contents over my head. Margalida is disapproving.

'That's the best way to get a chill.'

I wonder if the day will come when I meet with Margalida's approval, but then it doesn't seem to matter given that she humours me just the way I am.

'I have a bag of figs for you.'

She hobbles into the house, returning with a plastic carrier bag.

'Here, they'll give you energy.'

I give her a hug and hurry up the track. When I look round, I see her standing like a statue, her near sightless eyes following me as I go. Alan is out in the front garden hosing his herb patch as I puff into the courtyard.

'You won't believe it,' he seethes. 'Those dratted cats have dug up my new seedlings. It's taken me weeks to nurture them.'

Given that cats are becoming such a sensitive issue I mutter sympathetically and quickly slip away into the *entrada*. The windows and doors are flung open as Catalina makes her weekly assault on the house. Meanwhile, Ollie has returned to school, having complained as he left that three months' holiday simply wasn't enough.

'Come here,' Catalina is calling from upstairs. I find her in what we call the snug room, the only place where we actually have a sofa of sorts. She is leaning out of the window.

'Look at those stupid cats! They're sleeping on the roof.'

Following her lead, I peer out of the window and there, curled up on the hot clay roof tiles below us, are Minky and Orlando.

'They must have climbed out of the window. Do you think they're safe?'

164

'Yes,' she considers. 'As long as they don't fall.'

'Very funny.'

She bustles downstairs. 'Remember the mayor is coming in an hour. You'd better be ready.'

The Mayor of Sóller also doubles as the town's vet and has agreed to pop by the *finca* to assess whether our orchard could possibly house a cattery and if not, to discuss other options. With a growing population of feral cats in the town and the local villages, I'd also like to suggest a possible solution to the problem.

I am upstairs in my office writing my weekly column for the *Majorca Daily Bulletin* when a car draws up at the gate. Catalina is bawling up the stairs.

'It's the *Batle!* Come!'

The mayor is accompanied by Stefan, Catalina's brother who, I am pleased to learn from her, is securing an increasing amount of work with the local council. In the few years we have known him, he has risen from lone stone mason to respected building contractor, employing many. Without ceremony, the mayor strides into the *entrada*, greets Alan and me warmly and then proceeds to look around the gardens.

'What a nice house,' he exclaims. 'Your work?'

Stefan nods. 'There's still a lot to do though. Paving, installing a better irrigation system and then we've got to start on the *casitas*…'

Ah yes, the outhouses by the pool. Another little task we've yet to accomplish.

'*Poc a poc,*' I say, using the 'little by little' refrain that used to drive me to near insanity when I first arrived in the valley. Now I can look at wires spewing from walls, tiles unfinished, gaping sockets and turn a blind eye to it all because it will, as the locals say, be done in time. *Poc a poc.*

'You must explain to the mayor about your cattery course,' says Catalina.

Stefan is already leading the way down the stairs into the orchard. Excitedly, he shows the mayor the area that could accommodate a modest wooden agricultural building.

'You own all this land?'

'Ah, no,' says Stefan, answering for us. 'Only half, but they want to negotiate for it.'

Alan is chewing his lip thoughtfully and remains taciturn.

I tell the mayor about the cattery course, a phenomenon that he finds mildly curious, but he nods encouragingly.

'Look, in principle, I have no problem with the idea. In fact, it's a good one – especially if, as you say, you would also like to address the feral cat issue in the valley. We can discuss that further. However, first we need to check planning permits. We will be in touch.'

He heads off to the courtyard with Stefan. Alan trails behind with a troubled expression on his face.

'What's this idea of yours for helping the feral cats?' he asks suspiciously.

'Well, a sort of Pied Piper pilot scheme whereby we lure the cats away from the bins to central feeding points out of the main thoroughfares.'

'And who provides the food?'

'That's for discussion.'

He gives a cough. 'It wouldn't involve us by any remote chance?'

Catalina quickly interrupts. 'That was encouraging, wasn't it?'

'You think so?' I ask.

'Well, it's a start, but the first real step will be negotiating for that land.'

Pep is sitting at our kitchen table pouring over a large desk diary.

'OK, so tomorrow this nice British hen party arrive at eleven.'

166

Alan sits across from him with his own diary. 'I hope they're not as moody as those Swedes.'

'Well, they were all right in the end. Your handsome plumber told me they kept inviting him round even when the water was back on,' Pep chuckles.

'Poor Pere. He must be pestered by women all the time,' says Alan.

'You mean like you and me, *mon amie?*'

I give Pep a look. 'In your dreams.'

Alan doesn't bother to respond. 'After this lot, your flat's free until early October.'

'Yes, so you can have a little respite.'

'Respite? You must be joking. I might be up for another commercial.'

Pep looks up from the table. 'Another bank advert?'

'No, it's for shampoo.'

Alan leafs through his diary, refusing eye contact with either of us.

I can see that Pep is savouring the moment. 'Shampoo? No self-respecting *macho* would do a shampoo advert.'

'Not even for six hundred euros?'

He demurs. 'Admittedly, that's not bad, but how long will the filming take?'

'Half a day, apparently.'

'And he gets to kiss his co-star,' I add helpfully.

Pep drops his pen and grabs my arm. 'What? You're joking?'

Alan is coy. 'I only have to peck her on the cheek.'

'Why do you have to kiss her at all?'

'Because she buys me a bottle of shampoo.'

Pep gets up and runs his hands through his grey mane. 'That's ridiculous! No man would kiss a woman for buying him a bottle of shampoo.'

Alan strolls over to the sink area and impatiently plugs in the espresso machine.

'Calm down. It's probably just his excuse, you know, to kiss her.'

'*Per favor!* No Mallorcan would need an excuse to kiss a woman.'

'Oh God, why did we start this?' Alan battles with a packet of ground coffee and manages to spill a small heap of it onto the work surface. Messily, he begins to dab at it with a cloth.

'How do you work this wretched machine anyway?'

I get up and shoo him out of the way.

'I'll do it. Want a cup?'

Pep nods. 'So tell me the whole story line.'

Alan plonks down on a chair. 'Take one is a shot of me with my hair looking lifeless, then it focuses in on the worried face of my wife. It cuts to her returning with a bottle of shampoo which I use...'

'Immediately?'

'I've no idea, Pep. Anyway, then it shows me boasting a healthy, glossy head of hair and the final shot is me leaning across to kiss her on the cheek.'

Pep's mouth opens and closes like a drowning goldfish. 'So you'll have to wear a wig?'

Alan is indignant. 'Of course not! What's wrong with my own hair?'

'Well, it's not thick like mine.'

'Yours is long, not necessarily thick.'

I push a coffee in front of both of them.

'Any chance of you two actually carrying on with some work, or are you just going to bicker all afternoon?'

It's 8.15 a.m. I am sitting at my desk wrapped in a towel while Rachel speaks rapidly to me on the phone. I make a mental note that it's actually an hour earlier in the UK and that she's already in the office. Meanwhile, I had only just showered when she rang.

'So what are we going to do?'

Rachel, normally so calm and collected, has obviously been thrown by this latest turn of events at H Hotels. A triple murder is never good for PR purposes and I can imagine Manuel Ramirez must be in a state of complete anxiety. She is breathing heavily.

'Hang on, Rachel. Let me get this straight. A maid at the Paris hotel was shot in the lobby earlier this morning by her jealous boyfriend, the gardener, who was then stabbed to death by the husband.'

'Other way around,' she says irritably. 'The husband is the jealous gardener. He shot his wife in the lobby and the boyfriend, who's a concierge at the hotel, stabbed and killed him.'

'Got it. So who killed the boyfriend? There's no one left.'

'Yes there is. Apparently the mother of the jealous husband thought he was acting strangely this morning and followed him to the hotel. When she saw him dead in the lobby, she went into shock and used his gun to kill the concierge.'

'This could only happen in Paris. It's like a Feydeau farce.'

'Except that it isn't very funny.'

'Right, have you written a holding statement?'

'I've already emailed it to Manuel. There should be a copy on your system.'

'Excellent. I need to speak with Manuel and then we can put a crisis statement together.'

'He's expecting your call. I'm afraid he only wants you to speak to the press.'

'Fine. What about you?'

'I'm catching the next available flight to Paris. The girls from the French PR agency are meeting me at the hotel.'

'Goodoh, and who's liaising back at base?'

'Sarah's coordinating staff in the office. Everything's under control.'

'I wouldn't have expected anything less of you.'

She gives an enormous sigh. 'It's horrible to think three people died just a matter of hours ago. And for what?'

'I know, Rachel, but we can't think about that now.'

Her voice is shaky. 'You're right. I'd better get going. I'll call you when I reach Paris.'

The phone line goes dead. I am chilled at my own lack of emotion, the effect of handling numerous grisly client crises over the years. Wearily, I download my emails and open Rachel's file. Alan walks in with a cup of tea as I pick up the phone to dial Manuel.

'Crisis?' he says sympathetically.

'Yes, but nothing that a strong cup of tea can't solve.'

It's been a long day. I sit with my feet up on the kitchen table drinking a glass of red wine while Horatio, our adopted baby hedgehog, rustles behind the fridge. It's gone midnight and Alan is pottering around the garden watering his plants. With a sudden stab of compassion, Miquel, our water *siquier*, arrived this afternoon and opened up one of the water channels in the field, enabling Alan to revive his wilting vegetables and plants. The H Hotel saga has rumbled on all day and Rachel will remain installed at the Paris hotel until the crisis eventually subsides. I have spent the last ten hours glued to the phone, placating the press and coordinating with the police in Paris – not an easy task with my rusty spoken French.

The telephone begins blaring and I give a long groan. Now what? Please God the hotel chef hasn't killed his lover too. I answer warily. A screeching, drunken female voice demands to speak with Alan.

'Who is this? Jan from where? Hang on.'

I find Alan by the pond. 'There's some dodgy woman called Jan on the line.'

He looks puzzled. 'That's one of the hen party from Birmingham staying at Pep's flat.'

He follows me into the kitchen. The hose is left running.

'Hello? Jan?'

I watch as he pads about the kitchen, his brow becoming more furrowed as he listens.

'It is past midnight,' he says robustly. 'What did you expect?'

The voice at the other end is so piercing that I can almost make out the words.

'OK, OK. I'm on my way.'

He bangs down the receiver. 'Would you believe that? Bloody women!'

He has a murderous look in his eye.

'What's up?'

'It seems that our drunken hens have gone the whole hog. They're smashed out of their heads and playing God awful disco music. The *policia local* received a complaint about the noise from the neighbour upstairs and an officer is waiting to speak to me now.'

I put my head in my hands. 'This can't be happening. Shall we call Pep?'

'I don't think it's fair. He's paying me to look after his flat. I'll go.'

'Call me if you need linguistic back up.'

He plods outside, turns off the hose and briefly returns, fumbling for the driving keys in a pot by the front door.

'So much for a quiet life.'

I hear the crunch of gravel as the car turns out of the drive. Walking back over to the table I charge my glass and glance lazily at my book, an ancient copy of *The Bright Pavilions*. A scraping noise comes from behind the fridge.

'Be quiet, Horatio,' I yawn.

Inko stirs slightly on her cushion and regards the fridge with some suspicion. The strange sound gets louder and more frantic until the cat springs from the chair and wanders over to investigate. I flop my book down on the table.

'Do I ever get any peace?'

Behind the fridge all is revealed. Horatio's paw has somehow become ensnared in a metal catch and he struggles desperately to get loose. With difficulty I begin heaving the huge silver fridge towards me, a disgruntled army of bottles clinking within. Horatio regards me with dark, startled eyes when I peer down at him, my hand carelessly resting on his sharp coat of needles. I stifle a curse and after an intricate operation manage to release the tiny paw. He gives a relieved snuffle and creeps off into the gloom of the garden. As I walk over to the sink and run my grazed hand under cold water, the telephone rings. I am tempted to leave it to bleat into infinity, but finally remove it from its cradle.

'Hello?'

It's Alan. I can hear loud disco music thumping in the background.

'Hi. I'm afraid we've got a bit of a crisis.' He hollers down the line.

'What on earth's going on?'

'It's the Birmingham hen party. The girls are completely sozzled and refusing to cooperate with the police. It's chaos!'

'What are they doing?'

'Dancing wildly around the flat wrapped in tinsel and precious little else.'

'I think you need back up. Let me call Pep.'

'It seems a bit unfair at this time of night.'

'Quite to the contrary, I think the prospect of wild Bacchic women swathed in tinsel will set his heart racing.'

'You're probably right,' he says wearily. 'Whatever you do, don't wait up.'

The line goes dead. Something tells me that Pep and the Scotsman will be dining out on this cracking tale for some time to come.

ELEVEN

DIVA MOMENTS

Tuesday 7.30 a.m., the club, Mayfair

Bernadette is sitting on the end of my bed and cleaning her thick-rimmed glasses with an old hankie.

'Oh B'Jesus! What a hoot. A cattery course? You've lost your marbles, girl, and that's a fact.'

I'm still in my running gear, having managed ten miles around Hyde Park and just returned to the club. The dreaded date of the New York marathon looms nearer and I'm upping my training considerably even though my old leg twinge has returned. Bernadette had pounced on me as I opened the door to my room.

'It's not that funny, Bernadette. There are loads of people running catteries.'

She's still tittering. 'I can just see you now in your wee suit and shiny heels mopping up cats pee.'

'Great. Well I'm glad to be the comic turn this morning.'

'You always are!' Her shoulders are shaking.

'Any chance of my getting showered and dressed?'

She rises slowly and pads out into the corridor. 'I'm only pulling your leg, darlin'. You'll love it… all those nice little furry things, God love 'em. When do you go?'

'Thursday.'

I grab a towel and potter off towards the shower. Even as I reach the bathroom door I can hear Bernadette cackling with laughter as she clunks a vacuum cleaner along the hallway ready for a murderous assault on the threadbare carpet.

10.04 a.m., The Berkeley, Knightsbridge

I rush through the swivel doors of The Berkeley, only to find Rachel pacing around the marble foyer in some irritation. She struts towards me.

'I've been trying to reach you.'

'Sorry, I forgot to plug the mobile in last night. I'm only a few minutes late.'

She shakes her head with some impatience. 'Look, it's not that. We've got a problem. Mary Anne came down a few moments ago to say that our meeting's got to be postponed until Thursday because Tetley thinks it's not a propitious time.'

'Oh for heaven's sake! I thought she decided these things in advance of Dannie's trips?'

Rachel raises her eyebrows. 'Apparently, Tetley had a vision last night. She said that Dannie should stay in her room today and consume only coffee, grapefruit and almonds.'

I pinch my arm. 'Ow!'

'What are you doing?' hisses Rachel.

'Pinching myself to check I'm not in an asylum. Listen, there's no way I can see her on Thursday. I'm at the *Evening Standard* all morning and having a quick lunch with Ed before leaving for my cattery course.'

'I forgot about your cattery visit. Can't you just cancel it? You know my views on the whole thing.'

'Absolutely not. I wish you wouldn't gang up with Alan.'

Rachel runs a hand over her brow. 'Very well then, do you think you can talk some sense into them all?'

I call Mary Anne on her mobile and a few minutes later she descends in the lift to the lobby. As always she is dressed in a voluminous trouser suit, this one cyclamen pink. A small gold cross plays about her neck and her hair hangs lankly. She is harassed, but greets me with outstretched arms.

'Sugar, what can I say? When Dannie's in one of her moods, there's nothing I can do. She's refusing to budge from her suite and, between you and me, we had a bit of a nasty write-up in the *New York Times* today, so things are looking pretty ugly upstairs.'

Greedy George was right in his prediction. I have bitten off more than I can chew with Dannie, but I know that if I cave in to this madness now, we will forever be her slaves.

'If she won't leave her suite, we'll go to her.'

Mary Anne's lip wobbles. 'Impossible! She hardly lets anyone into her suite. She's still in her robe, and Rocky hasn't done her hair yet.'

I give her fleshy arm a little squeeze.

'Call her now and say I want to speak with her.'

She hesitates, staring at the mobile as if it's the trigger for a nuclear holocaust.

'Can't we do a meeting Thursday instead? She's tied up tomorrow, but...'

I shake my head. 'I can't do Thursday, Mary Anne. I have wall-to-wall meetings all day.'

Rachel flashes her blue eyes at me with the word WARNING emblazoned on them. I watch as Mary Anne, a film of perspiration on her top lip, makes the call. With a trembling hand she passes me the mobile.

'I'm afraid it's out of the question that we meet today.' Dannie's tone is surly.

'That's absolutely fine, Dannie. As you can't rearrange until Thursday and I'm busy all day, we'll wait till you're next over.'

There's a pause. 'But we urgently need to discuss the product launch at Conran. You'll have to change your meetings.'

'Sorry, Dannie, no can do. It's been difficult enough setting them up as it is.'

'You consider your schedule more important than mine?'

'Not at all, but like you I too have commitments.'

'But I'm not even dressed.'

'You're not leaving your room so does it really matter?'

Mary Anne is gawping at me with large, fear crazed eyes. I return the mobile to her.

'Oh my Gad. What did she say?'

'To come on up.'

Dannie greets us in a jade silk kimono and with her hair swept up in a towel. She is wearing big Chanel shades and there is a crimson sheen to her lips. Balancing a tortoiseshell cigarette holder between jewel-encrusted fingers, she ushers us in to her two room suite. The walls are salmon pink and the large windows, draped in crimson tartan, open out onto views of Hyde Park. On the walls are elegant framed pastel prints and vases of fresh flowers have been placed on occasional tables and on the dark mahogany desk. There are alcoves on either side of the window from which two white, stone figures gaze wistfully at the floral carpet. Beyond the salon, a door hints at the bedroom beyond, but all I can see is the corner of a gilt mirror and a soft green and rose patterned rug.

Dannie slams the window shut and shivers.

'It's awfully cramped in here. Mary Anne failed to book my normal rooms.'

Rachel gives a cheery smile. 'Oh, it'll be fine for our meeting.'

'That's the least of my concerns,' she snaps.

I ignore the sullen demeanour and sit with a business-like air on one of the crimson sofas. In front of me is a long mahogany coffee table on which are piled various glossy publications and a clutter of cups. Dannie follows my gaze and glares at her assistant.

'Get those cups cleared and order coffee and almonds.'

Mary Anne obediently scuttles over to the internal phone while Dannie collapses onto a comfy armchair and studies me for a few seconds, a thin smile playing on her lips. 'Do you play chess?'

'Not unless I have to.'

'You like card games?'

'They bore me to tears.'

She draws deeply on her cigarette. 'Russian roulette, perhaps?'

'Only on Fridays.'

Dannie throws her head back and laughs. 'What do you make of this?'

She plucks a newspaper clipping off the armrest of her chair and flings it towards me. I catch it mid-air, noting that it's the *New York Times* piece that Mary Anne forewarned me of. There's a photo of Dannie in a svelte black suit, her legs like long, thin liquorice sticks in dark tights, resting on the shiny desk in front of her. On the far wall is a portrait of Dannie and George Bush smiling together. The article headline reads: THE DEVIL WEARS CHANEL? I read on. It's a feisty feature, on the surface admiring of Dannie's business and charitable achievements, but underneath damning about her diva persona, lavish lifestyle, acrimonious divorce from a well-known senator some years ago and the terse treatment of her entourage.

There's a knock at the door and room service arrives. Mary Anne clears the table and pours everyone coffee. I notice she has ordered a huge plate of biscuits. A bowl of salted almonds have been placed in front of Dannie.

I hand the newspaper cutting back to her.

'This Sarah Harper certainly doesn't hold back.'

'She's a bitch. A pathetic, sniping little reporter devoured by envy and greed. They're all the same.'

I feel myself frown. 'Would you say that about Frankie Symons?'

'Of course not, dear. What she wrote about me in *The Telegraph* was the stuff of dreams. But she's a one-off. The rest are a pack of grubby rats out to ruin lives.'

Rachel chokes on the coffee that Mary Anne has offered her. 'Steady on, Dannie! Most of my friends are in the media.'

She gives her a crisp smile. 'I'm sure you avoid the savages, Rachel.'

Mary Anne chomps nervously on her biscuit and gets out a stack of files. I see her reach for another chocolate morsel which she quickly devours before clearing her throat. Absent-mindedly, she brushes biscuit crumbs from her lips which settle on her notepad. She waves her ballpoint in the air.

'OK everyone, let's get down to work. Now…'

Dannie glowers at her. 'Stop!'

She removes her glasses for a second and peers into Mary Anne's face. 'Haven't I told you to wax your moustache?'

Rachel's eyes pop out. I study my file intently.

'I've been too busy, Dannie.' Mary Anne is crimson.

The glasses are back on. 'Fix it today. You know I cannot abide body hair.'

Shakily, Mary Anne picks up her notes, swallows hard and reconvenes the meeting.

Wednesday 6 p.m., H Hotel, Mayfair

It's the weekly guest cocktail event at H Hotel Mayfair. Jennifer Griffin, the eccentric and wacky executive manager is stalking around the lounge chivvying staff to get everything ready before the first arrivals. We have had our meeting and now she has persuaded me to stay for a glass of champagne and sweet talk some of her guests. Apparently, her deputy's off sick and the marketing manager is on business in Sweden so my support is needed.

'They're usually deadly dull, darling. Do hang about.'

I stand on the whitewashed floor boards, glass in hand, examining some of the weird abstract paintings adorning the walls. The furniture is minimal and black and the slate grey walls give the place a moody atmosphere beloved of pop stars and Hollywood A-listers. Jennifer is drawing frantically at a cigarette.

'I thought this was a non-smoking lounge?'

'Oh is it? Thanks for telling me,' she grins, defiantly wafting smoke in the air. A receptionist hurtles through the swing doors.

'I'm afraid we have a situation, Miss Griffin.'

Jennifer smiles serenely and follows her out of the lounge to the reception. Several guests arrive by the same doors and are offered cocktails by the attendant waiters. Slightly awkwardly, I go to greet them, jabbering animatedly about the wonderful attractions London has to offer, and about the hotel and its services. A large Texan observes me with a dark smile.

'Forgive me, but my wife says the drapes in this hotel are a disgrace. Have you seen how dirty they are?'

'Well, I can't say I've examined them too carefully, but…'

'You do work here, don't you?' he booms.

Jennifer is back, a look of controlled panic on her face. 'Ah, there you are,' she gushes, prodding my arm. 'I have a little problem to deal with upstairs so could you hold the fort for a while?'

I'm about to reply when the Texan interrupts. 'Are you the manager?'

She introduces herself and gives him a winning handshake. 'Mr Herbert, isn't it? So lovely to meet you. I'd love to talk, but I have a teeny problem to sort out and then I'll be right back.'

He nods his head. 'That's fine by me, but later my wife would like to talk to you about the terrible state of the drapes in the hotel.'

Jennifer claps her hands together. 'That's marvellous, because this is Jane Kirby, our housekeeper.'

She pushes me towards him and rushes off.

'Why, you little cheat,' he guffaws. 'Giving yourself another name when we met! Boy oh boy, my wife's gonna take you to task. Here she comes now…'

I turn round, miserably acknowledging a vast trifle of a woman in red and yellow descending upon us. The huge jelly breasts wobble threateningly, and the hips, like lumpy custard, bulge inside the tight yellow satin skirt.

Some nightmarish minutes later, having promised to replace every drape in the entire hotel, I manage to extricate myself from the throng and head for the reception area. A siren is whining close by and a cluster of lugubrious staff are hanging around the dark lobby.

'What the hell's going on?' I demand of one of the concierges.

He beckons me closer, sweeping the room with his eyes before running a forefinger across his throat.

'Someone's done himself in. Room 208.'

'Oh my gosh,' I mumble. 'Is he still alive?'

'Course he's bloody not. It's a bloodbath up there. We'll have to drag him down the staff stairs. Heavy bugger too.'

He yawns and flicks idly at a copy of *The Sun*.

'You haven't seen the body, have you?'

He clicks his teeth. 'I was the one that found him. He never picked up his theatre tickets yesterday so I went up there myself. Had a funny feeling about him.'

'How awful for you.'

'You get used to it. We've had four this year. Pill poppers are the easiest, no mess, see?'

I return to the lounge and practically into the arms of the fat Texan diva. She dives at me with fury. 'You don't deserve your job, young lady! Look at the chandelier. I am astounded.'

A hush descends on the room. Waiters clutch protectively at their drink trays, their mouths down-turned like Pierrot half moons of dismay as they raise their eyes to the ceiling. In a daze I glimpse up at the ultra-modern light creation at the centre of the room. Like a skilful trapeze artist, a plump grey mouse is ascending the electric cable which links the light to the ceiling rose, its long, thin tail curling like ivy around the flex. I face the smouldering eyes of the Texan woman, and the rest of the subdued hotel guests.

'Well, what do you have to say for yourself?'

I shrug helplessly. As the housekeeper manqué what should I say? Suddenly a hand grips my arm. Jennifer has slipped into the room and is all smiles.

'Ah! There's Harold! I thought I'd lost him,' she trills.

'Who's Harold?' barks the Texan trifle.

'My pet mouse. Thank you so much for finding him. He escaped from his cage this morning.'

'You are kidding?' scoffs fat Mr Herbert.

'Not at all. He's the H Hotel mascot as in H for Harold?'

The trifle is speechless as is the entire wide-eyed company. Her obese husband gawps up at the pirouetting rodent and then at Jennifer.

'Blow me down,' he whispers. 'You English really are crazy sons of bitches!'

Swooping on two glasses of bubbly, I pass one to Jennifer and give her a knowing smile.

'Well, I suppose the only problem now is how to get the little darling down.'

Thursday 1.30 p.m., The Cavendish Hotel, Jermyn Street
Ed pushes his plate away from him and lies back on the deep plush sofa.

'That Club sandwich was divine. I could almost eat another.'

'Ed! Don't be a pig.'

He reaches into his MEK and takes out some small white pills.

'For my heart,' he says thinly, as he knocks them back with the remains of his water glass. 'So you think this trip to New York will be OK?'

'I think it's fantastic that Charlene has fixed up the trip for when I'm over.'

'Isn't November treacherously cold in Manhattan?' he whines.

'Oh, don't be a wimp. You'll have a great time.'

'I'm looking forward to seeing you run in the marathon,' he admits, and then, as an afterthought, 'Although I don't like crowds so we'll have to play it by ear.'

'If you're very good I might get you an invite for Greedy George's Pet Parade. It's going to be a huge media sensation in Bryant Park.'

He coughs frantically. 'With my cat allergy, that's the last place I'd want to be. The whole idea's insane. It could only happen in the States.'

'Spoilsport. Perhaps I can lure you to H Hotel's launch party in Tribeca instead?'

'Maybe,' he concedes. 'Tribeca's supposed to be very trendy, isn't it? Charlene would enjoy that.'

I flick my watch towards me and realise that I should be heading off.

'Well, cat duty calls.'

He lowers his head in seeming despair and grasping his MEK, stands up. 'Don't blame me if it's a nightmare.'

'It's going to be fun. I've never visited a cattery before.'

We descend the stairs and push through the hotel's glass doors into sharp sunlight.

He stands on the pavement looking glum. 'Actually, I bought you a little something to cheer you up while you're there.'

He fumbles around in the MEK and produces a plastic bag from WHSmith's which he hands to me.

'Go on, open it.'

I draw out the slim tome. The cover illustration is of a prostrate female lying on the ground. The title reads: *When Things Fall Apart*.

'That's great, Ed. I'm sure it'll prove excellent bed-time reading.'

He gives me an earnest nod of the head and together we head off along Jermyn Street.

4 p.m., on the train to Dorset
Rachel's voice sounds scratchy and she's speaking so fast that I miss half of what she's saying.

'Rachel, I can't hear you. Slow down.'

'Isn't it fantastic?'

'What is? Let me guess: you're calling with some good news?'

She doesn't trace the irony in my tone.

'Prince Charles is going to attend the launch of the Crown jewels book at the Tower of London.'

I catch my breath. This genuinely is fantastic news.

'They've just called from The Stationery Office. We'll obviously have to amend plans somewhat, but it's so exciting.'

The book launch is still four months away, but there is a great amount of logistics involved, especially now there will be royal presence.

'It's wonderful, Rachel. Thanks for letting me know.'

'Just think, if we pull this off well, the work will really flood in. You won't have time to dwell on wretched moggies anymore.'

If she only knew the truth. If we successfully pull off this project I may at last feel able to cut loose the ties of London and, in the spirit of departing politicians, spend more time with my family and of course other exceptional animals.

TWELVE

A CAT CALLED ZACK

5.30 p.m., The Cat's Whiskers, rural Dorset
There's a light drizzle of rain falling on the quiet country lane. The lush green hedgerows are full of wild flowers and tall weeds, dock leaves and nettles, reminding me that this is the rural England of my childhood. I am standing outside a substantial red brick manor house, watching the departing taxi dissolve in a mist of rain. There's no going back.

I look up and down the road. There isn't a soul in sight and apart from the rather shabby manor house peeping up from beyond extensive foliage, there's nothing but swaying trees, fields of skittish lambs and rolling countryside. Grasping my suitcase by the handle, I wheel it over to the black iron gate on which a perfunctory wooden sign announces that I have arrived at Grove House and The Cat's Whiskers. It doesn't mention the word cattery but perhaps that's self evident. I peer through the dusty railings to the gravel drive and courtyard beyond. The gate wheezes as I drag it open and make my cumbersome way over the gravel, the wheels of my case stubbornly buckling against the small stones. No sooner am I half way up the drive than a gigantic Dobermann comes hurtling towards me as if from nowhere, teeth bared and growling ferociously. I stop in my tracks, foolishly considering running for my life, although secretly acknowledging that the beast would be upon me before I'd even reached the gate. There's nothing for it. I stand my ground and attempt to muster an ounce of dignity before facing my adversary. For a split second the hound draws to a halt, tongue hanging from its jaw, as it sizes me up. Then with a sudden gallop, it leaps up with powerful front legs resting on my shoulders and begins licking my face. I stagger backwards, tripping on my case and muttering 'Good dog' inanely to the rain. A rosy faced, burly chap in old corduroys and wellies now appears on the drive, squelching through the gravel and grinning from ear to ear.

'Ah, you've met Beauty then? Come on, girl!'

The dog drops its paws and stands panting by my side.

'I think she mistook me for a bone.'

'Yeah, she's a right little bugger with guests, but she's as harmless as a fly.'

Try telling that to my Scotsman when I'm found mauled to bits in a ditch. I smile politely.

'I'm here for the cattery management course.'

'Sure you are. Let me take your case. I'm Willie Patterson, the glorified odd job man around here since I retired. My wife, Jessie, runs the cattery.'

I offer him my hand and pat the dog a trifle self-consciously. Willie stretches forward and effortlessly lifts the case off the ground, his eyes resting on my suit and then shoes. He gives a little titter.

'I hope you've packed some better kit than that because you'll get well and truly mucked up while you're here.'

Oh shucks, if only I'd known! As a dizzy PR all I've packed are a couple of ball gowns, some four-inch heels and a bottle of Evian. He waits for a response.

'Don't worry,' I say reassuringly. 'I had some business meetings earlier in London. I've got jeans with me.'

He gives a slight nod and walks jauntily back up the drive to the courtyard, the dog and I following in his wake. We enter the house by what appears to be the back door. A narrow scullery leads into a rustic kitchen, with an old cooking range and suspended iron hoop from which copper pans dangle, and beyond that a small dining room and long bright hallway.

'I'll show you to your room and then you can meet Jessie. She's looking forward to showing you the ropes.'

Yippee. I follow him up the creaky oak staircase and into a small room with buttercup yellow walls and blinds. The windows are wide open and the sound of loud baa-ing seems to echo around the gardens. I wonder if there are any escapologist ewes amongst them. Willie drops the case at the foot of the brass bed.

'Don't worry about the lambs. They just get a bit excited in the rain. Normally, they hardly make a sound.'

He potters over to the window, hands on hips, peering at the blur of green beyond.

'The bathroom's down the corridor,' he says dreamily. 'I'll see you in the kitchen in a few minutes.'

He plods off, closing the door behind him.

Some neatly folded yellow towels are piled on the bed along with a plump and efficient looking folder entitled, 'PRELIMINARY TRAINING COURSE'. Oh boy, what have I let myself in for?

9 p.m., dinner
'So you see, it all worked out in the end,' Jessie is saying, as she begins clearing away the plates. I watch as she loads a tray and disappears into the nearby kitchen. I find myself captivated by

the story of how she and Willie came to own a cattery. Having run a successful furniture business in Sunderland for many years, this intrepid couple decided to retire, up sticks and run The Cat's Whiskers from a new home in Dorset. They had a nightmare with planning permission but persevered and after a two-year battle with local authorities finally gained a licence. Jessie admitted that at times she'd nearly thrown in the towel.

I pick up a tureen, observing that only a few forlorn florets of broccoli remain at the bottom, and attempt to follow her into the kitchen.

'Oh, you stay put. It's enough with the blooming cats getting under my feet in there!'

I sink back into my chair. There's no standing on ceremony in this household.

'The thing is,' says Willie with a cynical grunt. 'I was never keen on the idea. Seemed like a lot of work to me.'

'He's a dog man, you see,' cuts in his wife.

'As I was saying,' he continues a tad impatiently. 'I thought it would be a lot of hard work for little return.'

'And was it?' I ask.

He passes his napkin over his face and slowly returns it to the table, folding it into a neat triangle. I wonder why he does this when, judging by the dessert spoons in front of us, we still have pudding to come. A ghost of a smile plays on his lips.

'Too darned right it was.'

His wife bustles back into the room carrying a crusty pie and a jug of cream.

She eyes her husband critically. 'The truth is that when I was growing up in Wales my old mum ran her own cattery and kennels so I knew what I was in for. It doesn't make you rich but it does keep you busy and that's good when you retire.'

Willie stares at his napkin with renewed interest and places it on his lap.

'Jessie's just potty about felines. Besotted.'

'It's true,' she concedes. 'The cats are our family. We don't have kids.'

A pause. 'I like dogs, mind, but they're not the same.'

'You always know where you are with a dog,' says Willie firmly.

'I'm sure,' I say, for want of anything insightful to add.

I watch as Jessie cuts into the steaming pie, placing hefty slices onto dainty floral dishes which she passes to us. It smells heavenly.

'Apple pie! That was one of my grandparents' treats when I used to visit them in Carmarthen. I love it.'

Jessie rests her gaze on me briefly. 'Well, you can't be all bad if you've got Welsh blood.'

'Actually, some Irish and Scottish too,' I counter.

'Oh, heaven help us!' mumbles Willie, dolloping thick cream onto his pudding.

'So, why do you want to open a cattery then?' He observes me with his rheumy blue eyes.

'I love cats and I've adopted countless ferals.'

'That's fine if you want to be Mother Teresa of the cat world but if you want to earn a living...'

'Give her a chance to speak, Willie,' hisses Jessie.

'I'd like to create the sort of cattery that I'd want to put my own cat in. A small oasis for cat owners who loves their pets. I'm not looking to make it my main income. More a hobby.'

Willie clicks his teeth. 'We'll knock all that rubbish out of you tomorrow!'

His wife gives a little giggle. 'Leave her be. The truth is, love, that it's no picnic, so you really need to be sure you're doing the right thing.'

Willie finishes his apple pie and licks his lips.

'You'll find out soon enough. If I were you, I'd get yourself plenty of sleep tonight.'

Ominous words. I offer to help wash up but Jessie's having none of it. She shoos me away from the table and so, wishing them both good night, I make my way upstairs to the bedroom.

'Remember, six o'clock sharp tomorrow morning,' Willie calls after me. 'And make sure you're wearing some decent clobber.'

Thursday 12 a.m., in bed

The laptop is purring like a contented cat, its screen basking in the bright rays cast by the bedside lamp as I tap away. Sitting cross-legged on the bed with a pile of pillows pressing against my back, I give a heavy yawn and decide to call it a day. Somehow I've managed to edit three press releases and put the finishing touches to a detailed planning document for the Crown jewels event. That'll keep Rachel off my back. I shut down the computer and rub my eyes. According to the energetic Jessie, we'll be cleaning out litter trays and doing the breakfast round very early so I must get some kip. A lorry rumbles by in the distance as I plod across the room and dump the laptop on the desk. Outside it is eerily silent and dark. There's not the braying of a donkey or the tinkling bell of a mountain sheep to be heard, and why would there be? Mallorca seems a million miles away from this picture of English rural bliss. Even the air smells different. I shiver with the chill and, turning off the bedside lamp, snuggle under the covers, my mind swivelling back to the curious evening just spent in Jessie and Willie's company. It's a pity Alan isn't with me. He'd have hit it off immediately with Willie and enjoyed his remarks about my Mother Teresa pretensions in the valley. The Scotsman is exasperated by the growing number of scraggy moggies hanging about our land and largely blames this phenomenon on Ollie and me for sneakily feeding them when he's not looking. Much as we hotly deny the accusation, he regularly stumbles across empty feeding bowls in the long grass so that our guilt is self-evident. Just recalling his recent outburst when a clumsy feral cat crash-landed on his shoulder from a lemon tree has me giggling. And that's how I fall asleep, laughing. A good thing, because I have a feeling it will be my two hosts, Willie and Jessie, who'll be having the last laugh over the next few days.

Friday, The Cat's Whiskers

I am installed in my blue work overalls at The Cat's Whiskers, a vast wooden outhouse with a corrugated iron roof situated in the field beyond the main house. This exclusive cat hotel consists of a small office and twenty indoor suites which run in a vertical line on one side of a long central concrete corridor, each one being capable of housing two or more cats. On the other side of the corridor is a low concrete wall above which is fine wire meshing, allowing gusts of cold air to infiltrate the building. The suites themselves are meshed on two sides for greater air ventilation and each has a cosy, heated sleeping zone tucked away at its rear and a sizeable exercise run for stretching the legs and paws. A bolted, wire-meshed door ensures the captive is kept in and any unwelcome visitors out. I am told that in a separate stone clad annexe in the garden are some large and luxurious duplexes for cat families and Dietrich diva moggies who *von- to- be- a- lawn* and whose owners are willing to pay for the privilege. The duplexes have special names such as Fishy Hall, Tuna Towers and Garfield Gables. According to Jessie, many cat owners fight for their chosen suites and book months, sometimes years, ahead. And I thought I was one cent short of a euro!

At six this morning Jessie shoved a cup of tea into my hands outside the bedroom door and told me where to find breakfast items in the kitchen. At that ungodly hour, prolonged sleep rather than breakfast was on my mind so I followed her like a sleepwalker out into the cool garden and through a wooden gate into the field where a path led up to the office of The Cat's Whiskers. Once there I had been swiftly delivered into the care of Emily, one of the cheery, young cattery assistants, while Jessie beat a hasty retreat back down the path. I had been given a nylon overall and set to work.

First of all we prepared cat food and fresh water for each of the sixty pampered inmates. And don't let's for one second think they all ate the same grub. Not a bit of it. Some felines liked dry pellets, others wet food, some a mix of the two. Then there were the fat cats on diets, the sickly ones on special medical regimes and the prima donnas who only ate fresh fish or chicken. Last but not least, in a league of his own, was Zack the Korat. This spitting bundle of fun only consumed lightly cooked tuna and a costly dried seaweed supplement. When I asked for an explanation, Emily just rolled her eyes and smiled indulgently. 'He's an actor, bless him!'

And she wasn't being ironic.

Having delivered food to all the feline guests by seven o'clock, Emily asked me to tag along with her for the next task, which was cleaning out the dirty litter trays. A treat was in store! If I ever thought my own cats made a mess with their litter, this lot could teach them a trick or two. Now, some cats were considerate, just as you'd find with the ideal guest at a hotel who folds back his bed covers neatly and doesn't leave toothpaste all over the sink, or loo paper streamers on the floor. These moggies did their business in their tray, covered it over with gravel and didn't leave a trail of devastation in their wake. Unfortunately, this wasn't the case with Marvin the Manx. His concrete run appeared to have been hit by a snow storm and tornado at precisely the same moment. Tiny fragments of white litter were sprayed all over the floor, in the water and food dishes and, in his tortoiseshell pelt, he'd even trailed it back into his basket. Squeaky rubber toys were strewn everywhere and he'd peed in a corner of the run. Emily had waggled a finger at him and then cheerfully offered to let me clear it all up.

'You're too kind,' I said.

'No bother,' she replied sweetly.

She had held him lovingly in her arms. 'You know they say that the Manx cat was the last animal to get on the Ark and when Noah shut the door too fast, its tail snapped off.'

I looked at the tail-less cat thoughtfully. 'Anything's possible, Emily. And what about the reason why the tails of Siamese cats curl upwards? The story goes it's because the Queen of Siam used to keep a precious ring on her pet Siamese's tail.'

She gave a little frown. 'Is that true?'

'Why not ask one of your Siamese inmates?'

'I might just do that,' she said.

By the time duty calls for the hosing down of a run in preparation for an incoming guest, I'm not in the best of humour. I've been on my feet for two hours and I'm beginning to wonder what a girl has to do to get a tea break around here. According to Emily, we don't break until eleven o'clock. On the dot. Inside the rubber gloves my hands are numb with cold as I fumble about with a mop and soapy water in the vacated cat run. My nylon overalls make a swishy sound every time I move, in much the same way, I imagine, as the crisp satin of a ballroom dress might do during a waltz. Having a ball I may be, but at a ball I am not. Emily issues instructions.

'That's right. Give it a good clean. Ooh! You've missed a bit over there.'

Well, of course I've missed a bit over there. It's hellishly cold and I'm in desperate need of a cup of warming tea. Does it really matter? As if she's read my thoughts, Emily folds her arms and views me sternly.

'Hygiene is really important in a cattery. It's the number one golden rule.'

'So you keep telling me.'

She drums a finger against her cheek. 'When I trained I found that KITTEN helped me. It goes, "Keep It Tidy, Totally Efficient and Neat".'

'A mnemonic,' I say gruffly.

She gives a little shrug. 'Whatever.'

I slop the mop over the area I've missed.

'That's better. Now, go and swill out the bucket and get going with the hosing. You remember how I did it?'

Does the girl think I'm a complete fool? I mean, how difficult is it to hose down a near empty space? She made it look simple enough.

I drag the green hose over to the run under Emily's steady gaze.

'Where's Jessie?' I say a tad impatiently. 'I was rather hoping we could go through some admin aspects of the job.'

'All in good time,' she beams, removing a soapy rubber glove to brush a stray blonde tendril back behind her ear. 'First of all, it's best to get to grips with the physical work.'

Harrumph. That's put me in my box. I go in search of the tap, dropping the hose on the floor. It spasms for a brief moment like a snake caught in its last death throes and then lies still.

'Hang on,' calls Emily. 'Where are you off to? Remember, all you have to do is pull the switch on the hose itself. You don't need to turn the tap.'

That'll teach me for not paying attention. I bend down to grab the hose and pull back the small lever at the nozzle.

I hear a strange gurgling sound but no water emerges. I wait. Emily is momentarily distracted by a call for help from her co-worker, Dawn, a sturdy lass with dark curly hair who is grooming a cat a few doors down. All I can see through the thick meshing of the various runs are her flailing arms. I wonder if she's being devoured by some psycho feline.

'Just a moment,' Emily says to me and strides out of the run. Impatiently I tap the hose on the concrete floor and closely study the errant nozzle. And then, in the best traditions of Laurel and Hardy, a fierce jet of freezing water squirts straight in my eye, splashes my face and drenches my overall. I give an involuntary shriek and drop the hose, allowing water to shoot all over the run and through the wire meshing. By the time I've taken control of it, Emily is back to see cascades of water pouring down the central corridor. She shakes her head. 'Deary me. What are you doing?'

I'm sopping wet and ice-cold. 'The stupid hose doesn't work,' I spit.

'That's not what it looks like to me.' Her eyes scan the puddles of water forming in the run.

'Well, we'd better mop up this mess.'

Miserably, I begin squeezing out the mop. She bites her lip, trying to inhibit a rogue grin.

'Go on, hop it,' she sighs. 'Get some dry clothes on and I'll finish off here.'

I falter. 'What was up with Dawn? She was waving her arms about in the air.'

She laughs. 'Oh, she was just wiggling strings for Dixie to catch.'

'Dixie?'

'Yeh, the blue Persian you met this morning. I've just had to help her get an enormous knot out of his hair. He's a right one!'

With what little dignity I can muster I turn tail and head back to the house in drizzling rain, icy water dripping down the back of my neck. In the distance there's a gentle baa-ing of a lamb, and from The Cat's Whiskers office the unmistakable sound of gales of laughter.

Saturday, pill popping
'It's easy, see? You just hold his head back like this and pop the pill in. Then you stroke his throat and it's gone.'

Emily calmly releases the struggling Persian and strokes his fur. He hisses at her and moodily saunters off to his refuge, a dark and cosy den with a cat flap, at the end of his run.

'We've got to give some pills to Zack later so you can have a go if you like?'

No thanks, I'll leave you to enjoy that mauling, Emily, my sweet. Zack, I have quickly discovered, is the original Exorcist cat. I haven't seen his head swivel yet, but it's only a matter of time.

'OK,' I hear myself say in a weak voice.

I can't believe it's only day two because it already feels as though I've been here a month. At six this morning, the bustling and energetic Jessie knocked on my door with a cup of tea and half an hour later Dawn and I were on the gravy train handing out food and water to all the inmates while Emily did the litter trays. We cleaned out the runs together and then got a fat tabby ready to be reunited with his owners, collecting his toys and blanket and unearthing his basket from the store cupboard. Visitors seemed to come and go throughout the day either delivering or collecting moggies and the telephone in the office rang incessantly. I managed to snatch a bite for lunch but I haven't stopped since.

'Great news!'

My senses are alert. I turn my head, half expecting it to be Rachel from my office, inventor of the 'great news' bugle, but it is Jessie. She is beckoning to me from the office door, her voice booming up the corridor.

'The vet's come to give some injections. I thought you'd like to watch.'

Emily gives me an encouraging smile. 'Gosh, that's good timing. It's your lucky day.'

I plod past her, too fatigued even for a witty riposte.

Monday, the great escape

Emily and I put clean water and a food bowl down in the run.

'So, did you have a nice day yesterday?' she asks.

'It was great to have some time off if that's what you mean. We did the feeds and cleaning out in the morning and then I had the afternoon free to sleep.'

She laughs. 'Oh, come on. You can't be that tired. I'm up at five every day, even Sundays.'

'Well, you're obviously completely mad.'

'No, I just like to make the most of the day.'

I gather up a sweeping brush and mop just as Dawn, in baggy blue overalls, arrives outside the run flipping a clump of mail about in the air.

'Got some post for you, Dribbly Dibbly.'

The object of her gushy overtures is the elegant, smoky hued Siamese now sitting disdainfully in his private den.

She looks at us through the wire meshing.

'Where's Dibbly boy?'

'Sulking in the back,' says Emily flatly.

'Oh shame! He's got a letter from the Lamberts, his owners, and a lovely postcard from Marrakech.'

I snigger. 'Is the card from the King of the Berbers?'

She examines the text. 'Nah, I think it's from the Lamberts' daughter, Cristobel.'

She leans in closer. 'I'll read them to him later. All right?'

I watch her potter off, swaying her hips and humming, 'What's New Pussycat?' to whichever long-suffering, incarcerated feline will listen.

Emily pushes her fair locks back with a rubber-gloved hand.

'Right, can I leave you to grooming duties in suites one to ten and then we'll do some admin and booking in of new clients together?'

I give a confident nod, already dreading the moment when I will arrive at suite ten, home of Zack the Korat. I've tried to make this silver blue menace more endearing by nicknaming him Borat the Korat, but it makes no difference. He's an evil bugger bent on vengeance and is in desperate need of a good psychotherapist. Motherly and good-hearted Jessie has given me the sob story – broken home, abusive parents, victim of a hit and run and near poisoning with Warfarin by a careless farmer, but I'm losing sympathy. A cat called 'It' he may be, but he doesn't do himself any favours. Twice he's lashed out when I've tried to clean his run and he bares his teeth and spits through his netting at the cattery old faithfuls. Despite my misgivings, Zack is held in high esteem by Jessie and the rest of the staff who lavish him with cuddles and grooming sessions. His owner is a famous British comedian and Zack is a star in his own right, having appeared in several TV series, and is soon to hit the big time auditioning for modelling and acting roles in LA and New York. Maybe if I offer him a bit of PR coaching he might change his attitude. I mean, we are both in the media business after all.

I methodically do my rounds, making sure to lock the door of each cat run behind me to avoid escapees. I have been assured by Jessie that should a cat give me the slip it wouldn't get very far given the tight circle of security in and around the building, but I'm taking no chances. A fat Burmese named Basil, ward of a London-based ambassador, yawns when I enter his run and rolls onto his back for a tummy tickle. Arnie the Abyssinian in suite seven, who arrived at the cattery two days ago in a chauffeur-driven limo all to himself, claws the mesh of his run with excitement when he sees me appear with his grooming brush, and as for Biscuit, the sybaritic ragdoll, we are the best of chums. At least he just sleeps all day, purring loudly (a sign of genuine appreciation) with every stroke of the brush.

Fastening the door of run nine behind me, I stare into Zack's pit, suite ten. He gives me a grimace and sinister, amber light radiates from his eyes as he sees me unbolt the door. With trepidation, I enter the narrow cell and am on the point of shutting the door behind me when without warning he flies through the air and lands on my neck with claws unleashed. I give a yowl loud enough to freeze the blood in my own veins. Neatly propelling himself off my head, Zack races out of the run like a bit part in a cop drama. Actors! I feel blood on my neck and scalp, but there's no time to have a diva moment. I rush after him down the corridor but, like a silver streak, he turns at the corner and begins scaling a set of high metal shelves. He scowls down at me, hissing furiously, his eyes now flashing a vivid jade green. Emily and Dawn have already heard the commotion and calmly enter the fray from the adjoining office, shooing me out of the way and standing by the shelf in reasoning mode like a pair of suicide counsellors.

'Come down, Zack,' says Dawn in soothing tones. 'No one's going to hurt you, sweetheart.'

He gives her a wary scowl, but I notice he's stopped spitting.

'We love you, Zack,' coos Emily. 'You're such a brave boy.'

I stand by the wall, redundant, like an inept social worker. Dawn has donned leather gloves and now reaches up to Zack. He scratches at her, but on the third attempt begrudgingly accepts her embrace.

'There, there, pet,' she croons, gently taking him back to his run and settling him in his basket.

Like a guilty school pupil, I follow Emily into the outer office. She rounds on me coldly.

'Didn't I warn you about leaving doors open?'

'It happened in a flash.'

She raises her eyebrows and nods slowly but is evidently disappointed.

'I'm afraid Jessie won't be pleased. She's very specific about security.'

I feel my hackles rise. 'He didn't get very far though, little psycho.'

She gives a loud tut. 'Actually, he's a highly talented and intelligent cat. When you gain his trust, he's a darling. His owner says he's in constant demand for TV work. Mark my word, it won't be long before he gets a Hollywood contract.'

'You mean in a Hammer Horror?'

Perhaps unwisely, I continue in goonish mode.

'That's right folks. Zack is back. He's dark, dangerous, deranged and he's in a cattery near you. Be afraid. Be very AFRAID!'

She doesn't smile. Instead she frowns at the dried blood on my neck and arms.

'You'd better clear up those wounds. It's a hygiene risk.'

'Give me a break,' I mutter.

Truculently, I open the first aid drawer and with some cotton wool dab a liberal amount of Dettol on my cuts. She gives me a sarcastic little smile.

'Well, if you thought running a cattery was a piece of cake, you'd better think again.'

Tuesday afternoon, sick as a cat

Jessie and I have just returned from the vet with a pair of sick kittens. They only arrived late the night before but have become increasingly poorly, throwing up their food and showing signs of listlessness. Jessie was taking no chances so immediately put them in an isolated run in the field away from the other healthy felines and booked to see the vet during the afternoon. Like her shadow I accompanied her in the car and helped carry one of the cat baskets into the surgery.

'New assistant?' beamed the nurse.

'She's a trainee,' said Jessie.

'Oh, well you've picked one of the best catteries. Having fun?'

I had thrown her an indulgent smile, thinking back to the vomit I had been cleaning up for the best part of the morning.

'A thrill a minute,' I replied.

The good news, the vet informed us, was that both cats appeared to have minor stomach upsets but were otherwise in fine form and apparently needed only rest, a 24-hour fast followed by a bland diet. We drove them back to the cattery in some relief.

Dawn bustles into the office as Jessie and I take off our jackets and slump into chairs.

'The kettle's just boiled. Everything OK with the kittens?'

'Yes, love,' says Jessie. 'Nothing untoward. Still, better safe than sorry.'

Dawn ambles over to the kettle and makes a pot of tea. 'Oh, by the way, that strange woman from London's coming in half an hour.'

Jessie turns to me. 'Now, this lady hasn't been to us before. She's got a Scottish Fold.'

'A what?'

'They're lovely cats. They have special ears.'

'In what way?'

'They're squashed flat, as if they're folded.'

Dawn slaps a mug of tea and a digestive biscuit down on the small table in front of me. Jessie reaches over and taps my knee conspiratorially.

'Between you and me, the owner sounded a bit neurotic when she rang so it might be interesting for you to meet her.'

In heaven's name, why? I've got enough neurotic clients of my own to last me a lifetime.

'Yeah, you've only met nice clients so far. It's good to know how to handle the difficult ones,' says Dawn. 'Jessie's got an appointment with a supplier so you and I can handle this woman together.'

'It takes all sorts,' murmurs Jessie, taking a sip of tea.

I take a bite of my biscuit, wondering what this client and her special-eared cat are going to be like. Forty-five minutes later I

A CAT CALLED ZACK

find out. The office doorbell rings and Dawn gives me a warning wink. She puts on her best smile and swings open the door.

'Ah, good afternoon, Mrs Buckley. We were expecting you.'

A middle-aged female as thin as a twizzle stick with peroxide blonde hair and perma-tanned skin barges in, tottering on towering stilettos. Her eyes blaze.

'The traffic was horrendous and this place is simply impossible to find! The directions were dreadful.'

She accentuates the vowels and rolls her 'r's in a clumsy attempt to sound grand. I wonder whether she's an actress. She shakes her long mane and after what appears to be a pause for effect, says, 'The Duke of Marlborough's in the boot.'

Dawn's brow buckles slightly. 'Erm... sorry, who?'

'It will probably take three of us,' Mrs Buckley rattles on. 'He weighs a ton.'

I shoot Dawn a wary look. Either I'm about to become an accessory to a murder or the woman's a complete fantasist. Either way, police presence might prove reassuring.

'Don't just gawp at me, woman,' she snarls in my direction. 'Hurry up. I haven't got all day. I don't like to keep the Duke waiting.'

I leap up from the seat and fumble for my jacket. I can see the sky is already dredging up some new tears but there's no time to search out an umbrella.

Dawn gives a little cough. 'Excuse me, but if we could just sort out some basic admin here first.'

Mrs Buckley flicks a gloved hand in Dawn's direction. 'I really don't have time for this.'

She drops her black handbag on the desk and begins throwing out various items. 'Here, this is the cash for the Duke's three week stay and these are his vaccination details. Right, let's go. I have a plane to catch tonight.'

She opens the door and sweeps out in her chic camel jacket with Dawn and me following in her wake. Gusts of

203

icy wind and spitting rain hit us as we head off through the field to the front drive. Dawn presses a hand in my back and I turn to see a furious expression on her face. We arrive at the sleek black Range Rover with its personalised number plate of BUCK O1 and watch as Miss Twizzle Stick uses her electronic key fob to release the boot's lock. Inside an enormous cream cat squats in a metal cage. I feel myself gasp. Dawn peers inside.

'I take it this is the Duke?'

'Who else did you think it was? The President of the United Bloody States?'

Dawn frowns. 'There's really no need for that tone, Mrs Buckley.'

I lean in and try to budge the cage.

'Get out of the way,' she hisses at me. 'I know how to slide this out. Here,' she pushes a massive holdall towards me. 'These are his toys and belongings.'

I take the bag while she, assisted by Dawn, removes the Duke from his confinement. He looks up at his owner and lets out a pitiful whine. I can't blame him. We stagger back to the office with the Duke of Marlborough and his bag. Once inside, Dawn rests his cage on the carpet and invites Mrs Buckley to take a seat. Irritably, she shakes her head in dissent and stands with arms folded by the desk. The Duke squats forlornly within his den, eyes darting nervously about him while we remove our soggy jackets.

'Would you like to settle him in?' asks Dawn stiffly.

'That's what I pay you people for, isn't it?' the woman's eyes flash. She is tapping a restless foot against the floor.

I'm beginning to think Daniella Popescu-Miller is a walk in the park.

'What does he weigh?' demands Dawn.

Mrs Buckley pushes an irritable hand through her fair tresses. 'He's perfect.'

'I'm sorry,' Dawn replies firmly. 'He looks significantly overweight to me, which means we'll want to get him checked by our vet.'

'More like you want to extract more money out of me,' she sneers. 'You people are all the same.'

I've had enough. 'That's completely untrue. Perhaps you and the Duke should take your custom elsewhere.'

Mrs Buckley narrows her eyes. 'How dare you! I could have you fired.'

'Actually, she doesn't work here,' says Dawn quickly. 'She's just a visitor.'

The woman is unsettled. 'Why did you carry my bag in from the car then?'

Dawn answers for me. 'She was just being helpful.'

Mrs Buckley sits down on the small sofa, smoothing her tight black skirt over her thighs. I notice that the tips of her stilettos are caked in wet mud. Her shoulders seem to droop and she gives a loud sigh. 'I'm sorry. I've been a bit stressed out of late.'

Dawn nods encouragingly. 'I see. Well, we all have those days.'

She gives us a plaintive look. 'The Duke does like his food.'

'Don't we all,' I exclaim. 'But he looks about to pop.'

Her eyes widen in alarm. 'Poor Dukie. He's my life. If anything should happen to him…' There's a theatrical sniff.

'Let's start from the beginning, shall we, Mrs Buckley?' says Dawn firmly. 'We can check the Duke over and get him on a slimming regime but first I do need to sign him in properly. Now, where's that pen?'

Wednesday 6 p.m.

I'm sitting on the concrete floor in Zack's run. With some irritation he looks up at the sound of a new arrival entering the cattery and gives a low growl. I stroke his ears and he lies back against my stomach in a state of contentment. My hands are covered in scratches, my neck still stiff, but Zack and I have miraculously come to an understanding. I have worn him down with kindness, turned the other cheek, and shown him who is boss. During the last two days I have, with grim determination and against the odds, administered his eye drops, fed him his pills and groomed him, even earning a begrudging nod of approval from young Emily.

Jessie appears at the doorway of the office and smiles.

'Your cab's here.'

I give Zack a final caress of the ears and grip his silky head between my two hands. His large amber eyes bore into my own.

'Now listen old buddy, if you want to have friends, you must make an effort, OK?'

He averts his gaze and gives a yawn. Stretching his long, silver blue body, he curls his paws up to his face as if he's praying.

'I'm serious, Zack. You can't go around mutilating people like some Mad Max doppelganger. It's just not cricket. I know about the past, but you've got to let it go.'

Jessie shakes her head.

'You really are a head case. I thought you'd never make it, but you've proven yourself to be a regular Mowgli.'

I look at her fiery red hair and big robust frame and marvel that she's humoured me for the last week. I've had my own minor diva moments, that's for sure.

'I'm tempted to bring him back to Mallorca with me.'

As I bolt the run and head for the office, she places a broad hand on my shoulder.

'And what did I say about becoming attached to other people's cats?'

'That it's a no-go area.'

'Precisely. Anyway, he's one of my rising stars. His owner makes a mint out of him.'

'It's a crazy old world.'

She gives a husky laugh. 'Well, it's been a tough week, but you've made it.'

'I still haven't tried giving a cat an injection yet.'

'Well, you can practise with a syringe on all those juicy oranges in your field. Then get the nice local vet you told me about to show you how it's done.'

She hands me a certificate, proof that I have undergone my cattery management training. With a degree of satisfaction, I pop it into the side pocket of my case.

'And don't forget,' she says. 'If you want your builder to come and see how we constructed our own cattery, we'd be delighted to put him up.'

'Stefan doesn't speak much English so I'd have to come too and maybe even bring his sister along.'

'The more the merrier – then we can put you all to work on the rounds.'

Willie opens the outer door for me and Emily and Dawn lean forward and both give me a little hug. I step inside the cab and wave as we make a slow retreat down the gravelly drive. I wonder what will become of psychotic Zack, but can only hope that a Hollywood career really does beckon and that one day I'll see my furry friend's name up there in blazing lights.

THIRTEEN

CATALAN FOR BEGINNERS

Sóller's *plaça* is dark save for the yellow haze cast from the dim
street lamps and the soft glow emanating from Cafè Paris and
other bars nestling around the square. Huddled together by
the stone wall of the bandstand a group of teenagers chat and
idly kick at a discarded coke can while thin and mangy cats lie
curled up at the side of the town hall, their eyes ever watchful as
I stride past. It is nearly eight o'clock and I am on my way to my
first free Catalan lesson. Thanks to the goodwill of Sóller town
council, foreign residents are offered complimentary lessons
in the local dialect. The lean, cobbled streets are deserted as I
hurry along. I don't want to be late for the class and I am yet to
find its location within the town's music school. Before long
the silhouette of the school rises before me, a rather fanciful
filigree stone edifice on three floors with a Gaudiesque spire
and row upon row of small windows. Beyond spiky black
railings and a paved yard a set of stone steps lead down to a
glass-fronted, arched door. The wood is scuffed and a dreary
light beckons from within. Pushing it ajar I find myself in a

sparsely decorated hallway from which there are flights of concrete stairs running upwards and downwards. Beyond are thin white corridors peeling off to both right and left. There are no signs or notices so I stand gormlessly at the intersection trying to decide which to take when a cheerful, booming voice greets me.

'You've finally arrived! What kept you?'

The face is round and full of fun, the dark hair razor spiked. Behind thick lenses a pair of chocolate brown eyes sparkle, studying me with some bemusement. It is Guillem, owner of Can Gata restaurant in Calle sa Lluna, who also doubles up as the local Catalan teacher.

'I've had one of those days.' I give him a grimace. 'Don't tell me I'm the last to arrive?'

He chortles merrily. '*Sí*, you are the last, so now you can make a dramatic entrance.'

'I was planning on slithering in, actually.'

'Come on. Let's get cracking!'

I follow him down the corridor and through a labyrinth of classrooms until we reach a small cell in which desks are tightly packed practically one on top of the other. I view the sea of faces, about twenty in all, and with some relief spot Judy, an Australian friend from my Pilates class, who is waving from the back of the room. I squeeze into one of the only available seats near the front of the class next to a smiling woman of about my age. While Guillem busies himself at the blackboard she tells me in Spanish that her name is Jutta and that she is from Germany and can only speak faltering Catalan. I tell her mine is almost non-existent. We giggle in complicity. Guillem now claps his hands together and begins passing round individual folders and books. He tells us that we should each introduce ourselves in Catalan and patiently acts as a guide telling us that *'Jo sóc'* in Catalan or *'Jo som'* in Catalan Mallorcan dialect both mean 'I am' and conjugate from the verb to be, *ésser*. Now, to complicate matters one can't just say, 'I am Frank' or 'I am Jenny' but must add *'en'* or *'na'* in front, hence *'Sóc en Frank'* or *'Sóc na Jenny'*. In the case of a name starting with a vowel such as Anne, it becomes *'Sóc n'Anne'*.

'Qui ets?' he says loudly. Who are you?

'Sóc en Helmut,' bleats his first German victim, a tall blonde man with a deep voice.

'Sóc en Marc,' says the man in the first row sitting next to him.

He continues questioning each of us in turn, explaining grammatical points as he goes. We move on to where we live and come from. We're a motley crew of Bosnians, Germans, Australians, British, Spanish, Argentineans, French and Belgians, not to mention the talkative Venezuelan contingent.

Guillem turns to me. *'Ets anglesa?'* Are you English?

'Som d'anglaterra,' I reply, sheep like.

Jutta gives me the thumbs up. A meek woman sitting directly in front of me makes a complete bish of things and has to start again. My heart misses a beat for her. I look at the clock. Another hour to go. Guillem spends a considerable time trying to help us get to grips with Catalan vowls. This is no meant feat given that they sound completely different from their British equivalent.

'Ahhhhhhh,' he intones loudly, 'ehhhhhhhhh…ooooooohhh… urghhhhhhhhhhhh.'

There's an enormous temptation to yell back impertinently 'Bahhhhhhhh…' but I'm trying to keep my ewe preoccupation under control, so keep shtum. We are given screeds of vocabulary sheets which would give hope to any aspiring British yob with linguistic ambitions. Next to some of the Catalan words and their English translation, I decide to add my own unofficial puerile list of British Yob Equivalents.

Here's my hot list:

English translation	Catalan	British Yob Equivalent
to throw	*git*	git
night	*nit*	nit
woman	*dona*	donner (kebab)
to sting	*punxar*	punch her
puncture	*punxada*	punch harder
fire	*foc*	fuck
seal	*foca*	fucker
floor	*pis*	piss
cough	*tosa*	tosser
radish	*rave*	rave
let's fight	*lluitem*	you-hit-'im
to place	*poseur*	poser
bang	*bum*	bum
naval dockyard	*arsenal*	Arsenal
beaks	*becs*	Becks

The Venezuelan party at the back of the room are breaking out into giggles as they attempt to pronounce Catalan greetings on the first page of the text book we've all been given. Guillem claps loudly and says in Spanish.

'OK, now we will learn how to greet each other.'

A young woman in front of me doesn't seem to understand. '*En Français*?' she pleads.

I dredge up some rusty French. '*Regard le livre. Maintenant apprendrons salutations.*'

She turns to face me. '*Ah, d'accord! Merci. Je suis Florence.*'

211

I wonder how Guillem is going to cope with us. It's not as if he's just dealing with a bunch of Brits or Germans. This class is a United Nations all on its own and not everyone can speak Castilian Spanish, let alone Catalan.

'*Bon dia!*' shouts Guillem. Good day. So far so good. He gives me an encouraging smile. '*Va Bé?*'

Be. I'm sure *be rostit* is roast lamb. Maybe he's heard about my sheep encounters or am I just becoming paranoid?

'*No tenc un be.*' I don't have a sheep, I say.

Guillem looks puzzled. Then the penny seems to drop. He chuckles to himself while the mystified class look on.

'You mean "*be*!" I'm talking about "*bé*".'

Well that's as clear as mud. He shakes his head with mirth and removes his glasses, wiping his eyes with a hankie. 'We are both right. You see an accented "*bé*" means well and "*be*" unaccented means lamb. It all comes down to correct pronunciation.'

The class enjoys the confusion and various would-be lambs begin baa-ing loudly. We reach the end of the lesson on a wave of laughter and Guillem, undaunted by the huge task ahead of him, energetically picks up his books and bids us farewell until next week. '*Bon vespre!*' he yells cheerfully. Good evening.

In some exhaustion, I leave the music school with two of my fellow students in tow, Jutta and Julia, a larger-than-life Venezuelan. We weave along the street, lamenting our dismal first serious attempt at conquering the local lingo and decide to pop into a local bar for a well earned nightcap.

I walk home through the dark country lanes, the shiny new Catalan file and grammar book in my arms. A screech owl circles overhead and a few scurrying rats crash around the hedgerows. I reach my track and in the sootiness of night vaguely make out the shape of Llamp in his run. He barks when he sees me and snuffles up to the fence, wagging his tail. In the obscurity I see the Scotsman striding towards me across the courtyard, a *puro*, its tip smouldering orange, gripped in one hand and a limp hose in the other.

'I've just been watering the vines.'

'I got a bit waylaid.'

He grins. 'Well, I was on the point of calling out a search party. So how was it?'

'It's going to be quite a challenge, but you know Guillem. He's such a character.'

He smiles. 'That's why his restaurant's always full. Here, I want you to see something.'

I follow him into the front garden where, between dark rocks and leaves, there is a huge flare of white light. Alan crouches down and slowly pulls back a leaf to reveal a glow worm snuggled within an earthy hollow, the first I've ever seen in our garden. As soon as it is exposed, the light dims.

'Extraordinary,' I muse. 'Quite beautiful.'

We stand in the stillness of the garden, listening to the methodical trickle of water from the pond's fountain. Alan yawns loudly.

'I'm off to check on the hens.'

As if in anticipation of his visit, Salvador crows discordantly and there's a sudden low braying from a distant donkey. Llamp howls mournfully and the nocturnal creatures of our valley seem to suddenly come alive. I sit on my favourite rock by the pond, lulled by the music of the water and the creaky croaking of the frogs. On a jagged rock, obscured on one side by wild rushes, I see the lumpy silhouette of Johnny the toad.

'Are you still angry with me?'

He puffs up his throat and blinks at me, before crashing with a loud burp and a huge plop into the treacly black depths below.

Someone's tooting at the front gate. Catalina wipes her hands on a cloth and strides over to the entry phone.

'It's Llorenç,' she tells me. 'You ordered more wood?'

'We're getting a bit low.'

'Yes, good idea to stock up now. Winter will be here soon enough.'

'It's only October.'

She breathes heavily. 'They say next month will be very cold.'

'Just as well I'll be in New York for half of it then.'

Llorenç mischievously slams his hand on the horn until we come out to greet him. Catalina swipes him with her tea cloth.

'You're a bad man.'

He grins at her and gives me a cheeky wink.

'Where's Alan?'

'He's gone to welcome some new holidaymakers at Pep's flat. He should be back soon.'

'Always an excuse not to help me with carrying the wood.'

'We'll help you.'

He gives a snort. 'I'd be quicker on my own. A cup of coffee would be more useful.'

'Another *macho*.'

'*Si,*' he smiles. 'Mallorca's full of them.'

I slip back into the kitchen and put on the espresso machine while Catalina resumes her ironing.

'Are you going to Nancy's exhibition tonight?' she asks.

'Yes, after Ollie's football practice. I have my eye on a painting.'

'Me too. I love her work. She's amazing to be painting at her age.'

Llorenç ambles into the kitchen and watches as I pour him a cup of coffee. He pulls up a chair and observes us both.

'So, how's the Catalan coming on?'

'Poc a poc,' I reply facetiously.

'Of course, lessons are one thing, but the real test will be trying it out in the town.'

'Just you wait and see, Llorenç.'

A car draws up in the courtyard.

'Perfect timing,' says Llorenç, slapping his empty cup down on the table.

'Now your Senyor can give me a hand with the wood.'

Pueblo Español in Palma, the venue for Nancy Golding's exhibition, is a vast complex of buildings which replicate some of the most famous landmarks in Spain. It has a lavish exterior with turrets, towers and spires and has the look of a medieval castle, although it's really no more than a glorified convention centre. Parking the car in one of the steep and unprepossessing side streets, we cross the cobbled front entrance and descend sweeping steps to the courtyard. A local estate agent has sponsored Nancy's show and its logo is prominently displayed on flags and posters. Twinkling candles brighten the dark courtyard and amidst the throng we see Pep and Juana waving to us. Ollie runs towards them, only interested in catching up with Angel who is hanging back by one of the tables gobbling olives and drinking Coca-Cola.

'You're late!' yells Pep.

'No they're not,' quips Juana, helping herself to some canapés from a passing waiter.

'Thank heavens you didn't dress up either,' I say, noting that she's in jeans and a red sweater.

She shrugs. 'Nancy wouldn't expect me to. Mind you, the moneyed set from Portals is here tonight.'

Puerto Portals hugs the bay a polite distance along the coast from Palma. It's the yachties' dream hang-out and a must zone for designer babes who pose and pout on the terraces of chic cafes fronting the marina.

Juana views the pretty courtyard with a critical eye. 'Lots of foreigners.'

Catalina and Ramon join us, together with her parents, Paco and Marta. I take in Catalina's stylish ensemble of tailored black trousers and exotic Moroccan jacket. Her short dark hair is streaked with henna and a stunning amber stone rests on her neck.

'You look amazing,' I tell her.

She gives a little grin. 'That's only because you always see me behind an ironing board.'

'True,' says Alan. 'You're a real Cinderella.'

Ramon shrugs his shoulders. 'Women will find any excuse to buy new clothes.'

I give him a poke in the ribs. 'Watch it, or I'll set a genet on your chickens.'

'What news of your cattery?' says Marta with a sweet smile.

I wince as Alan gives an involuntary frown.

'Oh, we're getting there slowly. We need to wait for the council to come back to us about planning permits.'

'Is it taking up a lot of your time?' she says.

'To be honest, I'm frantic with new clients and some big projects so I haven't had time to give it much thought of late.'

'She's organising a big even with Prince Charles!' blurts out Catalina.

'Really?' Marta looks impressed. 'Did you hear that, Paco?' she says to her husband. Paco nods impatiently.

'And how is the worm hotel these days?' he asks quickly, keen to get back to agricultural matters.

Alan cheers up. 'Touch wood, the Mallorcan worms are settling in well. I've had some wonderful compost this month.'

Paco smiles and nods. 'It's important to be patient in life.'

'Indeed,' says Alan. 'Where's that wretched waiter gone? I could murder a drink.'

I grab two flutes of cava as a waiter floats past, and push one into the Scotsman's hand. Coming towards our group is a stream of local friends from our valley.

'It's a Sóller invasion,' yells Pep. 'Where's Nancy? We need her here too.'

'She's showing some clients round the gallery. Wait a minute,' I tell him.

Ollie has already found Nancy in the interior of the building and holding her hand leads her over to us.

'If it's not all my favourite friends hanging out together! What is this, a private meeting of *Sóllerics*?'

Pep gives her a robust hug. 'We don't want to mix with too many wealthy foreigners. It's bad enough being infiltrated by the Scots,' he gives a pointed stare at Alan, 'without this Palma mob.'

Juana elbows him hard. 'Keep your voice down or we'll all be thrown out.'

There's a wave of raucous laughter from the group and we find ourselves being studied curiously by several elegant guests, all in expensive cocktail attire.

'Hopefully some of these *ricos* will cough up for some paintings,' says Catalina.

'I've kept back your favourite,' Nancy whispers in my ear.

'I may have to pay you in instalments.'

She giggles. 'It's not that much. Special price for special friends.'

The main sponsor, a tall German, now stands in our midst and delivers a welcome speech. Nancy, smiling sublimely, waits until he's finished and then makes a simple yet moving address which is greeted with thunderous applause. I accompany Pep and Catalina into the gallery where we are greeted by Tolo from our local Banca March, Xavier and Teresa from Colmado sa Lluna and a whole host of locals. Our Australian friends Jack and Sarah from Fornalutx are great art lovers and are considering a purchase, while Victoria and Robert Duvall talk with our two local mayors, from Sóller and Fornalutx. I find it touching that so many from our valley have come to support Nancy on her big night. Judging by the number of confirmed sales, it appears that she will be able to survive another cold winter in Sóller.

'Don't spend it all at once, Nancy,' cautions Pep.

'Life's for living, my friend. I'm not a hoarder.'

'Well, I believe in living and hoarding,' jokes Pep.

The evening rolls on until gone midnight at which point the *Sóllerics* begin to wend their way back to their cars, happy to be heading out of Palma and into the hills.

It's a cool day in the valley and across the Tramuntanas the harsh, resonating sound of gunfire can be heard, indicating that it's the start of the hunting season. I am never comfortable with the hunting of *tords*, the thrushes that are highly prized by Mallorcans and used in soups and *arròs brut*, a popular and hearty local rice dish. Still, as Pep always reminds me, it is not for us foreign residents to interfere with local customs and I agree with him wholeheartedly. Alan is down in the field planting broad beans and peas and shaking his worm compost over the soil. I watch as clouds of grey smoke rise from the forests up in the mountains and my heart goes out to the unsuspecting birds whose lives are to be snuffed out so unceremoniously. Sighing, I jog over to the open front gate and head off for a run. It's Saturday and at this early hour of the morning the roads are peaceful and the valley is quiet and swathed in soft cloud. Margalida is sitting outside her chalet praying to herself but as I approach she drops the wooden rosary to her lap and calls me to her.

'When are you off to America?'

'Next month.'

She holds my hands between hers and lets out a small cry.

'Are you sure it's safe? I've heard that everyone has a gun.'

'Don't worry, I'll be running too fast to get shot.'

She doesn't laugh.

'I shall pray.'

I shudder with the sudden chill. 'I'm relying on you.'

She brightens. 'At my age that's all I can do – watch the world go by and pray.' She pats my hand and rises. 'You go. I'm waiting for Jorge.'

'The postman?'

'*Pues,* he's such a nice young man. I promised to pick him some oranges.'

A bulging bag of fruit lies at her feet. I hear a toot toot at the end of the road and there, in a state of excitement is Gaspar with a huge pile of newspapers strapped to the back of his bike ready for delivery.

'Aha, thought I'd see you! Hurry up and I'll give you a race to the *Puerto*,' he yells.

As I set off along the road with Gaspar tootling along next to me, I ponder on Jorge's latest conquest. The man must surely be a god to win over my elderly neighbour, Margalida. Perhaps it's to do with his smile and the length of his hair.

Catalina and her brother, Stefan, are in my office poring over the architectural drawings in wonderment.

'You mean this is the actual size of the cattery?' asks Stefan flatly.

'Yes, but this is the one I visited. Ours can be much smaller.'

He exhales deeply. 'There is a new planning law coming in which could affect *horta* land.'

'What do you mean?'

'Well, I doubt you'd be able to build something this big in an orchard.'

My heart sinks.

'In fact, the mayor has warned me that the new law might prohibit all buildings in orchards, even non-permanent structures like this.'

Catalina tries to be positive. 'Let's wait and see. The most important thing is to look at what is possible. You must remember, we don't have catteries here. Cats usually live off the land.'

'There are Brits running kennels and catteries all over the island,' I argue.

'I know, but for us it's a strange British concept so it's hard to explain to the planners at the town hall.'

I tap my fingers fretfully on the desk. Having passed my cattery course with flying colours and worked on a preliminary business plan, I'd be sad if it all came to nought. My time at The Cat's Whiskers has convinced me that it could be an enjoyable little business to run from home. The problem I have at present is trying to juggle all my PR work and journalistic assignments while keeping the cattery idea afloat. I rub my eyes and yawn.

'Sleepy?' asks Catalina with a smile.

'Oh, I was up till gone midnight doing client work for Rachel and I've still got heaps more to do on the Crown jewels event, so I'm a bit the worse for wear today.'

She jumps up from her seat. 'I'll go and make us some strong coffee.'

She stops at the office door.

'Stefan, what about if we visited the cattery in England and worked out how we might create a smaller version here? You know, more manageable.'

He gives a tentative nod. 'OK, but I'm flat out with building projects until January. Anyway, by that time we may have news on the planning situation.'

'That suits me,' I say. 'I'd rather get my Crown jewels event over with in January before concentrating on cattery business.'

The door opens and Alan strides in.

'So, how's it going? Is it feasible?'

Stefan shrugs. 'In truth, I don't know. There's a new law stopping the building of any structures on orchard land. We may be unlucky.'

I give the Scotsman a sardonic smile.

'So, are you happy now?'

His face drops. 'Actually, no. I've studied your initial business plan and decided that it really is a workable idea. I totally support you.'

Despite the gloomy silence, I study his face and in that moment feel a huge swell of gratitude.

He puts his hand on my shoulder. 'Come on, chin up. You're not one to give up.'

'Yes, we know nothing yet,' says Catalina.

'After all,' the Scotsman rejoins. 'This is just round one. There's plenty of time to put up a fight.'

'In the meantime, I've got plenty of work to keep me occupied.'

'You can say that again,' says the Scotsman. 'And let's not even mention all the work I have to do, what with filming, chickens and keeping an eye on Pep's flat.'

Catalina laughs. 'That's not work. That's fun!'

He attempts to remonstrate just as Inko strolls in followed by Minky and Orlando. They look up at me expectantly.

'Ah,' says Stefan. 'Here's the planning committee. They envisage no problems.'

We all troop downstairs for some coffee. For now there's nothing more any of us can do but wait. *Que será será*. In the interim I shall just keep busy and take counsel from Stefan and my eminent committee of cats until such time as a decision by the council is made.

I'm on a ladder under one of the lemon trees with mobile glued to ear.

'Anyway, what are you doing up a damned lemon tree?' Rachel is tutting.

'Picking lemons?'

'Oh, very funny. Don't you ever relax?'

'Actually, Rachel, I do. The other night I went to a wonderful exhibition and bought myself a painting.'

'Hallelujah!' she squawks. 'Good to know you're living dangerously.'

'Hardly.'

'I expect Alan gave you grief over the price?'

'Thankfully, the artist is a friend so it didn't break the bank. I've hung it right above the bed. Even the Scotsman thinks it looks fantastic.'

'Good, you should get out more.'

'Well, when you stop piling on the work, Rachel, I might.'

'Touché!' she gives a laugh. 'Anyway, where were we?'

'Discussing the number of guests for the Crown jewels event.'

'Ah yes, well I think we'll have three hundred in total,' Rachel drawls.

'What? But the events people at the Tower said two hundred and fifty, max.'

'Too bad.'

'I'm not sure, Rachel. Don't forget the guests won't just be in the White Tower. They've also got to visit Waterloo Barracks to have a quick look at the Crown jewels collection during the evening. It could be a logistical nightmare with so many guests.'

She yawns. 'We can't cut the list down. Besides there'll be no-shows on the night, as always.'

'I suppose we can do drinks in the White Tower with Prince Charles, then take guests to the Jewel house in small groups.'

'Exactly.'

'What does Jim at the Stationery Office think?'

'He's fairly laid back.'

'I hope you're right, Rachel.'

'Listen, don't get so stressed out. I really appreciate all the work you're putting in just now but we've still got plenty of time on our hands.'

'Maybe, but don't forget I'm juggling a lot of other projects at the moment so I'd like to think this one's on course.'

'It is, don't worry. By the way, Greedy George is thrilled with your marketing plan for his dog and cat wear range. That was fairly inspired.'

'You know my penchant for pets.'

'Hmm... well, I certainly know about your absurd preoccupation with moggies.'

I draw the conversation back to the Tower. 'By the way, can we display the Crown jewels book up in the White Tower?

'I'll make sure that'll be fine with the Palace.'

'OK, but please check back with the Tower as well.'

She gives a guffaw. 'You're like a mother hen over this event.'

'I want it to work like clockwork.'

'It will. Never fear.'

I have agreed to meet Sabine Ricard for a coffee at Cafè Paris. On a Saturday she likes to visit Sóller market with Veronique and, although making few purchases, believes that she is fundamental to the thriving economy of my local town.

'Tell me,' she says, as we sit at a table waiting to be served. 'What would these people do without us?'

'I think they'd survive fairly well, Sabine.'

'Rubbish! We are the life blood of the island economy and should be treated with respect.'

I wonder sometimes why people like Sabine choose to live in Mallorca. They rarely have a good thing to say about the island or its people. Veronique is playing with a hideous Barbie doll and twisting her golden curls with her chubby little fingers. José catches my eye and saunters over. I've been waiting for this moment. He asks if I want my usual order, but I stop him mid track.

'Jo vull un cafè tot sol i un aigua sensa gas.'

He claps his hands. *'Fantàstic!'*

Sabine narrows her eyes. 'What did you say?'

'I asked for an espresso and a mineral water in Catalan.'

'Why?' she sniffs in disgust.

'Because I've started having lessons and need to practise.'

She looks horrified.

'I'm getting a lot of homework too, on top of all my other work stuff.'

'I can't believe what I'm hearing!' She gives me a pained expression.

José disappears, rushing over to Senyor Bisbal's table to tell him and some of his other regulars about my debut. They smile and applaud. José returns to take the rest of our order.

'I'm proud of you,' he says. *'Poc a poc.'*

'Maman, I hate Catalan. It sounds so ugly,' Veronique whines in French, scowling unpleasantly and twirling her hideous, emaciated doll across the table. José looks affronted, given that he speaks excellent French, but smiles stiffly and heads for the bar.

'But you live here now so you should try to speak the local language,' I say.

'Maman says I shouldn't,' she replies in perfect English.

Sabine eyes me frostily. 'I have no intention of speaking Catalan, nor shall my daughter.'

'That seems a little silly.'

José places our coffees in front of us and gives Veronique her cola. He returns to Senyor Bisbal's table for a chat.

'It is my decision. Besides, like you, we will always send her to an international school so there is no need.'

I decide to bait her. 'To be honest, we're thinking of sending Ollie to a local school next year.'

She thumps down her cup so hard that the teaspoon cries out, a small rattle of protest in the saucer.

'Are you insane?'

'Probably, but that has nothing to do with our decision.'

Senyor Bisbal stands like a vision before us, his tall, slightly hollowed frame blocking the few rays of sunlight that have found a path to our table. I attempt to rise, but he politely indicates that I should remain seated. He takes my hand in his.

'So now you can speak Catalan?'

'I can just about order a coffee, so don't get too excited.'

He laughs softly and smiles over at Sabine. Veronique talks to her mother in French.

'Ah, you are French. We Mallorcans have much in common with you.'

'Really?' she says, eyebrows haughtily raised.

'In Sóller we traded our oranges for years with France. I suppose that's why our languages are so similar.'

Sabine gives a little gasp as though he's squirted her with a water gun, but old Senyor Bisbal seems hardly to have noticed, bowing low and walking slowly to the door. For a brief second he glimpses back, a mischievous smile playing on his lips and then, with a little wink in my direction, he is gone.

FOURTEEN

RUNNING AROUND MANHATTAN

Sunday 5 a.m., midtown Manhattan

A leaden grey sky hangs over Manhattan as we walk the quiet streets en route to the New York Public Library, the pickup point for marathon runners. From there we will be shuttled by bus to the start line on Staten Island. It's cold and windy and I feel rather conspicuous exposing my bare knees to the world at such an ungodly hour. On either side of us, immense sleek tower blocks shoot up into the crowded sky, their charcoal glass shells reflecting an eerie glow from the gloomy street lights. A dog patters past, keeping flush with the dark walls, his eyes darting nervously about him as he heads determinedly in the direction of Times Square. Ollie and Alan stumble along beside me yawning and discussing where they might find a place open for breakfast once they've waved me off. As we approach the intersection of 42nd Street and 5th Avenue, a vast, inky black building like a great Egyptian temple rises up before us, flanked by an imposing flight of stone steps. Now, seemingly from every direction we are joined by runners grasping small plastic kit bags and water bottles. On the broad pavement in front of the library cheerful officials in bright NYC Marathon T-shirts beckon us forward and direct us to the coaches forming a line along the empty street.

'OK, honey,' yells a woman, 'Move along please.'

I step back to let others pass. Ollie is mesmerised by the sheer scale of everything around him and the number of runners trundling past.

'How's the leg?' Alan asks.

'I've got some pain killers if it gets really bad.'

'They say you shouldn't pop pills to mask the pain.'

'Who's they?'

'Medical experts.'

'Too bad.'

'Don't forget to warm up,' pipes up Ollie.

'Well, I've got about four hours until the start so I'll have plenty of time for warming up.'

'Just think, there'll be 40,000 of you at the start line.'

'Am I supposed to find that comforting?'

He laughs. 'At least you won't be suffering alone and there'll be millions of spectators.'

I feel dwarfed standing in the shadow of the library and rather homesick for the Sóller Valley. Pathetically, I'm dreading the moment when the boys take their leave. We walk aimlessly along to the coaches, distracted on our left by a large bronze statue of a woman. She's kneeling and her hands are placed close together on her knees. Alan studies the inscription.

'That's a good omen,' he says. 'It's a memorial to the American writer Gertrude Stein, frequent visitor to Deià and friend of Robert Graves in her day.'

That heartens me a little. I bid Ollie and Alan farewell and join one of the anonymous queues waiting to mount a bus. A few runners are travelling together but I feel rather downcast and alone. I am already fretting about my leg and the added pressure from Manuel Ramirez of finishing the race in less than four hours. I mount the bus and sit staring out of the window into the gloom. A moment later and a swarthy young man slumps down next to me. He is studying the route map, occasionally observing the runners filing past him with large, troubled eyes.

'Perdona,' he suddenly blusters. 'I am alone in New York. Do you speak any Spanish?'

12.35 p.m., Upper East Side

The last twenty-five miles have passed by in a mad blur of colours, smells, faces, wild cheering, majorette parades and music. I remember the mad rush at the start line, adrenalin thumping through my body as I surged ahead in an enormous bubble of humanity. Runners pushed and elbowed, laughed and whistled. Sidewalks became wild, undulating waves of moving bodies, and above our heads helicopters whirred and dipped. With an air of misplaced cockiness I soared through Brooklyn, slowed down in The Bronx and began limping in Harlem. I recall the five hellish bridges I crossed, my body part of a huge tangle of sweating limbs and reeking sportswear as we pounded along the narrow tracks in unbearable heat. In Harlem, the sudden loss of power as my right leg flared with pain infuriated me and soon I was grappling with pain killers that I had secreted in my pocket. I knocked them back with warm water from a plastic bottle and stubbornly blundered forward, furious with myself for acknowledging the pain.

Now we're on the last lap, the home run. The crowds are screaming and flying flags on either side of the broad street. Along the pavements well-wishers have set up small stalls offering free Pepsi, oranges and chocolate. God Bless America! An elderly American, who has shadowed me from the start line, hobbles up alongside me, perspiration running down his face.

'Still in pain?'

I squint at him in the burning sunlight, in such acute agony now that I'm not sure I can spit out a word without blubbing.

'Agony,' I blurt out.

He nods and pats me on the back as we jog along. 'Control the pain, girl. We're about a mile off. Look ahead, there's Central Park.'

'I think I'll have to rest a minute.'

He shakes his head. 'NO! If you stop now, you'll seize up. I should know. I've done ten of these darned marathons.'

Somehow, as we curled into Upper East Side, the pain had numbed to a dull nagging sensation, but now, with just a mile to go, it has become intolerable. I look at my watch and see that I have been running for three hours and forty-nine minutes. The face of Manuel Ramirez floats before me. *You will run in under four hours, a second over and you fail me.*

My elderly companion cocks his head towards me. 'You OK?'

'No. My leg is on fire.'

He pulls the baseball cap from his head and wipes his brow. 'We've gotta keep on trucking. Let's finish together. I'm Barney by the way.'

I feel my eyes moisten. This man has become my last hope. I nod and tell him my name.

'Sorry to be a wimp.'

'Recognising your own frailties is a sign of strength,' he says determinedly.

I find myself giggling. 'Kind of you, but I'm actually just a wimp.'

'Come on! There's the finish line. We're gonna make it.'

He grasps my fingers and pulls me forward. His frail, mottled hand is, like mine, slimy with sweat. I want to laugh and cry in helpless relief when I see in the far distance balloons and banners with the words, 'FINISH'. We are now in Central Park and the massive swell of spectators on either side of us are yelling 'RUN! RUN!' Tears are coursing down my face and there, bobbing up behind bunting and scores of spectators on the right side of the course, is Ollie with Alan at his side. They are screaming and punching the air and giving me the thumbs up. So very un-British. In a split second I can see Ollie's puzzlement that I am running with an old man, hand in hand. I begin laughing uncontrollably. Maybe it's the effect of the pain killers. Barney lets go of my hand and throws his arms up in joy as we practically throw ourselves over the finish line. He surveys his watch.

'Nice going, partner. Three hours and fifty-nine minutes.'

I give him a hug. Medals are thrust at us and soon I find myself wrapped in a metal foil sheet and caught in a tight embrace with Alan and Ollie. Barney is carried off on a wave of jubilant runners and the park is seething with foil-clad heroes and doting friends and relatives.

'You looked as if you were really suffering,' says Alan quietly.

'I can't begin to describe the pain.'

Ollie presses my hand. 'But you did it!'

'Did Ed make it?' I ask.

'He came, saw the crowds and bowed out gracefully,' says the Scotsman wryly. He leads me across the grass and towards one of the park's entrances.

'Right, do you want the good news or the bad news?'

'Go on,' I say, limping between them.

'The good news is that you've won Manuel's bet and there's some cold bubbly in the hotel fridge. The bad news is that we've got to walk all the way back there.'

I shrug my shoulders. 'A girl's got to do what a girl's got to do.'

Leaning heavily on Alan's arm, with Ollie dancing at my side, we head off along the street, the lure of iced champagne, a hot bath and a massage quickening my pace with every step.

Sunday 11 p.m., somewhere in the Manhattan grid
'Are we lost?'

'Of course not! It's just that we've walked further from the subway than I thought.'

Following a recuperative bath and massage at the hotel, I venture out with Alan and Ollie to try a restaurant recommended by a London journalist friend. We manage to find our way around the subway and even locate the restaurant and have dinner, but now it is late and cold and a taxi seems like the best option to whisk us back to the hotel.

'I think we're only about fifteen minutes away from the subway.'

I give Alan a warning look as he squints at a street map.

'Ah, maybe not a good idea. Probably your legs are feeling it a bit.'

Ollie tuts. 'Let's just get a cab.'

We lurk by one of the main intersections until a yellow cab finally rolls up.

'Hello, I wonder if you could take us to –' Alan's words are cut short.

'Get in.'

The door slams and we're off, skidding round corners and eating up 7th Avenue as if it's a hot dog. I catch the eye of the driver in the darkness and am startled to see that it's a warrior of a woman. A metal grill separates us, for which I'm grateful.

'Erm, we're going midtown to the Millennium Broadway Hotel.'

'Where? Never heard of it,' she barks at me.

'Do you know Times Square?' I say helplessly.

'She says do I know Times Square!'

I observe the silhouette of her shoulders heaving, her mahogany paws manipulating the steering wheel. She gives a hoot of laughter. Alan shifts around his seat ignoring us both while Ollie drops off to sleep.

'You guys from outta town?'

'London, England,' I say.

'That figures.'

She gives a coarse cackle. We're coming up to some lights.

'Do you often drive late at night?'

Her black eyes glower at me in the driver's mirror.

'What's it to you?'

'I just wondered, as a woman, if you ever got scared driving a cab late at night.'

'Scared? *Me?*'

She suddenly screeches to a halt mid street. It's empty.

'Crikey!' I say absurdly.

Alan throws an arm protectively over Ollie's slumbering form.

Our driver ducks down under the front seat, turns round and through the metal grill points a gun directly at me. For a second I'm too shocked to move. Alan appears white and frozen. In a split second she lowers the barrel and breaks into a huge grin.

'Hey listen, lady, I'm from Jamaica and I know how to deal with trouble. No one's ever gonna mess with me.'

With a heavy thud she hurls it back under the seat and roars off.

'Now where was it you folks said you was going?'

Monday 12 p.m., the Fountain Terrace, Bryant Park

Under a pale blue sky, the New York Public Library, its Beaux-arts, white facade bleached in sunlight, jostles for space in the concrete jungle. Mobbed by towering, lean and mean skyscrapers, it sits elegantly, like a learned professor, on the edge of Bryant Park, enjoying the attention it garners from the city's academics, students and visitors alike. Nestling behind this grand old boy is the park itself, an idyllic oasis in the cut and thrust of city life. It is here, the scene of many a fashion and PR event, that Greedy George has chosen to preview his new pet fashion range, Hot Dogs and Even Cooler Cats. It seems almost impossible to believe that only yesterday this was the very place from which I set off to compete in the marathon. Today, it's as if it was all just a dream. There are no banners, no jolly officials with loud hailers, no crowds of men and women in numbered bibs, no rows of coaches forming one long, illuminated caterpillar under the uncompromising gaze of Gertrude Stein.

In front of me, in agitated mode, is Greedy George, pacing about the lawn with his mobile glued to his ear.

'No, Alfonso, you listen to me,' he yells in his affected *sarf* London accent. 'I want the delivery by tonight or I'll stick peas up your nostrils, *capiche?*'

He snaps the phone shut and shoves it sulkily into his pocket.

'Peas?' I enquire.

'Whatever. It gave him a turn. And don't give me one of those looks.'

'I think we should get back to the guests. We'll just tell the press that there's been a short delay in availability.'

'Yeah, but on the press release we said all the stuff would be in the store today. That lazy skunk should have a good hiding.'

I grab his arm. 'George, just concentrate on the show. Alfonso's cocked up and that's the end of it.'

He strides, with a thunderous look on his face, across the grass towards the distant fountain terrace. This is the third time Alfonso Mario has failed to deliver Havana products to the store on time and Greedy George is not amused. Excited New Yorkers will now have to wait until tomorrow to purchase their pet trinkets from the shop. I walk stiffly behind Greedy George. My legs still feel bruised and battered like a pair of badly damaged bananas, but with the flexibility of dried concrete. Milling about the circular terrace which runs in a giant loop around the spectacular pink granite fountain at its heart, I see a throng of a hundred or more media guests. Most are sipping at cocktails and glancing at press material while a curious few examine, with some bemusement, the bright vermillion carpet that runs around the fountain. This is the official 'catwalk' on which Havana's new pet range will be modelled by various spoilt and well-trained pooches and moggies. A wooden reception desk has been set up, manned by five staff from George's New York PR company. Sweetly and with sickly smiles, they tick off names and hand out press packs and goody bags. George snaps into happy chappie mode as soon as he's approached by the event organiser.

'Everything on cue, Barbara?'

A tiny crisp of a woman in salmon pink chiffon and a helmet of peroxide, she prods at his big right paw with bony, insistent fingers.

'Another fifteen minutes, George,' she squeals. 'We've had a little problem with Roxanne the rotweiller, but she's shaping up.'

'What kind of problem?'

'Oh, nothing serious. She keeps shaking off the dog bolero and cape, but her agent and trainer are on the case.'

'Christ, diva dogs, that's all we need, guv.'

I notice Barbara's unsmiling and intense aspect and smother a grin.

'But the rehearsal was a dream. The guests are going to go wild, trust me.' She clasps her hands together in paroxysms of pure joy.

'They're not getting very wild on those fruit cocktails. Dreary lot. Come on guv, let's get a glass of bubbly and show these Yanks what's what.'

Barbara gives a little gasp as George whisks up two glasses and pushes one in my hand. She slips away, presumably to calm the stage nerves of her furry protégés.

'Your Barbara seemed a bit disapproving about our drinking champagne at this hour.'

George waves a hand in the air. 'Oh, bugger that. Bloody Puritans. These Yanks don't know how to live, guv.'

'How's your dodgy leg today?' he barks.

'Still dodgy. Can't you tell?'

'Thought you always walked like the Tin Man.'

'Ho ho ho. Anyway, where's old Bryan?'

It's a while since I've seen my client, Bryan Patterson. I'm rather hoping he hasn't brought Tootsie, his pet bunny, along to this event.

George points rudely over to the other side of the fountain.

'There he is with Rachel and your vampire mate, Dannie.'

I stare across. Rachel is rolling her head back and laughing politely. I'd love to know what they're discussing.

'Bryan's rabbit's in the show.'

'Tootsie? Please tell me you're joking?'

He gives a little whinny. 'I thought he could be the parting shot. I made him this cutesy little kid jacket and leather baseball cap which his ears hang through.'

I shake my head. 'Thank God I live in Mallorca.'

He wallops my arm. 'You love all this tosh as much as I do. How else do people like you and me get our kicks?'

'These days I'm finding new avenues.'

He breaks into silly giggles. 'Come on guv, let's go and upset some press.'

A tall, painfully thin woman in shades, a semi-transparent blouse and minuscule miniskirt is snacking on some snap peas from a plastic sandwich bag.

'Hi Francine. Forgot your skirt?'

She pats her concave chest nervously. 'Oh George, darling! Don't be so uncouth.'

I extend my hand which she holds limply like a dead fish.

'Oh, I am SO happy to meet you! Let me give you my card. I'm with *Vogue* USA.'

'Fabulous,' I gush.

George waits until she's ferreting in her voluminous Prada handbag, then opens his mouth and pokes his finger towards his throat. This is his unique way of conveying that he finds someone a) irritating, b) insipid, c) tedious or possibly all three. I bare my teeth at him. Francine hands me a card.

'Isn't George just fantastic? He's like the new tsar of fashion around here.'

'And do you have a pet?' I ask.

She takes a sip of water and gives a little cough. 'Oh, absolutely. I have a chihuahua named Lucy Belle. Like George, I am a great dog lover.'

He stands nodding with a beatific smile on his ample chops. A gaggle of women join us, all from top New York glossies. They introduce themselves graciously, only showing genuine fear and bad humour when a waiter approaches with a tray of canapés.

'Do the British still offer liquor at daytime press events?' asks a sweet girl from *Jayne* magazine.

'Well, yes it's normal in London to offer champagne or wine.'

She gives a loud tut. 'Really? Oh my Gad that's terrible! It's so unhealthy and besides it makes you put on so much weight.'

I'm about to reply, but am swooped on by Rachel. Given that she only flew in during the early hours of the morning, she's looking remarkably perky and bright eyed. She smiles indulgently at the small coterie of press and pulls me aside.

'I've schmoozed Dannie to death, but Bryan's in a flap about Tootsie's debut on the catwalk. God, I need a drink.'

I beckon a waiter over and with delight he passes her a glass.

'Well done, you. Now, once this is over, we'd better get over to H Hotel in Tribeca pronto to help out before tonight's event.'

'What have you done with Alan and Ollie?'

'They're having a ball at F. A. O. Schwarz and Central Park Zoo.'

'It's all right for some. I don't know if I can face Manuel tonight.'

'All I care is that he gives me my two thousand dollars.'

She reaches out for some canapés from a bored waiter. 'Just shadow us.'

He shrugs and hangs about, relieved that he's found an enthusiastic taker.

'Do you think your legs will hold out tonight?'

'If I zap them with enough champagne.'

Barbara is now welcoming us all from a small platform, her voice piercing through a crackly sound system on the terrace. Greedy George has wandered over and stands at her side.

'So, finally, let us have a few words from the maestro himself.'

Guests gather closer, surrounding the circular red catwalk.

'Great to see you all in your lunchtime glad rags,' booms George. 'And welcome to our presentation, Hot Dogs and Even Cooler Cats. [polite titters] If any of you fancy buying any of the models, we'll be selling them off after the show [gasps of surprise]. Only kidding [more titters]. And now without more ado, let the show begin.'

There's enthusiastic applause as from all sides as tall, skeletal women in black Lycra stroll down the terraces and onto the red carpet, each dangling a dog or cat from diamante red leads. Rachel watches in a trance as Afghan hounds, chihuahuas, terriers, pugs, Great Danes and slinky cats of all colours and breeds kitted out in minute leather apparel strut their stuff around the catwalk. In a mad moment I could swear I see Zack the Korat in a billowing red leather cape, swirling elegantly along the length of the red carpet.

I grip Rachel's arm. 'I think I know that Korat!'

'That WHAT?'

I call out his name.

She eyes me coolly. 'You really need help!'

CAT ON A HOT TILED ROOF

For a fleeting moment the Korat turns his head in my direction, nose tilted to the wind. I wave enthusiastically as he strolls on by. A woman next to me does a subtle little side step to distance herself but I take no notice. I feel sudden pride. Perhaps Zack made it. This could be his big debut in the heart of New York and here I am to witness it. Rachel is shaking with laughter.

'You really are a complete headcase.'

I shrug in agreement. A cheer goes up as a British bulldog makes his appearance wearing a Union Jack on his leather jacket. I am transfixed when, at the end of the show, a young fair-haired girl dressed as a fairy in a white floaty dress and translucent wings appears holding Tootsie. His big, floppy white ears emerge from holes in the black baseball cap, and he surveys the assembled throng in some bewilderment. Guests begin whooping and camera lights flash. Greedy George is looking pleased as punch and revelling in the applause. He is soon surrounded by adoring photographers. Rachel steadies herself on my arm.

'Tell me I wasn't dreaming.'

I sink my teeth into a tiny salmon roulade and contemplate the spectacle before us. 'I think we should get out of here before Bryan's reunited with Tootsie.'

We weave through the crowds and gesticulate at Greedy George, trying to get his attention. At last he sees me and gives the thumbs up. *See you tonight,* I mouth. He nods.

Even Manuel Ramirez can't better this.

3 p.m., somewhere in the subway

The old train screeches and grumbles as we snake round the dark, grimy tunnels. Somehow our adventure on the New York subway hasn't been as successful as planned.

'Rachel, remind me why we're down here?'

She ignores me and continues to scour the subway map in an attempt to find out where we've gone wrong. Around us tight-faced New Yorkers stare ahead, their eyes boring through the windows and murky darkness beyond. I fidget in my plastic seat. I've had enough. Lurching with the movement of the train, I get up and approach a small whippet of a man in a raincoat sitting opposite me. I shout because the hum of the engine and the squeaking of the wheels is deafening.

'Excuse me, can you help us? We're trying to get to Tribeca.'

His nostrils flare and he glances with panicked eyes around the long, bending carriage. We have only seven companions in here aside from the whippet. There's a big, fierce looking, hot mama balancing a plastic shopping bag on her lap, two cool Rasta dudes, a young, pasty faced man with multiple facial studs, a wistful elderly couple and a businessman. The whippet doesn't reply, but instinctively flinches and rises. I watch him scuttle to the far end of the carriage. Rachel gives a snort of laughter and returns to her map, her long hair sweeping the page. The two Rastas are watching me with sly grins on their faces. Dare I? Oh, what the heck. I get up and sway over to them. They nudge each other. Rachel is regarding me with curiosity. I notice a smug little inflexion of the eyebrows.

'Excuse me,' I boom. 'We need a train for Tribeca. I wonder if you'd be sweet enough to…'

They laugh inanely.

'Where you from, lady?' asks the tall one.

'England.'

More laughter. 'You on the train to Brooklyn, man. You want One or Nine.'

I beckon to Rachel who furrows her brow. She stumbles over and plonks herself down next to the skinny, grinning companion.

'Can you show me on my map?'

He pulls it from her and then indicates with his finger where we should catch the train.

'You've been very helpful,' I say.

The skinny guy explodes into giggles. 'Where you learn to speak like that?'

'England?' I suggest.

The train draws into the next station.

'You get off here, girls,' says the tall Rasta. 'And watch yourselves. Don't speak to no one.'

3.45 p.m., Canal Street, Tribeca

With relief we find ourselves in trendy Tribeca, with its huge lofts, cobbled side streets and hot bars. The last time I visited, it seemed more run-down, but with the likes of Robert De Niro moving his studios here and some of the smartest restaurants setting up home, it has taken on a new mantle.

'We just turn left at the next intersection and H Hotel should be halfway down the street.'

'Thank heavens. Let's take a cab next time.'

'Remember it was your idea to get the subway?'

My mobile rings. 'Hello?'

It's Greedy George. 'Fab news! Tootsie escaped in the park and security staff have only just found her.'

'What's good about any of that? Poor Bryan must have been distraught.'

'Great PR though. We should get some diary snippets out of that.'

Rachel leads me across a set of traffic lights. A massive highway unrolls before us with multiple lanes of traffic.

'Anyway, are you still all right to meet at the store tomorrow?'

'Aren't you coming to the launch tonight?' I ask.

George groans. 'Got a lot on. I'll do my best.'

A sudden thought strikes me. 'You didn't plan it, did you?'

'What?'

'The lost bunny thing in the park?'

'Not exactly,' he guffaws. 'What d'you take me for? Remember, I'm an animal lover.'

8 p.m., H Hotel, Tribeca

H Hotel is tucked away down a cobbled street, its exterior anonymous save for a discreet H stamped into a slab of oxidised metal on the left side of its entrance. Sliding glass doors open onto an airy, chocolate, leather-panelled lobby with a wide rich oak floor, library alcove, and simple reception desk. H Bar, a temple of cool in steel and glass, is located down in the basement while on the upper levels brick-walled loft rooms offer stunning views of the Empire State Building and New York skyline.

Sitting on one of the deep leather sofas in H Bar, Dannie clasps my hands between hers and smiles like a seraph.

'What a glorious day it's been,' she says dreamily. 'George's show was a triumph and as for Manuel – what a handsome, intelligent man.'

Mary Anne is knocking back a dry martini and eyeing up one of the Latino waiters. I extricate myself from Dannie's grasp.

'It's always good fun putting like-minded people together.'

She nods sagely. 'You waved your wand and Manuel, George and I found each other.'

Rachel coughs wildly and, apologising, makes her way over to a table of press. Dannie grows restless.

'Well, if you'll excuse me, darling, I'll go and talk with the editor from *W*. She's been waiting so patiently. It's a shame George couldn't make it tonight.'

I watch Dannie squeeze through the throng of partygoers and scanning the minimalist dungeon that serves as H Hotel's new funky bar, then espy Alan and Ollie in deep conversation with Charlene, Ed's new Internet babe. They all seem to be getting on famously as they munch on mini hamburgers and chips. I'm pleased that she and Ed came along and even more relieved to see that he's managed to find someone normal. Ed suddenly appears at my elbow.

'Scatters, there are some awfully strange people down here, and I'm not sure about that Ramirez chap. He keeps giving me dark looks.'

'It's all right. He doesn't like anyone carrying bags. It creates uncertainty.'

He absorbs this information carefully, holding the MEK close to him.

'The barman's nice. He's called Randy. He says he suffers from claustrophobia so this isn't the best venue for the poor chap.'

I look around the windowless room. 'Listen, I've got to talk to Manuel. Could you chat up the press over there for me?'

He gulps. 'OK, I'll tell them about my life at the BBC.'

'Great. That should have them riveted.'

I push through the crowds. The bar is air-conditioned, but the air feels sticky. My legs have seized up and my knees ache. Manuel is smoking by the bar and looking almost relaxed. He gives me a crocodile smile.

'Psst…come here.'

I see that his forehead is beaded with sweat and his eyes marinating in their own juices. Heaven knows how many whisky chasers he's consumed. He grabs my hand.

'Come outside. I want to you show something.'

I watch him lurch slightly as he attempts to ascend the under-lit wooden staircase to the lobby.

'Are you OK, Manuel?'

'*Seguro,*' he growls.

In the lobby he pads across the vast expanse of wood and out into the cool night air. A lone doorman doffs his cap, but Manuel only has eyes for me. He walks into the silent road and buttons up his expensive jacket.

'Shoot!' he bawls.

'Pardon, Manuel?'

'Shoot me!'

I notice that two limo drivers ensconced in their cars by the hotel are discreetly averting their eyes. I decide to play the game, whatever it is.

'Sorry, I forgot my gun.'

'Come on!' he yells. 'You can do better than that!'

I stick out two fingers the way Ollie always does when he's playing cops and robbers with his chums and shout, 'BANG! BANG!'

He laughs manically. 'Here,' he says, drawing me closer. 'This jacket can take a shot from a 44 Magnum or a 3.57 revolver and I wouldn't feel a thing.'

His eyes are bloodshot. 'Feel it. It's only about a kilo in weight.'

I touch the course fabric. It feels neither heavy nor cumbersome.

'That's marvellous, Manuel.'

He sways on his feet. 'My Colombian tailor is Mr Caballero in Bogota. The world's best kept secret.'

I smile indulgently. In a flash he sobers up.

'Now, I must go. Please, take this cheque.'

He thrusts a folded piece of paper into my hand, and with a clap of his hands commands one of the attendant limos and speeds off into the dark night.

FIFTEEN

COLD TURKEY

Christmas is upon us and yet the air is warm and the cobalt sky streaked with long wispy clouds that curl round the Tramuntanas like ghostly white fingers. In the highest peaks of the mountains small tufts of snow hint at the cold weather to come, but for now the sun is the colour of ripe corn and the valley is giddy with the scent of lavender.

Alan puffs up from the field carrying a large pannier brimming with the first of the season's oranges. His shirt sleeves are rolled back and he is singing one of his crusty old Scottish ballads.

'What a glorious vision!' he says contentedly. I follow his gaze past the front garden and up to the tiered terraces which overflow with wild clematis and lavender. In a few days time it will be Christmas Day and I wonder whether this year, with such heavenly sunshine, we'll be carving the turkey out on the terrace. My eyes rest on the pond and with a tinge of sadness I acknowledge that my toad and his croaking companions will be gone until March. Absurdly, I worry that Johnny and I had not parted on the best of terms. There's a toot at the gate and

244

Llorenç arrives with a delivery of wood. Alan strolls over to the gate and with a flourish guides him in. The van shudders to a halt. Llorenç gets out and straightens his back.

'All this wood cutting will be the death of me.'

'You need a good massage,' Alan says.

'Any offers?' He winks in my direction.

'Sorry, Llorenç, I'm off to town to pick up the turkey.'

He gives a hefty tut. 'Typical woman, eh?'

Alan nods.

'And what about your Catalan lessons?' he yells.

'We've stopped for Christmas.'

'Any excuse.'

'If you must know, Guillem's given me a stack of homework to do over Christmas.'

'A likely story!' he quips.

Since getting back from New York, I've had a fair bit of catching up to do on my Catalan. I've missed a lot of lessons, which was borne out by the rather modest result I achieved in our first surprise *examen*, a few weeks ago. I had sat looking at the verb tables as the clock ticked by, realising that I hadn't got a clue about the imperfect and conditional tenses of *menjar*, to eat, neither was I able to fill in the blanks on a picture of a living room which required Catalan vocabulary. Rather desperately I had made up words combining French and Castilian vocabulary, to disastrous effect. Still, Guillem was full of smiles when he gave me the result, telling me that I'd somehow managed to pass, which was a good start. I've decided that some serious swotting up is in order over the holidays but when I'll find the time in between Christmas shopping, cooking and entertaining, heaven knows! I look at my watch. I've a mountain of shopping to do and am still to pick up some extra little under-the-Christmas-tree, gifts for Ollie. I jump into the car and start the engine. Alan taps on my window.

'Don't forget to pick up Ollie from football practice at noon.'

I roll down the window. 'Yes, and don't forget to collect the Christmas tree. Ollie's desperate to hang the decorations.'

He gives me a self-satisfied grin. 'Actually, the nursery has kindly offered to deliver it this morning, so I don't have to pick it up.'

'Great, so you'll have the tree up and ready to decorate by the time I get back?'

He shakes his head. 'Never a moment's peace.'

Llorenç catches the drift. 'Don't worry about her. We'll have a relaxing coffee when we've unloaded the wood.'

'Good idea,' says the Scotsman brightly, waving me goodbye.

Driving along the track proves hazardous this morning. Wolfgang and Helge arrived late the night before and are now in the midst of transporting their luggage into their house. Helge comes over to the car for a chat and to catch up on news. No sooner have I set off again than Llamp comes charging towards the car with a frowning Rafael following in close pursuit. I roll down the window.

'What's the matter?'

'He's wild this dog, and now he kill one of my chickens!'

I draw to a halt outside his *finca*.

'He can't have killed a chicken. He's just a pup.'

He places his hands flat against the car door as if he's about to do a press up and juts his head towards me, eyes ablaze.

'I caught him with it hanging from his mouth. The bird fly into his run and he catch it.'

I fear this might herald the end of Llamp's days with Rafael and that the poor mutt will be packing his kennel and bones just as Franco the boxer did before him.

'Give him a second chance. It's Christmas.'

Rafael thumps my car. 'Crazy woman!'

I reach the end of the track expecting to see the bustling form of Margalida, but the house is silent and shuttered. Perhaps she's staying with relatives today.

The town is heaving with excited shoppers stocking up on Christmas fare, for eating in Mallorca is a serious business and each and every fiesta is embraced like an old friend and plied with as much wine and culinary delicacies as can be mustered. I stroll along in the sunshine, greeting various acquaintances on the way. In the main *plaça* children are playing with balls and weaving between the spiky trees on bikes. Rows of tiny lights have been strung across the trunks and branches of trees, waiting to be illuminated once darkness falls. At this time of the year the *plaça* looks magical at night, resembling a rather refined grotto with tiny twinkling white lights clustered in the dark trees surrounding the floodlit town hall. Throughout Christmas, standing tall on either side of the town hall, is a *gegant,* an enormous wood replica of a female and a male folk dancer in traditional and historic garb, while from the depths of the building Catalan carols are blasted out from huge speakers. It all adds to the festive atmosphere and it is impossible to walk by without humming one of the tunes. As I walk up Calle Sa Lluna, I spy Antonia sitting in her store like a spider in its web, smoking and contemplating a mountain of boxes around her. She calls out to me.

'Tomorrow we finally move!'

HiBit's business is thriving and they are about to locate to larger premises. Albert and Antonia have found a well-lit store a hop, skip and jump from Café Paris. With a touch of nostalgia I remember back to my first months here in the valley when, without Internet access, I came to rely on this store as a home from home. Although I now have my computer connections functioning in the *finca*, I still need Albert's technical support and I continue to buy all my supplies here. It's always a good excuse to catch up on gossip with Antonia.

'It's all very exciting,' I say encouragingly as I enter the small store.

'You're kidding, right? I have the whole family for Christmas lunch, cooking and cleaning and now this move. Too much stress.'

I lean on one of the cardboard boxes.

'Once you've moved, it will all fall into place.'

'Ha! You got a good sense of humour, girl, I give you that.'

'Where's Albert?'

'Kitting out the other shop. No electricity, no water over there… we're going crazy!'

She wanders through the heaps of boxes, tutting to herself.

'Oh, before I forget, I've got your boy's *Football League* DVD. You better take it now or I'll never find it again.' She fumbles in a box as if it's a lucky dip and pulls out a disc.

'Ollie will be ecstatic! One more Christmas present for the pile. How much do I owe you?'

She waves me away. 'Pay me later… the till isn't working and I trust you by now!'

Out in the street, I bump into Nancy Golding, as always dressed in black and wearing her chic fedora hat.

'Have you hung my picture yet?' she asks.

'It's above our bed. It's so beautiful when it catches the light.'

She gives a coy smile. 'That makes me happy.'

'And what are you doing for Christmas?'

She fiddles with her meagre shopping bag. 'Oh, you know, hanging out at the flat, I guess. Some friends are planning to take me out for lunch on Christmas Day.'

My heart sinks a little. 'Can we come over?'

'Well, if it's not too much bother. Rosie and I would like that.'

Nancy's daughter lives in the States and work commitments prevent her visiting her mother at Christmas.

'How about Boxing Day?

She gives a little shrug. 'Suits me.'

I watch her potter off along Calle sa Lluna, no doubt en route to Art I Mans to order some picture frames or new paints. At Ca'n Matarino, the butcher's, a swell of people crowd into the small interior so I decide to pop into Colmado Sa Lluna before returning there to pick up the turkey. Xavier is busily slicing chorizo while Teresa is diligently packing customers' bags. Bustling out from the *magatzem*, the store at the back of the shop, Xavier's mother greets me, her arms cradling two huge legs of *jamón Serrano*. She dumps them down on the counter and wipes her hands on her apron. Although there's a queue, I don't have to wait too long and soon I am ordering everything from *jamones* and *salchichones*, spicy sausages, to kirsch, *dàtils*, dates, and rich Manchego cheese. Then there are the walnuts and chestnuts and special artisan biscuits and *dulces* from Barcelona.

'How are you going to carry all this?' enquires Xavier. 'Shall I drop it off at the house?'

'Are you sure?'

He laughs. 'Do I have a choice?'

Back in Calle sa Lluna, I grab my chance and dash into Ca'n Matarino's to collect the turkey. With relief I see that it's a far more modest size than the one we had for our first Christmas here. Ramon had reared us one of his own turkeys, but it grew out of all proportion and we couldn't fit it in the oven. I'm hoping this Christmas will be less eventful. Cheekily, I nip back to Xavier's shop and ask whether he might carry my turkey back home along with the other purchases. He dumps the heavy bag behind the counter and with hands on hips shakes his head theatrically and addresses the queue of customers.

'I suppose she'll want me to cook it for her too?!'

General titters and guffaws follow me out onto the street. I pop into one of my favourite haunts, Calabruix, run by Margarita and Margalida. This is Sóller's version of a good old-fashioned British bookshop where nothing is too much trouble and any title, however obscure, can be ordered swiftly and without fuss. The owners will spend precious time discussing the merits of one Catalan dictionary over another and they have a wonderful Aladdin's cave at the back of the shop housing many more titles. I select a few children's paperback novels in Catalan and Castilian Spanish and dump them on the counter.

'These look a bit difficult for you,' jokes Margalida with a glint in her eye.

'Too right! They're presents for Ollie.'

'Poc a poc!' she replies with a grin.

Tolo, our friend and guardian at the local branch of Banca March, greets me as I walk back across the *plaça* and pulls one of his bank's Christmas calendars from his bag. This is an annual tradition, and so I take it with some ceremony and promise that Alan will hang it above his desk. I have two more stops to make and I'm fast running out of time. Bel greets me as I squeeze into her tiny shop, Cavall Verd, which rather curiously means The Green Horse. The interior is crammed full of boxes of gifts and toys. Wooden mobiles, Christmas decorations and streamers hang in profusion overhead and scented candles line the shelves by the door. I look at my watch.

'Bel, I'm in a hurry. Can you suggest some small toys to put under the tree for Ollie?'

She catches the eye of a customer, a robustly built elderly senyora, and they have a brief word.

'I have just the thing! This lady says her grandson's favourite toys are a spinning top and a *diabolo*. They're all the rage now in schools.'

'Diabolo, as in diabolic? That sounds a bit dubious.'

Bel rustles around at the far end of the shop and hands me a small funnel shaped, wooden item with grooves which is attached to a long piece of string. I look mystified.

'What do you so with this?'

'It's a traditional spinning top,' she replies.

The elderly lady comes over and, taking it from my hand, bids me follow her into the busy street. Once outside, she winds the string around the base and then with great dexterity unrolls it quickly in the air and watches it tumble onto the pavement. It spins round and round at speed, attracting an immediate crowd of on-lookers, mostly children.

'Wow! *Fantàstic!*' I exclaim.

She smiles modestly then shows me how to accomplish the task. The children laugh as I make several lousy attempts at it, until finally getting the wooden top to spin. She then bustles inside, returning with the second strange object, the *diabolo*. It appears to be a twin-headed top made of plastic. She carries two wooden sticks with a string attached between the two.

'You have to juggle the top on the string between the two sticks,' she explains. 'All these toys have been around since I was young. You know, *diabolo* means devil on two sticks.'

I watch as she spins the top deftly between the two sticks which she joggles from side to side. It amazes me that a woman of her age has the agility and patience to perform these tricks. The spectators applaud and, panting a little, the senyora takes a small bow and re-enters the shop. Bel is delighted with the sudden attention her little boutique is attracting. Before it's mobbed I pay for my spoils, thank the senyora and leave. Now, I just need to make a brief stop at Rullan, the toy shop, and I'm done.

It is nearly noon as I leave Rullan with gifts for Catalina's twin girls and head for the car. Just as I pass Cafè Paris , someone touches my arm. It is elderly Senyor Bisbal. He greets me cordially.

'I'm glad to see you today. *Venga*, I want to buy you a little Christmas gift.'

I remonstrate but it's no good. He leads me into one of the main *patisserias*, Forn de Campo, and buys an enormous, family-sized *ensaïmada*, the popular Mallorcan sweet pastry, filled with custard cream. It is ceremoniously packaged in a large carrying box which Senyor Bisbal hands over to me, before doffing his cap and disappearing into the street. I stagger out of the shop with all my wares and hear my mobile trilling. Oh no, now what? I manage to extricate the phone from my bag. It's Pep.

'Hey, where are you, lazy woman? I picked up Angel and Ollie from the football pitch. You left the poor boy stranded.'

I look at my watch. 'I'm afraid I'm running late.'

'*Tranquil.la!* What are friends for, eh? We're in Cafè Paris . Come and join us for a coffee.'

Never has an invitation to coffee sounded so good.

We arrive back at the *finca* laden with bags. Ollie nibbles nervously on his bottom lip. In his hands he twirls his sealed football report. An interesting phenomenon in Mallorca is that football reports are treated with almost as much respect as their school counterparts. These typed documents are lengthy and detailed, focusing on the student's psychological state, response under pressure, alertness to trainer instructions, team spirit, tactical ability and attitude. Finally, there is a handwritten paragraph from the trainer himself, noting any special attributes and commenting on the student's overall rating. Ollie takes it all very seriously and I hope one day he'll show the same gravitas when it comes to his school reports.

The Scotsman helps carry bags from the car.

'I thought you'd have more stuff.'

'Actually, Xavier's coming up with the rest.'

His shoulders sag with the weight of the load. 'I might have known.'

He glances at the huge cardboard box. 'Whatever's in there?'

'A giant *ensaïmada*, a Christmas gift from Senyor Bisbal.'

He shakes his head. 'Trust you!'

He strides into the house in conversation with Ollie and plonks the bags down on the kitchen table. Some minutes later I find Ollie and him absorbed in the football report.

'Excellent, Ollie. All 'A's and 'B's.'

I lean over the paper.

'An '*A*' for psychological state? They've slipped up there.'

Ollie gives a loud grunt and splays his legs out in front of him at the table. 'I'd rather have got an A for striker skills.'

'You can't win them all.'

He raps his fingers against the table. 'By the way, when does Alex arrive?'

Alex is my nineteen-year-old nephew whom Ollie considers the epitome of cool. On Christmas Eve he and my sister, Cecilia, will be arriving to take possession of a house in Fornalutx village. Having completed the deal last month, they will be camping out at the sparsely furnished property for three weeks and spending Christmas itself over at our *finca*. When Alex returns to university, my sister will begin her new life in the valley, gradually renovating the house and commencing work as a language consultant in Palma.

'They'll be here the day after tomorrow.'

Ollie looks deflated. 'That's ages away.'

Alan folds up the report. 'How about helping me in the garden?'

He rolls his eyes. 'No thanks.'

'All right then, what about decorating the Christmas tree?'

Ollie's eyes light up. 'It's here? Where is it?'

Alan taps his nose. 'It's outside. Come and see. It's enormous.'

Ollie rushes out into the back patio, closely pursued by his father.

I start unloading the food into the fridge, a task I dread at this time of the year because it's nigh impossible to squeeze everything inside. A few minutes later they return.

Ollie is bubbling with excitement. 'It's awesome! I'm going to start sorting out the decorations.'

He patters off in the direction of the cellar where the decorations are stowed away in an old wooden chest.

I turn to Alan. 'I saw Nancy in town. I said we'd pop over to see her on Boxing Day.'

He looks up. 'Good idea. We can bring her Ollie's present then.'

Two days earlier, while Christmas shopping in Palma, Ollie had found a marcasite brooch of a cat which he deemed a fitting gift for his beloved Nancy.

'Talking of old friends, Margalida's chalet is shuttered up. D'you think all's well?'

He gets up and stretches. 'She's probably staying over at Silvia and Pedro's for Christmas. I wouldn't worry.'

Despite Alan's reassurances, I find it odd that Margalida would sleep at her daughter and son-in-law's home when she only lives across the track from them. Something doesn't add up.

There's a loud tooting at the gate. Xavier has arrived.

The wind is blowing wildly, petulantly throwing garden pots about the garden and rippling the cats' fur. Alan slams the kitchen door behind him, unzips his Barbour and peers out at the sky.

'The rain's starting again.'

It is Christmas Eve and the rain has been falling solidly for two days. Cecilia and Alex are arriving later tonight so Ollie and I have been busy placing presents under the Christmas tree, putting up decorations around the house and cooking. He's an enthusiastic sous-chef, and between us we have made the chocolate log and brandy butter and baked several batches of mince pies and sausage rolls. Tomorrow, Pep, Juana and Angel, will be spending Christmas Day with us all so I am trying to prepare as much as I can in advance. Their kitchen is being renovated so it's impossible for Juana to do any cooking at their house for another week.

A final batch of mince pies are in the oven and with the washing up finished Ollie and I sit at the table munching on some chocolate biscuits. I take a gulp from my mug of tea, contemplating what I need to prepare for dinner.

Ollie frowns. 'The oven's making a bit of a funny noise.'

'Well, we've been doing so much cooking. Poor thing probably needs a rest,' I reply.

He shrugs his shoulders and starts flicking happily through a comic.

'I think this is going to be the best Christmas ever!'

'I hope you're right, Ollie.'

I listen to the rain on the window pane, pleased that we're warm and cosy inside the kitchen. Alan suddenly looks up from a gardening book he's reading.

'Aren't you supposed to be seeing your chum at the port this afternoon?'

I give a groan. Indeed he's right. I have agreed to meet Julia, my Venezuelan friend from the Catalan class, for a festive coffee but I'm not relishing the drive in heavy rain.

'I might as well set off soon. With all this rain, the roads will be bad.'

'Good idea. When will you be home?'

'About five. By the way, can you keep an eye on the mince pies? Just turn them off in about ten minutes.'

'Fine.'

We stand by the sink, looking out at the rain which is now falling in heavy white sheets on the patio.

'So much for Christmas lunch al fresco,' the Scotsman sighs. 'You can't even see the mountains.'

A cloak of silver grey mist has descended over the Tramuntanas and there's a chill in the air. I pull on my jacket and am on the point of opening the front door when there's a tremendous bang from the oven. Ollie and Alan both yelp in unison and rush over to the stove. Smoke billows from its sides and there's a strange crackling sound. I rush back into the kitchen.

'Please don't tell me it's blown up,' I cry.

'I told you it was making a funny noise,' says Ollie.

Alan carefully opens the door, fanning away a plume of grey smoke, and rescues the semi-cooked mince pies.

'God knows what's wrong with it.'

'Great timing,' I mutter.

'Maybe it's just a fuse,' he says doubtfully.

He potters off to the basement and returns with a long face. 'Hmm, it's not the fuse. Maybe it's an electrical fault.'

I watch as he plods off again, this time to get his toolbox. When he returns he removes the front panel encasing the temperature dials and examines the electrical circuit and wires behind.

'I think it's completely buggered. The wires seem to have melted. We'll have to get the engineer up.'

'You're joking? On Christmas Eve?'

He is silent for a second.

'Were you planning on using it tonight?'

'That's not the issue. I'm thinking about the turkey tomorrow,' I groan.

He gives a sigh. 'What about microwaving it?'

I cast him a scornful look. 'Of course we can't. It would never fit in there.'

'There's always Pep and Juana's house,' he says.

'Aha! That's true,' I say brightly.

'But their kitchen's all upside down,' says Ollie.

'Damn, I forgot.' Alan plods over to the espresso machine. 'Look, you go to the port and I'll have a ponder. I'll try getting hold of an engineer.'

Inko and the grey twins cautiously re-enter the kitchen. They had bolted under the piano when they heard the bang. Despondently, I pick up the car keys and an umbrella by the front door. How can the fates have conspired to wreck the oven the day before Christmas? Let's hope nothing else can go wrong. Alan suddenly calls after me.

'Before you go can you remind me how to work this blasted coffee machine?'

The Faro bar sits up high on a hill above the busy shops and restaurants of the port, and offers breathtaking views of the wild sea below. A narrow track runs beyond its entrance to a path with a steep cliff face on one side and the lashing sea on the other. Inside, cheery amber flames leap from the hearth and the wooden tables are festooned with holly and berries. Behind the bar, Marga, the waitress, wipes glasses and stares out at the rain. Julia is sitting in front of the fire and warming her hands. She drains her cup of coffee.

'You poor thing. As I said, if I didn't have twelve Venezuelans arriving for Christmas lunch, you could have come to me.'

I shake my head. 'Don't worry, we'll work something out. One of life's little challenges.'

She brightens up. 'If the rain stops, you could maybe spit roast the turkey in your field.'

Some time ago, Alan reliably informed me that in his youth he was a Queen's Scout, an honour apparently bestowed on boys able to perform the most difficult of scout tasks, so I now have visions of the Scotsman erecting a precarious pyre, losing control of the flames and reducing the turkey to ashes whilst

257

setting the entire field on fire. We get up to leave and I glimpse the bill.

'I'll go and settle up at the bar.'

As I take my change, the front door springs open and three rain-sodden creatures hurtle inside. The woman's glasses are misted up and her jumper is heavy with water. A teenage girl looks out miserably from under a thin hood while the man shakes an umbrella and stands against the door.

'You speak German?' she asks forlornly.

Marga shakes her head in the negative.

'English?'

Marga looks at me hopefully.

'Can I help?' I ask.

The woman seems exhausted and her face is pale and drawn. 'We desperately need somewhere to stay. We only arrived yesterday late evening at a rented flat, but in the night the roof collapsed with the rain and now we are out on the street.'

I thought I was the only one with problems today. Julia doesn't understand what the woman says so I translate. She puts a hand over her mouth and makes the sign of the cross.

'Can't the owner of the flat help you?'

She runs a distraught hand through her unruly grey hair. 'No. We called her and she just told us to leave. She gave us the money back and left us stranded with our belongings.'

I feel indignant on the German lady's behalf. 'I'll see what I can do.'

I bid Julia farewell and call Victoria Duvall, knowing that she has many contacts renting property in the area. By luck she answers immediately and promises to come right back to me. It's five-thirty and the weather is getting more bleak by the second. To keep spirits up, I tell them all about my cooker blowing up. The woman tuts sympathetically and then with a big smile taps my hand and says, 'I have a great German recipe for poached turkey.'

'Poached?'

She is yelling above the wind. 'You boil it tonight with onions and have it cold with boiled potatoes tomorrow. It's delicious.'

I try to look enthusiastic. 'Thanks, I'll think about that.'

The mobile phone trills.

'You're in luck!' says Victoria. 'I've found them a *finca* in Fornalutx. Tell them to come over now.'

'She can help us?' the man asks hopefully.

The Germans are ecstatic. 'We had wanted a nice Christmas by the sea but perhaps with this rain, mountain views are best, *ya*?'

They break into hysterical giggles, reminding me yet again that German and British humour genes are at times quite at odds. In their situation I'd be blubbing into a double vodka and contemplating a brisk walk off the edge of one of the nearby cliffs.

I scribble down Victoria's details as the woman enthusiastically hands me a card from her handbag.

'Here, take this and if you want my recipe, just call me.'

I wave them goodbye and study the card in the rain. She is a professor from Heidelberg University. I can only hope her lectures are a tad more inspiring than her cookery tips. Whatever happens, one thing's for sure: we shall not be eating poached turkey tomorrow. Imbued with the spirit of Christmas I feel certain that, in the immortal words of Charles Dickens' eternally optimistic Mr Micawber, *something will turn up.*

It is Christmas morning and I have risen early to dress the turkey. Heaven knows why when I still don't know how I'm going to cook the wretched thing. Ollie was awake at some ungodly hour, desperate to investigate the fireplace downstairs for evidence of Father Christmas's visit. With delight he discovered a pillowcase in the grate stuffed with booty and at its side a half-eaten carrot and some mince pie crumbs presumably left by a litter lout reindeer. He now sits cross-legged on the rug in the *entrada* enthusiastically tearing at wrapping paper and whooping with joy at every item uncovered. A large tree, smothered in white fairy lights and decorations, sits in a far corner by the French windows underneath which Orlando and Minky play with a string of small gold stars. I hear someone plodding down the staircase and my nephew, Alex, appears in the *entrada*, hair dishevelled and yawning.

'Alex!' screeches Ollie, launching himself on his cousin. 'Come and look at my presents.'

'Wow. You're one lucky piglet.' He grabs Ollie under his arm and then spins him round.

'Let go, Alex!' He gurgles with mirth. They fall on top of each other in a heap.

'Fancy a coffee?' I yell above the din.

Alex untangles himself and stands up to give me a hug, taking the mug at the same time. 'Wonderful! Now you know why you're my favourite aunt.'

'You've only got one.'

'That's very true,' he says contemplatively. 'Now, in the night I had an inspirational idea about our turkey problem.'

'Am I going to like it?'

'Hmm. I'm not sure but it's worth a punt. I was on the *YouTube* website at about three this morning…'

'What?'

'It's all right, that's what teenagers do, and I found a brilliant way of cooking a turkey on a clamp lamp.'

I digest this information slowly while Ollie happily carries on unwrapping gifts and playing with his toys. Alex potters into the kitchen and sits down at the table, his long legs splayed out in front of him. I notice he's wearing a black Armani T-shirt and black pyjama bottoms. He's apparently stylish even in bed.

'Do you have a clamp lamp lying around?'

I give him a frown. 'I don't even know what it is.'

'Ah well, it's simple enough. As long as you've got any kind of light source we can cook the bird.'

'How?'

He gives me an old-fashioned look. 'Well, you cook the turkey above a bowl which contains a clamp lamp and some DVDs. The reflected light creates heat which cooks the meat. All very simple.'

'Have you done this before?'

He tuts. 'Of course not. Law students don't cook.'

My sister wafts into the kitchen, Ollie attached to one arm. 'You just live on kebabs in Manchester, don't you?'

'Your son is proposing that we cook the turkey over a clamp lamp, which I doubt we even have in the house. I'll have to ask Alan.'

Cecilia relinquishes Ollie's hold on her and fills the kettle with water. 'I'll play in a minute, sweetheart. I desperately need tea.'

'It was that third bottle of wine we had last night.'

'Don't remind me,' she groans, slumping at the table.

Alan potters in from the garden.

'A happy Christmas to one and all! Who's for breakfast?'

'Do you have a clamp lamp?' asks Alex hopefully.

The Scotsman eyes him curiously. 'Down in the *abajo* I have an old one.'

'Excellent. Then all we need are some containers and a few DVDs.'

'Are you doing an experiment?' asks Ollie.

'Yes, he's going to blow up the house,' I rejoin.

Alex squeezes my arm. 'Have faith, auntie dear. Now Alan, let's get to work.'

A weak sun is shining in the sky and we all feel in good spirits as we huddle around a large tin bowl in the garden waiting for a miracle to happen.

'Well, it's starting to smoke,' says Alex.

'Are you sure it's safe?' I ask.

'Well, if it blows up at least we're outside,' says Alan. 'Running the flex out from the kitchen was a good idea.'

'I'm full of them,' says my nephew with a huge grin.

Cecilia and Ollie nudge each other and then creep off inside. 'Tell us when it's cooked,' my sister says. 'We're off to eat the chocolate tree decorations.'

Smoke soon begins billowing out of the sides of the lid covering the turkey.

'That's good, Alex,' says Alan. 'It must be cooking.'

We stand back.

'How long do we wait?' I'm not convinced this is going to work and I'm very concerned about my old *Die Hard* DVDs being used as turkey bait around the clamp lamp.

'We just leave it for about an hour or so, I think,' says Alex.

Cecilia potters out with some mince pies. 'Here, have one of these to keep you going.'

We all swoop on them.

'What time are your friends coming over?' she asks me.

'About two o'clock. Remember, no one eats early around here.'

'That's great. We've got bags of time to get the turkey cooked and…'

At which point there's a strange sizzling sound followed by a loud pop like a champagne cork going off and the clamp lamb bulb explodes. We all leap back and exchange looks.

'Perhaps we should move on to plan B?' beams Alex.

'And what is plan B?' I say with irony.

'Well, I've just had an idea,' he says.

262

COLD TURKEY

Alex and I are picking at a plate of smoked salmon blinis and slurping champagne while Ollie sits drinking cola and eating olives.

'I feel a bit guilty about Alan and Cecilia doing all the relays up to Fornalutx while we're stuffing ourselves back here.'

He stretches his arms out in front of him. 'Look, I can't drive and you've got to be here to welcome Pep and Juana so we had no choice. Feeling guilty is a complete waste of energy.'

'I suppose you're right,' I say, thinking about the turkey which at this very moment is hopefully cooking in the oven of my sister's new home. Alex's plan B was actually rather clever. He remembered that a gas cylinder had been delivered to their new house for the oven – piped gas not having reached our mountains yet – and suggested that we ferry the bird and potatoes up to their village for cooking. The Scotsman and my intrepid sister offered to take it in turns to baste the turkey at intervals and check on the roast potatoes. The mobile phone rings. It's Alan reporting that Cecilia's on her way down the mountain and that he will stay put until the bird's cooked.

'That's good, Alex. The turkey's nearly done. We'll have to eat as soon as Alan returns or everything will go cold.'

'That's OK,' he yawns. 'Pep and Juana can have a drink and by the time Alan gets back it'll be time to eat.'

There's a loud tooting at the gate.

'That must be my mother.'

But it isn't. Catalina pulls up in the courtyard and comes bustling in to the kitchen with presents.

'Hey, where's my glass of cava?'

Alex flips open the fridge, ever grateful to have an excuse to open a bottle.

'So, your mother and Alan are cooking the turkey, and what about you, Alex?'

'I'm needed here to keep my aunt plied with cava.'

She pokes him in the ribs. 'You're a bad boy. *Molt dolent.*'

Many years ago, Catalina au-paired for my sister in Kent, and was the one who persuaded us to first visit the island on holiday. Little did she realise then that she'd be the catalyst for our complete change of lifestyle. She has a special fondness for Alex whom she looked after when he was a toddler.

'I love Christmas,' sighs Catalina. 'So much food and chocolate. I'm at my aunt's restaurant with all the family for lunch today and then dinner with Jack and Sarah at Es Turo this evening. What a crazy day!'

Alex gives a smirk and refills her glass.

'Don't get me drunk, Alex. I have to drive back up the hill.'

There's more hooting at the gate and within minutes Cecilia arrives in the kitchen.

'Thank God I don't have to drive up to Fornalutx again. That's my third trip.'

'Have a drink, mother,' says Alex cheerfully.

Having given Catalina a hug, she takes a glass and we all stroll out into the sunny garden.

'Look how beautiful it is today,' says Catalina.

'Maybe we'll be eating al fresco after all,' I add.

'Why not?' says Cecilia. 'Let's transfer all the dishes outside.'

'Christmas under a Mallorcan sun,' I sigh. 'Now whoever would have thought that possible?'

Pep is lying back in his chair at the table, puffing on a huge Havana, a gift from Alan. A paper hat is slung lopsidedly on his head.

'You know, that was one of the best turkeys I've ever tasted,' he says. 'An interesting temperature too.'

I give him a warning look. 'Watch it!'

'What do you mean? I love cold turkey...' he giggles.

Cecilia shakes her head. 'Is he always this objectionable?'

'Always,' says Juana with a wry grin. 'Now you're coming to live here, you'll see how bad he is for yourself.'

'I think I've seen enough,' she jests, throwing her arms wide as if to embrace the hot sun above.

'Thank you for a wonderful lunch, all of you,' beams Juana.

'Hear, hear!' says Pep, unleashing a party popper over my head.

Alex grabs one from the table and fires it at Pep.

'Children!' laughs Juana. 'I swear my husband gets worse as he gets older.'

'This is just the beginning,' I say, giving Pep a kick under the table.

Alan arrives from the kitchen with flutes of chilled champagne and chocolate truffles.

'Yummy!' shriek Ollie and Angel in unison, interrupting a game of swing ball to come over and help themselves to chocolates.

'I don't think I can eat another thing,' I declare. 'Mind you on second thoughts…'

'What a perfect Christmas,' says Alan. 'Good food, friends and family and blissful weather.'

'To a perfect Christmas!' says Alex, raising his glass to us all.

'To a perfect Christmas!' we say in unison.

'To the best Christmas ever,' says Ollie and with a cheeky grin he takes a swig of my champagne and runs off into the field with his friend, Angel.

It's Boxing Day. Rachel is full of Yuletide cheer.

'I'm glad you managed to have your Christmas lunch in the end.'

'So am I. Yours sounded a lot less chaotic.'

She laughs. 'Yes, M&S did us proud. We didn't have to do very much at all.'

'Well, I hope you can switch off from work for a few days now.'

'You must be joking! I've already had Manuel on the phone. He's going to ring you later about the Cuba H Hotel opening and Greedy George called about the Crown jewels book launch.'

'They rang you at home?'

'I don't know why you're so surprised. You know those two never let us off the hook.'

'It is an international holiday!'

'As if they care!' she titters.

'So what is George after this time?'

'He wants an invitation to the Crown jewels launch.'

'What a cheek!'

'It gets worse. He thought he and Dannie could come together.'

'Did you explain it's by invitation only?'

'I did, but he sounded so keen. Let's talk about it later.'

Despite her robust exterior, Rachel can be a marshmallow when it comes to Greedy George. She often caves in to his boyish charms.

'Well, we've only got a month to go now. Is everyone at the Stationery Office happy?'

'Cock-a-hoop. Oh, there's just one thing. The editor of the Crown jewels book queried a small detail on the draft news release you sent him for the press conference.'

'What's that?'

'You gave it the headline, "BLAIR TO UNVEIL CROWN JEWELS".'

'So? His name is Mr Blair.'

'But he's a little concerned that some media might think he's the *other* Mr Blair and that we're talking about the *real* Crown jewels.'

'Exactly, Rachel. This way we'll be guaranteed to have a spectacular press turn out.'

COLD TURKEY

It's early evening. Nancy is sitting in front of a tiny electric heater with Rosie at her feet. She was somewhat taken aback when we arrived with a bottle of champagne and a meals-on-wheels Christmas dinner for one, especially as it is Boxing Day. We were going to invite her to join us at our own bizarre Christmas feast but were pipped to the post by some mutual friends. Given our disastrous turkey relay-run luncheon, I'm glad she had safe harbour elsewhere.

Nancy gives me a big smile. 'I shall heat it up for my supper later. Rosie and I will have a feast.'

Ollie hands her a small packet together with a handmade Christmas card. He has lovingly painted Nancy's favourite animals – two sea otters on the front – wearing Santa hats.

'Well, I guess with all this drawing you're going to be putting me out of business soon.'

He puffs out his cheeks. 'In my dreams.'

She coughs and pulls her black shawl closely around her shoulders. With difficulty she fumbles with the tightly packed gift, finally unwrapping it and holding the marcasite cat up to the light.

'Why, Ollie this is divine! I mean, I'm going to feel like a queen walking down the street wearing this.'

She plants a big kiss on his cheek. He is flushed with pleasure.

'They're not real diamonds though.'

She dissolves into laughter. 'Didn't you know that marcasites are far more special than diamonds? They've got real character.'

He studies her face closely.

'Really?'

'Sure. Just like your card is so much more valuable than any trumped-up thing you could buy in a shop.'

He gives a satisfied sigh and potters off to draw a picture at her desk.

She smiles serenely for a few minutes, absorbed in thought, and then grasps my hand.

'I have some news.'

I take a sip of champagne. 'Great. Is it about the exhibition?'

Alan is eating a truffle and sitting back in an armchair, listening intently.

'No. Actually, it's about my move.'

'What move?' I say sharply.

She releases my hand and fiddles with one of her amber rings.

'Well, you know I've been finding things a little difficult of late, what with my health and money issues and this infernal cold. My daughter has suggested I move back over to the States to live near her.'

Alan sits up in his chair, his face expressionless. Ollie has stopped painting.

'You're going away? For how long?'

She gives him a gentle smile. 'I don't know, Ollie. Some time, maybe. You know, until I get back on my feet.'

I feel hollow at the thought of Nancy leaving the Sóller Valley. Her incredibly vibrant abstract art hangs in our home, a daily reminder of how lucky we are to have her as a friend.

'How do you feel about that?'

She gives a little shrug and touches my hand.

'I don't know. It's kinda sad to be going, but California has great weather and I'll be near my daughter. It sort of makes sense.'

Alan exhales deeply. 'When are you thinking of leaving?'

'The spring, I guess. I'll need a few months to get packed up.'

'It's going to be quite a wrench for you and for all of us.'

She gives me a flash of her pearly teeth. 'Come on, why the long face? Ever heard of email?'

We arrive at the mouth of the track and to my relief I see a light on in Margalida's chalet. We are all feeling rather sombre at the thought of Nancy's departure but, given her difficult circumstances, know it makes sense. For some time now I have wondered how much longer she would be able to cope all alone with the winter weather and her increasingly bad health. I ask Alan to stop the car so that I can check up on Margalida.

'Well, don't be long. Remember we're cooking for the troops tonight.'

Cecilia and Alex are back at the *finca* and tonight Catalina and her family will be joining us for supper. Thankfully, an engineer drove up from Palma earlier in the day to fix our oven, telling us that the wiring had been wrongly connected and we were lucky not to have been burned to cinders. I relish passing that news on to our local electrician, but he'll no doubt throw his hands melodramatically in the air shouting *'Joder!'*, a favoured Spanish expletive, and tell me the man is a buffoon and it is all the fault of the manufacturer. At least it's fixed. I watch as Alan passes me up the track, the car tail lights fading in the dusk. I knock softly on the door and wait for the sound of Margalida's stick clumping along the corridor. Eventually the lock turns and a sliver of bright light squirms through the partially open door. She is squinting up at me.

'Ah! I thought it might be you. I haven't been too good.'

I enter the house, closing the door behind me. Using my arm for support, Margalida leads me into her kitchen.

'What's up?'

She gestures for me to sit at the table. Once settled, she blows her nose and with trembling hands sips at a glass of water.

'It happened so quickly. One minute I was picking oranges, the next I was lying on my back under the tree.'

'How much *herbes* had you been drinking?'

She gives a little smile and tuts.

'So there I was alone in Silvia's orchard and I couldn't move. Just like a *centpeus*.'

I deduce that this must mean centipede. A new word for the old memory bank.

'Were you there for some time?'

She flutters her hands in the air. 'Thankfully not very long. My son-in-law found me and helped me into the house, but my hip was badly bruised. I've been staying over at Silvia's ever since.'

I shake my head. 'Thank heavens you didn't break any bones.'

'God is merciful,' she mutters, fingering the cross on her neck. 'I'm glad to be back home.'

'Yes, but don't overdo it. Do you need anything?'

'Just good health and considerate neighbours.'

I get up and give her hand a little squeeze. 'I'll pop over tomorrow with some mince pies.'

'What are they?'

'They're little fruit pastries we have at Christmas time.'

'*Pues*, if you're not too busy.'

As I walk back up the track in the thick, velvety darkness, I gloomily reflect on Nancy's news and the growing frailty of Margalida. In London I seldom had cause to ponder the passing of time and aside from my ninety-year-old aunt tucked away in a nursing home in Kent, rarely came into contact with elderly people. Now these two feisty women, whose sagacity and unconditional friendship I have come to rely on in so short a time, are encountering the fickle and unyielding pressures of old age. I am passing Rafael's open front door and at the sound of my tread he shoots out of the house in merry mood with Llamp in tow.

'Hey, why so sad?'

I force a smile. 'Oh, I was just reflecting on old age.'

He gives a hoot of laughter. 'You don't look so old! Besides, it's Christmas. Cheer up and have a glass! Old age is just an attitude of mind.'

I look at his manically cheerful face. In this valley it's impossible to stay glum for very long.

SIXTEEN

A BLESSING IN DISGUISE

There's a cacophony of noise in the *plaça*. The big-hearted Saint Francis of Assisi, lover of all things whiskery and furry, and Noah, that noble architect of the great ark, would be proud. For today, 17 January, is Beneides de Sant Antoni, the day when animals everywhere are invited to be blessed in the presence of the local priest and an appreciative audience of townsfolk. Sant Antoni, who was born around AD 250, may not have enjoyed the same status over the centuries as good old Saint Francis, but a patron saint of animals he became nevertheless. In fact, his signs are a bell and a piglet. Now, in medieval times it was popularly believed that the bell warded off the devil, hence its popularity as a saintly symbol, but the piglet is a different matter. It seems that Sant Antoni adopted a starving piglet which he overfed to such a degree that it began waddling and soon became so utterly obese that it couldn't get up at all. Forever after Antoni was regarded as the patron saint of beasts, though animal lovers today might have taken him to task for not putting his beloved pig on a strict regime when it began to totter on its trotters. Aside from the annual animal blessings held in his name, Sant Antoni also presides over a series of public bonfires and spectacular displays of dancing devils presented during the same week across the island.

From all sides of the sunny square come donkeys, bulls, pigs, goats, small yappy *ca rater* dogs with their spindly legs and quivering black coats, cats in baskets, horses, exotic birds and mice in cages, reptiles and fish in glass containers and, oh no, ewes too. Their owners wait patiently in turn as the holy man in his black cassock raises his hand and makes the sign of the cross above the head of each and every creature. With closed eyes he utters a prayer while the animals neigh, honk, tweet, bark, yowl and splutter, some pounding the paved floor with their hooves but all showing remarkable restraint on this most celebrated of holy days.

This morning we have spent precious time trying to persuade Inko and the grey twins, Orlando and Minky, to attend the event. With some bad grace all three wriggled under Ollie's bed and refused to be unearthed until drastic measures were taken. With one blast of the vacuum cleaner they shot out from under the bed and, quick as a flash, we had them snapped inside carrying baskets ready for the brief car journey into town.

So, this morning the cafes are bulging and a throng of locals pour into the *plaça* with their pets and livestock. At long wooden trestle tables, red and white wine is served in plastic cups and huge platters of *coca* are spread out for all to share. As a general rule, *coca,* one of Mallorca's best loved pastries, is served at every fiesta in squared slices. It's the Mallorcan equivalent of pizza and is topped with peppers, onions, spinach and other vegetables. As with the *ensaïmada* spiral shaped pastries, it's easy to become a little *coca-d* out given that both are served liberally at most events, so it's often wise to have a break from it in between celebrations. At another table a swarm of guests cluster like excited bees, tucking into *sobrasada* sausage which is offered on slices of dense, locally baked brown bread. This meaty Mallorcan delicacy is made from pork cured with paprika and salt, although other local ingredients such as honey are often added.

Like one of Cleopatra's slaves, Ollie struggles to carry the Empress Inko up the cobbled street to the square. Supine within her carriage she allows her head to tilt occasionally towards her subjects in the street with eyes that denote total disdain and ennui. Meanwhile, I wrestle with the twins' basket. Inside they huddle together emitting little meows whenever a passer-by dares to peep inside their den.

We wait to receive blessings from the priest and all is well until Alan suggests opening the baskets to allow the anointing of our captives' heads. We reach the front of the queue, watched on by many a beatific, furry face. Tentatively, Ollie opens Inko's cage. She rolls over onto her front and allows the priest to touch her forehead before inching back into the safer recesses of her basket. Carefully, I undo the catch of the twins' cage but just as the priest bends to touch them a very unholy *ca rater* breaks rank and comes snarling up by my side. The priest and I swerve to avoid his tight little jaws while his owner lunges forward and secures him with a lead. It's too late. Opportunistically, the twins leap from the basket and slink off at speed across the *plaça* in the direction of Calle sa Lluna. The priest looks helplessly on and shrugs while a grubby Rasta sheep with long matted dreadlocks kicks at one of the pigs. In all the brouhaha, Ollie yells for me to find the twins while Alan stands with hands on hips tutting at the unholy din around him.

'Hurry! We must get them back,' cries Ollie.

Indeed we must. Hastily handing Inko's basket to his father, Ollie grabs my hand and off we dash in pursuit of our dynamic duo. It is Sunday so the shops in Calle sa Lluna are closed but lots of happy families are ambling along the narrow street to join in the festivities.

'Have you seen two grey kittens?' calls out my son as he runs along the street. People shake their heads and look about them in confusion. There isn't a meow or a streak of grey fur to be seen. Out of breath, we stop in our tracks mid street and begin yelling their names. Nothing.

'I know,' says Ollie in a burst of sudden hope. 'Why not sing their favourite song? You know, the one they like.'

I gather my thoughts. 'Ah', I whisper, 'You mean, *"Oh we'll drink, we'll drink, we'll drink, to Inko the pink, the pink, the pink, the mistress of the feline race…"*'

He holds up his hands in frustration.

'That's Inko's song. They're hardly going to like that. No, the one you sing about Slinky Minky and Orlando the fattest cat in Sóller town.'

A small group of children has gathered around us, all helpfully looking in doorways and bins for our beloved moggies.

I hiss at Ollie, 'We're in a crowded street. People will have me certified if I start singing the communists anthem.'

'Sing it!' he commands.

'Well, you join in then.'

He views me with impatience. 'OK, OK.'

So, feeling more than a little silly, I begin singing a ridiculous and rather irreverent version of The Red Flag while local children view me with a mixture of pity and humour. Ollie plucks up the courage to join in and soon, with much giggling, our young onlookers attempt the tune too. I'm concerned that it might be misconstrued as a young communist rally. We do several repeats to a small applause from some parents who seem to mistake us for child entertainers, but it's to no avail. The kittens appear to have gone.

'Don't give up,' says one of our small backing group. 'I lost my dog a week ago, but he showed up last night.'

Ollie nods bravely, but he is full of despair. We slump against a wall considering our options when a little girl screams out, *'Moix! Moix!'*

We follow her pointed finger and there surveying us from a tiled roof are the twins. The children give a cheer and so with finger to lips I tell everyone to be as quiet as mice while I try to lure them down. After much coaxing both cats at last descend and stand at my feet. Ollie gathers Orlando up in his arms while I clutch hold of Minky.

'Well, thank you everyone for your fantastic help.'

The children step forward to stroke the miscreants.

'*Es un miracle!*' squeaks a little girl.

'*Si, es Sant* Antoni!' says another with gravitas.

'Are they right?' asks Ollie. 'Is it really a miracle that we found them?'

'Who can say, Ollie, but God does seem to work in mysterious ways.'

We head back to the square where the Scotsman is deep in conversation with Albert and Antonia from HiBit. I notice he has a large cup of red wine in his hand and a piece of *coca* in the other.

'Ah, there you are!' he beams. 'Put the little devils in their basket before they run off again.'

We pop the kittens into one of the baskets at his feet.

'I guess this is the last time you'll be taking them to a blessing,' laughs Antonia.

'Yes, I think we might just be spectators next year,' I reply.

'Here, have some wine,' says Albert with a grin.

I gratefully take the cup from him. I look around me, at the same time exchanging greetings with various acquaintances. The *plaça* is full of locals enjoying the warm sun and delicious fare provided by our town council. Most of the animals have been led away and those that haven't find themselves the centre of attention with children who fondle their ears and slip them leftovers from the tables in the square. The old priest is sitting on a bench in deep conversation with a couple of farmers who stand with their backs to their donkeys. What a scene of bucolic bliss. It's at times like this that I realise there's really nowhere else I'd rather be.

The Scotsman is down in the field digging his vegetable patch. It's the end of January and yet the heavens display no ill humour and the sun smiles weakly through the kitchen window as I finish preparing lunch. As it's the weekend we are entertaining some Mallorcan friends, Inès and Jaume from Palma and their two children, Lluc and Neus. Lluc is one of Ollie's buddies from school, an impish boy who spends much of his free time conducting quasi-scientific experiments – much to his parents' dismay – and playing football. While our son regards him as the epitome of cool the same cannot be said for his poor sister Neus, whom he largely ignores because she's a girl. Their father, Jaume, is a lawyer and his wife, Ines, a civil servant. They speak excellent English, although insist that we practice our Spanish and Catalan with them which invariably has them guffawing with laughter when one of us makes some linguistic howler.

Ollie sits up on the work surface and with concentration draws his finger around a discarded mixing bowl, licking up the remnants of chocolate mouse until there's hardly a trace remaining. It's gone half one, but I'm not the least perturbed. It's unusual for Spanish friends to turn up much before two at lunchtime. Alan appears at the kitchen door with a muddy trowel.

'The soil's rock hard. It's going to be a few days before I can loosen it up.'

'Let's hope it rains.'

'No way!' cries Ollie. 'I've got football practice tomorrow, thank you very much.'

I scan Alan's attire. 'You'd better get changed out of your Boy Scout shorts. They'll be here in a minute.'

'All right,' mumbles the Scotsman. 'Give me a second.'

He places the trowel outside the back door and sets off up the stairs to change. Some time later a car toots. I open the gates via the intercom and am slightly confused to hear two vehicles crunch in to the courtyard. Ollie frowns.

'That's odd. Why would they come in two cars?'

The awkward answer soon presents itself. Ollie and I skip over to the porch and find our four friends emerging from their blue jeep. From the second car appears another quartet I've never seen in my life. Jaume rushes to greet me.

'*Hola!* It's so good to be here. The air is so fantastic. Please let me introduce you to my mother and father and two of my sister's children, Ignasi and Llora.'

I grit my teeth into a manic smile. '*Hola!* Lovely to meet you all.'

Inès wanders over with the party and we exchange kisses. 'It's OK we all come, *si?* I nearly rang, but it's only a few more people.'

'When I told my mother about you, she said she'd like to visit too but my sister's kids were staying with her so I thought they could all come,' says Jaume without the slightest embarrassment.

'*No problema!* I'm sure we'll manage somehow. I'll just get Alan.'

I lead them into the garden and fix drinks. Ollie takes the four children up to his room while the adults walk around the gardens marvelling at Alan's horticultural prowess. I scurry upstairs.

'Alan, we've got a problem. They've brought four more people.'

'What? That's all we need.'

'I know. I can rustle up a big pasta for the kids, but I've not got enough chicken pieces for the adults.'

'What about the starter?'

'I'll just have to give them lots of garnish with the prawns. Listen, I'll call Pep and see if he can lend me some chicken breasts.'

He looks horrified. 'Poor Pep! You can't do that. He's probably in the middle of lunch.'

'I can drive round. You keep the troops plied with drink.'

Alan dashes downstairs to play host while I call Pep. He listens in some bemusement.

'You never learn. Why do you think we Mallorcans always cook everything in a big pot?'

'To save on washing up?'

'No. So that we can feed endless guests. You never know how many people will ever turn up so make sure you over cater.'

'It's not quite like that in England,' I grumble.

'Of course, you British are so civilised,' he says, mimicking a snooty English accent.

'So can you lend me some chicken breasts?'

'You could always kill your cockerel. Live entertainment.'

'Don't be horrid.'

'All right, as it happens we do have some frozen chicken breasts. I'll come round.'

'No, don't worry, I'll pick them up.'

'It's easier for me. Juana's at her brother's house so I've got nothing to do.'

'Have you had lunch?' I ask warily.

'As it happens, no.'

I give a groan. 'Would you like to join us?'

'Well, with such a gracious invitation, how could I refuse?'

Alan and Pep are smoking *puros* and drinking *herbes* on the patio while I huddle opposite them warming my hands on a mug of freshly picked mint tea. We are wearing jackets because the sun is waning and a light chill descends on the valley as early evening approaches. The Tramuntana range still holds the glow of the departing sun, its craggy features displaying a rosy sheen while the verdant forests pepper its rocky surface like dark stubble on a chin. Alan's gaze rests on the landscape before him and then returns to Pep.

'We can't thank you enough. It was like feeding the five thousand.'

Pep sniggers. 'My pleasure. Don't forget I got a free lunch out of it.'

'The chocolate mousse didn't go very far though.'

He gives me a smile. 'No one noticed. Besides, it was better for our waist lines.'

Despite my initial misgivings, the day turned out to be a great success. Everyone mucked in, serving out the food and clearing up while the children, rosy cheeked, careered around the garden and field, climbing trees and yabbering to one another in a mix of English, Spanish and Catalan. Jaume's mother insisted on my giving her the chocolate mousse recipe, which I took as a great compliment, and then patiently described how to make the perfect tortilla, the potato omelette that is part of the staple diet here. Jaume spent time discussing the parcel of land we want to buy, and on his departure offered to oversee the final contract. All in all, it was a wonderfully relaxing and spontaneous day.

'So, how are the German walkers staying at my flat?' Pep exhales a long plume of smoke into the cold air.

'Nice, quiet people. I wish all your clients were as easy.'

'Luckily, we've got a lull for a few months. You can concentrate on your acting career.'

Alan puffs at his *puro*. 'After the shampoo debacle it's amazing they've offered me this latest insurance ad.'

'Don't blame me. You shouldn't have made that joke.'

The Scotsman's film career was nearly cut short some months ago when he tried to be jocular with a member of the Focus

Films team. When asked if he'd mind kissing his co-star in the shampoo advert he retorted that it depended what age she was, what she looked like and where he had to kiss her. The young executive was rather po-faced about it and Alan found himself dropped from the ad, much to Pep's relief.

'They thought you were a sexist pig, Alan.'

'I think you're more deserving of that title, Pep,' I say.

He kicks my foot under the table. 'How can you say that when I gave up my Sunday to help you cook?'

'Remind me which bit of the meal you prepared?'

'Offering moral support is as good as performing the actual deed.'

The Scotsman throws the stub of his expired *puro* into the bushes and stretches.

'Time to water and feed the chickens. Salvador's making a racket.'

Ollie runs out of the kitchen, depositing his book on the table.

'I'm coming too.'

Pep rises and with alarm looks at his watch. 'I'd better get back before Juana calls. If she gets home and finds the chickens aren't fed, she'll be mad. Then I'll have to walk the damned dog.'

The two men exchange martyred looks.

'It's a hard life being a male,' says Alan.

'It certainly is, *mon amic*. We never stop working.'

I don't bother to stifle a guffaw. 'Send Juana my best.'

'I will.' Pep just about reaches the porch when his mobile begins bleating.

He hands it to me wearily. 'Better still, why don't you tell her yourself?'

It's early morning and I have just returned from dropping Ollie off at school. It's a bright cold day and the wind rattles the doors and sends gusts of icy wind down the chimney. Catalina sits opposite me at the kitchen table munching a monster muffin. Her hair has been cut very short and streaks of henna run through it like flashes of amber.

'You sure you like my hair like this?'

'I do. It's very hip.'

She momentarily surveys her own hips.

'Not that kind. What I mean is trendy, fun.'

'Ah, OK. That is good, but Ramon says it's too short.'

'Well, that's men for you. He'll get used to it.'

She sighs and rises to her feet, stretching across the table to pick up a bundle of brightly coloured plastic strings.

'What are these things? Ollie has them all over his room.'

'They're called Scoubidou, the latest fad at his school. You weave them together to make bracelets and key rings.'

She nods slowly. 'But he's got so many.'

'Yes, he's decided to make a load of key rings to raise money for the Sri Lankan orphanage. The tricky part is that he's suggesting we hold a fete in our field and invite local kids to buy his wares.'

She digests this information thoughtfully. 'Why tricky? I went to a fete in England when I au-paired for your sister. They had sack races and stalls with English cakes and tea. I loved it.'

'I don't think I've got the energy to organise one here.'

She begins filling a bucket with soapy water.

'Don't be lazy! We can do it. Just think of all the money we could raise – I can help bake and we can have lots of stalls.'

She has a point. It would be a great way of raising money and besides, it would be fun to stage an English fete in the Mallorcan mountains.

'We'd need time to plan.'

She nods. 'Let's do it in a few months before you go off to the orphanage in Sri Lanka. When do you leave?'

With all that's been going on I haven't given too much thought to our impending trip. It's about time I did.

'My friend, Noel, is organising our flights. I told him to get us the cheapest tickets in April.'

'So we do the fete in March. A Sunday would be good.'

I'm not too sure how I'm going to juggle this event on top of everything else. In the next month I have the Crown jewels launch, a pile of work to do for Rachel and my American-based clients and have just agreed to write a five-page feature on Mallorca for an in-flight magazine, aside from my weekly *Majorca Daily Bulletin* column, oh, and revising for my next Catalan exam. I must be mad. Catalina begins cleaning the kitchen windows. She turns to me, soapy sponge in hand.

'You know, I banged into Rafael today. It's sad about the dog, but better he goes.'

She is referring to the imminent departure of Llamp, Rafael's dog. Following the chicken killing episode my neighbour decided to find his Labrador pup another home and today the new owner will take him away.

'I'll miss him.'

She tuts at me. 'He'll get another dog, don't worry. Forget Llamp.'

I take a gulp of tea, realising, not for the first time, how sentimental I have become about animals since living here.

Catalina gets out a diary and pen from her capacious handbag.

'Right, let's discuss our trip to Dorset.'

Ah. The trip to Dorset, yet another thing on my agenda.

'There's not much to sort out. I've booked our flights and we'll be staying with Jessie and Willie, the couple who own The Cat's Whiskers.'

'Why they call it this? It means something?'

'It's a double entendre. The cat's whiskers is just a way of saying something's the best. You know, like the bee's knees.'

'I never hear this. Do bees have knees?'

'I haven't the foggiest. Look, it's just a silly expression.'

She regards me with some scepticism. 'So where will Stefan and I meet you when we arrive?'

'Paddington Station, but don't worry. I'll find out the train times to Shaftsbury and we'll agree a time and place to meet.'

She nods. 'And you'll spend some days in London beforehand?'

'Don't forget that I have the Crown jewels event that week.'

Her eyes fill with excitement. 'Will you meet Prince Charles?'

'I doubt it. I'm just the event organiser.'

'You never know. I'll keep my fingers crossed.'

Alan strolls into the kitchen in a smart blue suit. Catalina and I exchange winks.

'Oh, look at him! Are you off to meet the Prince too?'

'Not today, Catalina. I'm going to Focus Films in Palma for this insurance ad.'

'Well, it still sounds glamorous.'

He straightens his tie and takes a seat next to her.

'To be honest, all I have to do is pretend to be working at a desk in an insurance office. I don't get to utter a monosyllable.'

'Your time will come,' I say chirpily.

'Anyway, they pay me well and it gives me a break from gardening.'

I get up and deposit a bag of chocolate muffins in front of him.

'Drop these off at Margalida's on the way.'

'How is she now?' asks Catalina.

'In pretty good form, but I've noticed she's much more frail since the fall.'

Catalina shakes her head. 'Old age can be hard to bear. And what about Nancy?'

'I popped round yesterday to see her. God knows how she's going to sort out and pack all her stuff. She's such a magpie,' I reply.

Alan rises and picks up the bag of cakes. His eyes stray to a forlorn, miniature, empty tank sitting by the sink.

'What's happened to Ollie's sea monkeys?'

I run a finger across my throat. 'All dead.'

He picks up the plastic container and studies it. 'Is he disappointed?'

'Not really, he seems to be happier catching minnows in his net.'

He rests it back on the draining board and shrugs.

'I'd better be off to Palma. Remember, I'm taking Ollie straight from school to tennis. Don't forget to feed the hens.'

These days, on top of my mounting workload, I seem to spend my life cleaning out and feeding the hens, but they do at least oblige us with eggs. The only way I can get everything done is to rise at half six every morning and even then I run out of time. There just aren't enough hours in the day. Alan picks up the car keys and strides off. We hear the revving of the car engine.

'What are you doing this afternoon?' Catalina asks, getting up to start on some ironing.

'Working in my dugout of course.'

'How about you come olive picking instead?'

'Are you starting already?'

'*Segur.* My mother and father will be up in the grove today.'

It is always a jolly affair picking olives, hovering precariously aloft a wooden ladder, sharing jokes and a *copa de vi negre,* a glass of robust red wine, with Catalina's family and feeling huge satisfaction when a wicker basket is filled to the brim.

'I shouldn't really. I've got a mountain of work.'

She smiles. 'Work can wait, but the olive season can't.'

'Good point.'

'We can have a little wine and *pa amb oli.*'

She sees a greedy sparkle in my eye. *Pa amb oli*, literally bread and oil, forms part of the staple diet of the Mallorcans and is one of my weaknesses. The magic lies in the additional ingredient of *tomatiga de ramellet*, a local tomato that is threaded with string and hung in rows in either the kitchen or cellar and used all year round. Rich olive oil, sea salt, tomato and a whisper of garlic on rich Mallorcan bread is the closest one might ever come to earthly heaven.

'I'll come.'

Well, that took a lot of convincing.

'Five o'clock at my house,' she beams. 'And don't be late.'

I rise to my feet and gather up my diary and pen. 'Right, that's my incentive to get cracking. I'm going up to the office to wade through all my work in peace.'

'What if anyone calls?'

'Just say I'm busy or better still that I'm up an olive tree somewhere and unavailable for comment.'

It is late January and we are experiencing what the Mallorcans term 'the January calm'. There is little wind and the weather is mild. As I sit outside Cafè Paris reading the *Veu de Sóller,* our local Sóller newspaper, I see Antonia from HiBit approaching.

'Have you seen the postman lately?'

'No, but he seems to be having secret trysts with my elderly neighbour Margalida.'

'Really? Well, I haven't seen him for more than a week. Another man delivered the mail today.'

'Don't lose sleep over it. I'm sure he'll tire of Margalida's sweet oranges and return to his duties.'

She laughs. 'By the way, it looks like the new shop will be ready in a week's time.'

'Fantastic. Will you have a little fiesta?'

'Sure thing. Some wine and *coca* for all the clients.'

Of course. Where would we be without *coca*?

'You skiving off work this afternoon?'

'Give me a break. I'm just reading the *Veu* to practice my Catalan. I've got an exam tomorrow.'

'You poor thing. I don't think my written Catalan would be very good now. You know, under Franco we learned everything in Castilian Spanish in school.'

'So Margalida tells me. At least you've got an excuse.'

She laughs. 'So how's Ollie?'

'Actually, I'm waiting to pick him up from football practice. Sometimes I think it might be easier to make up his bed on the pitch.'

'I thought he was into tennis now?'

'Both. In fact, he's sport mad. He obviously doesn't inherit it from me.'

'I don't know, you did the marathon.'

'My body was in protest, remember. I'm not a natural.'

She gives me a grin and wanders off up the road. A moment later, Senyor Bisbal stands by my table. I jump up to greet him.

'*Tranquil.la, tranquil.la,*' he says, patting my arm. 'I wonder if I could introduce you to a friend?'

'Of course, please join me.'

With a polite nod of the head he turns and beckons to a small troll of a man in battered brogues and worn attire. His snowy hair and withered skin denote that he must be well into his eighties. When they have sat down, Senyor Bisbal leans forward conspiratorially and takes my hand.

'My friend is Xisco. He has a good eye for land.'

He sits back and taps the forefinger of his right hand against his nose. Xisco shapes his mouth into an oblong smile, unveiling a set of blunted teeth, chipped and greying like ancient tombstones. When he opens his mouth to speak, I notice the two incisors are missing and that a gold filling is winking from somewhere at the back of his mouth.

'I know of some good fields.'

Unsure of exactly how I am supposed to respond to this riveting news, I give an enthusiastic nod.

'Marvellous. Good for you.'

Senyor Bisbal takes over.

'I hear that you are looking to breed livestock.'

'Not exactly, Senyor Bisbal. *Un hotel pels moixes*.'

The snowy troll spits on the floor and clicks his teeth. He studies me in the way a lab technician might an alien species.

'*Moixes*, you say? You joke, *si?*'

Senyor Bisbal's face is clouded with confusion.

'In England we have places where cats stay when their owners go away.'

'Are you serious?'

'Of course. They pay maybe twelve euros each night, sometimes more.'

Xisco hunches his shoulders and honks loudly.

'You English are completely *loco!*'

Senyor Bisbal is utterly baffled. 'Why not just leave the cats to find their own food like we do?'

I realise that nothing I say about cattery philosophy will ever make sense to these hoary, rural veterans so I give up.

'Look, we just do things differently, that's all. Now, might you have some land if I needed it?'

Xisco puffs out his bottom lip.

'*Pues*, maybe, but how much land would this hotel need? Don't tell me the cats have beds?'

He pulls a *puro* from his pocket and is laughing so much at his own wit that he's quite incapable of lighting a match. Senyor Bisbal throws him a warning scowl and offers his own lighter.

'Excuse my friend. *Per favor*, if you give us the specification, we will try to help. What materials would you use?'

'Timber.'

He looks reassured. 'Good, because you'd never get planning for a concrete structure.'

'And how many cats would you have?'

'Maybe twenty.'

Xisco erupts into hysterical laughter again, his small roly-poly form practically leaping from the chair. I sneak a look at my watch and call for the bill.

'No,' says Senyor Bisbal, 'This is my treat. Next time we meet, give me the spec you need.'

I thank him and get up to leave.

'By the way, who told you I was looking for land?'

Senyor Bisbal is inscrutable.

'You must remember that nothing is secret in the Sóller Valley.'

SEVENTEEN

THE CROWNING GLORY

Thursday 9.50 a.m., the club, Mayfair

It's a wintry day in London. Even after some invigorating laps around Hyde Park I still feel the bitter chill of the wind as it slaps my face with a frosty palm. Back at the club, Bernadette is bustling about on the third floor, a stack of clean white sheets in her arms.

'Tonight's the night!' she jabbers as I walk past the small laundry.

'For what?'

'That famous politician, you know the one with the funny hair and the glasses? Well, he's speaking at the club this evening about his book.'

'Which side of the house is he?'

'God only knows, my lovely, but he was always hanging round with that there Lady Thatcher. I'm sure he'll have some tales to tell.'

'I shall miss it.'

'Shame, and what will you be up to?'

'Launching a new book about the Crown jewels.'

'Jesus, Mary and Joseph. You never are?'

I offer her a further morsel. 'Prince Charles will be there.'

She balances the sheets on the top of the washing machine. 'Never! And will you be meeting his nibs?'

'Very unlikely, but it'll be fun anyway.'

'And where will it be?'

'The Tower of London.'

She puts her hands to her voluminous chest. 'They'll all be there in their finery and jewels. And what will you be wearing?'

A good point. What will I be wearing? The fact is that I'm still undecided. Should it be the trusty woollen suit or the overused little black dress? The suit would allow me to wear low heels whereas the dress would require something more substantial. Given that I'm a hobbling disaster in anything higher than an inch, it's probably best to play safe and wear the humble suit.

'Just a suit.'

She turns down her mouth in disappointment and picks up the sheets once more. 'Never mind, Cinders. Enjoy it anyway.'

I watch her lumber along the corridor with her load, gingerly descending the creaky old spiral staircase. To my dismay, Dannie has requested that we hold a brief meeting about Miller Magic at my club because she thinks it sounds quaint and very British. My entreaties about it being a little tired and shabby for the likes of her cut no ice with Dannie so I had little choice but to succumb.

Downstairs in the library a waitress has set a table with a clean cloth, coffee cups and a plate of custard creams and bourbons, as instructed. The poor woman has a look of terror in her eyes whenever anyone approaches the library door for I have warned her of Dannie's bite.

'She'll be fine,' I say. 'It's just that she can be rather particular. If she asks for anything strange, just humour her.'

She listens carefully. 'I'll do my best.'

I sit down and examine my notes. The Conran launch of Miller Magic products was a great success and at last we're getting Dannie column inches in the newspapers, but it's been an uphill struggle. Three interviews in the glossy press were cancelled when Tetley informed Dannie that they were inauspicious. According to Tetley, the journalists' names all ended in 'y', which didn't bode well at all. It took Rachel and me some weeks to reschedule them all with different writers who weren't called Penny, Jenny or Kelly.

The door swings open and Rachel, followed by Mary Anne Bright, strides into the library.

'Oh, wow!' shrieks Mary Anne. 'This is awesome. You know, it's like a Dickensian film set. Dannie's going to explode.'

I sincerely hope not today.

We sit around the table while Mary Anne's eyes dart about the walls, taking in the tall, dark wooden bookshelves on all sides and the oaken floor.

'How have you been?' I ask.

She pulls out a handerkerchief and sniffs. 'I'm having a bit of a heavy time right now. My older son's gone to college, but the younger one's still at home. '

'Is he missing his brother?'

'It's not that. I'm divorced and with all this travelling, I'm not at home to keep any eye. A lot of kids are doing drugs in New Jersey.'

Rachel pricks up her ears. 'How old is your son?'

'Sixteen, so it's not like he's that young. I mean, he can get takeaways at night and everything. If I'm away he can look after himself.'

I feel for this boy without family around him, living on a diet of fast food and solitude.

'Can't you tell Dannie that you can't travel so much?'

She gives a hoarse laugh. 'Heads up! Can you imagine what she'd say?'

292

Rachel sighs. 'Pretty much.'

'Besides, I need this job and I get paid well. So what if there's a bit of abuse? I can handle it.'

The waitress pours us some coffee.

I turn to Mary Anne. 'Is she coming soon?'

'Any time, I guess. By the way, Rocky's got flu and couldn't come over this time. Can you recommend a good hair stylist for Dannie?'

'One that does big hair?'

'Whatever.'

'I can ask mine.'

'He'd have to come over tomorrow morning.'

'No problem. I'll sort it out.'

There are voices in the corridor. Dannie, accompanied by the club's receptionist, appears at the library door. She gives a gracious smile to her companion.

'Thank you, darling. That'll be all.'

With arms outstretched she wafts into the room on a cloud of Chanel.

'Oh my god! This is so incredible. I love it.'

She wanders about, feeling the bookcases and smelling the covers of leather tomes. Casually, she strolls back to the table.

'A plate of biscuits? Oh, I'm so glad you won't starve, Mary Anne.'

Her assistant gulps down what she has in her mouth and wipes away the evidence with her serviette. Dannie scrunches her nose and smiles.

'And where's this secret panel you told me about?'

Rachel and I lead her over to the faux bookcase. With genuine delight she pushes the false panel and shrieks when she finds herself in a small, hidden anteroom. Rachel waits till she's inside and whispers to me, 'Any chance of sealing her in?'

I push Rachel away and try to maintain some sort of composure.

'Come and have some coffee, Dannie.'

She steps back out of the tiny room and perches on a wooden chair at the table, spellbound by her experience.

'Do you know, darlings, this has to be one of the most special days in my entire life?'

As always, Dannie the actress knows how to deliver a line crackling with fake sincerity, but on this occasion I'm somewhat puzzled to see her eyes brimming with tears. Perhaps, I ponder, even spoilt divas like Daniella Popescu-Miller occasionally recognise that simple pleasures really are the best.

11.30 a.m., in a cab en route to the Tower of London
'Mahogany, how can I help you?'

'Please, get me Richard, it's urgent.'

'Just one moment. Who's calling?'

A few seconds later, Richard comes on the line.

'What's up?'

'Can you do big hair?'

'That depends. I don't like big hair. Who's it for?'

'My client, Daniella Popescu-Miller. It's sort of Mr Whippy cum Cruella de Vil.'

'Urgh.'

'Please, Richard. I'm desperate. She needs someone tomorrow morning at The Berkeley, suite 319.'

'How much is it worth?'

'A Mr Whippy 99 ice cream?'

2 p.m., Tower Hill underground station
Rachel and I are standing at the entrance to the underground station with the Tower of London forming a perfect Legoland backdrop before us. It is cold and crisp and office workers on their way back from lunch hurry past in small clusters, heads to the wind and clutching at their coats. The vast Tower, white

and serene, with its endless turrets and spires jutting up into the sky like jagged teeth, disgorges several coach loads of Japanese visitors. Obediently, in small groups, they scuttle behind tour guides who brandish garish umbrellas raised high in the air, and then one by one they mount humming, impatient coaches, only to be whisked off to yet another British must-see sight. We have spent the last few hours tucked away inside the Tower's great belly of grisly dungeons, towers, cobbled yards and gardens, trying to convince the British media that the definitive guide to the Crown jewels is a book worthy of a one thousand pound price tag. We had set up the press conference in the Keeper's Lodge, a special privilege granted us because of the nature of the book, and more than fifty journalists had attended. There had been the usual small but manageable hurdles. A Chinese film crew had asked whether they could purchase a copy of the book together with an actual trinket from the Queen's private jewels collection and a regional newspaper reporter had wanted to know whether the timber used for printing had come from sustainable rainforests. Heaven only knew but I certainly didn't have time to find out there and then. I managed to give a long-winded response that confused the journalist to such a degree that she forgot the original question altogether. Always a good media tactic. A few of the press had been a bit miffed to discover that Claude Blair, the esteemed editor, was not in fact the Mr Blair they had been expecting, but admitted it was a good ruse, albeit a joke at their own expense. Of course, had they bothered to check with the Labour apparatchiks at ten Downing Street in advance, they'd have known it was a prank.

When the photocall and interviews were over, the press drifted off towards the main exit while Rachel and I cleared up the debris with the Tower's event staff and did a final recap of plans for tonight's big event. In a matter of hours we will be back here again. I swear I could find my way to the White Tower blindfolded, so many recces have we done.

Rachel yawns.

'Well, that went off pretty well. I think I'll have a few hours' kip before we come back tonight.'

'What?'

'Just kidding. Were you happy with it?'

'So far so good, but maybe we should just do one final run through with the staff.'

She pats my arm. 'We've done endless rehearsals. Everything's under control. Nothing can go wrong.'

'Famous last words.'

'Shall we head back?'

'Not before we've had something to eat. I've a feeling this is going to be one heck of a long day.'

4 p.m., the office, Berkeley Street

'I've got George on line one.'

The tiny white light on the telephone face flashes hysterically. Now what's up.

'Watcha guv?'

'Hi George. Whatever it is, make it snappy. I'm about to leave for the Tower.'

'All right, all right. Keep your hair on.'

'So?'

'Just wanted to wish you luck. I'll be coming with Miss Dracula.'

'Thanks, well just behave and keep her happy. I'll see you tonight.'

'Just one other thing. A little bird mentioned something about you opening a cattery.'

'Did it now? It wouldn't be a stork with long hair and an obsession for heels and red suits?'

'Spot on. Rachel just mentioned it in passing. Got me thinking.'

'Oh no. Look, it's just a tiny germ of an idea.'

'I like it. Seriously. Nice little sideline and it would be good for me to have a European outlet. Have to be exclusive though.'

'What are you talking about?'

'For my pet range of course!'

'Sorry George, you've lost me.'

'Think about it, guv. We could create an exclusive outlet of my cat and dog gear attached to your cattery.'

I decide to humour him for fun. 'I don't suppose you've thought about the heat angle? I mean leather capes and cat suits might not go down too well.'

'Yeh, I know that. I'm thinking linens, Egyptian cottons, cat and dog shades…'

I erupt with laughter.

'I'm serious, guv.'

'I know, that's what's worrying me.'

'Let's have a serious heads up when you're through this event.'

'You're incorrigible.'

'I know. So what do you say?'

11 p.m., McDonald's, Charing Cross Road

Rachel wipes her mouth with a paper serviette and takes a sip of her coffee.

'Do you know, I just can't believe it's all over. What a relief!'

I pop a chip in my mouth and nod in agreement. Once again we're sitting in a fast food restaurant dressed up to the nines and attracting unwelcome glances from other diners. The plastic seats are uncomfortable and the fierce strip lighting is making my eyes water.

'Why is it that after any major bash we end up in here or KFC? You know I hate fast food.'

'That's because it's late and we need somewhere to sit and recover.'

'I'd prefer The Dorchester bar.'

'Yeah, right. Dream on if you think it's coming out of the company budget.'

She takes a bite of her burger hungrily and gives me a disapproving look.

'Well, we deserve the odd treat. I mean, it was a resounding success. Everyone said so. The Stationery Office was ecstatic.'

Rachel licks a finger. 'It was brilliant but that doesn't justify blowing a hundred quid at the Dorch.'

I think back to just a few hours ago when together we had welcomed hundreds of guests in their finery to the floodlit White Tower. The event had been spectacular, with stylish waiters in sleek black carrying silver platters groaning with the most delectable canapés. The champagne flowed and trickles of laughter rose high into the wooden rafters of the elegant building as clusters of guests poured through the great arched doorways into the hall. Daniella Popescu-Miller swathed in a mink stole and with diamonds the size of olives in her ears, had arrived on the arm of Greedy George, attired understatedly in a black silk nehru jacket and trousers. Roger Katz from royal warrant bookshop, Hatchards, and the cream of the publishing world had turned up in force, as had the world's top gemmologists. There in the centre of the Tower was the focus of everyone's attention, a colossal, red leather-bound book with thick gilt-edged pages, the culmination of forty years of research: *The Crown Jewels*.

At some point during the evening Prince Charles had to make his way over to the book for a photo opportunity. We had positioned the photographers behind a red cord at a discreet distance but with a perfect angle to film proceedings, but alas! At the last minute a zealous attendant at the Tower had altered the plinth's position so that the Prince's face was obscured when he viewed the book. The press photographers seethed behind their rope until I felt I had no option but to sidle up to the Prince and request that he turn towards them while I stealthily manoeuvred the plinth. He kindly obliged and the press, thankfully, got their shots.

Rachel is giggling. 'Oh, I did crack up when you went up to the Prince and whispered in his ear. God knows what everyone thought!'

'Desperate situations require desperate actions, Rachel.'

'Well, it made all of us laugh. You won't live that down in the office!'

'I'm always the comic turn.'

She sniggers into her serviette. 'That's why we like working with you! So, what was it like to meet Prince Charles?'

'Very nice.'

She thumps a hand down on the table. 'Is that it?'

'What do you want me to say? He was charming, of course.'

Rachel bursts out laughing 'Well, what did he say to you?'

'Oh, this and that.'

She puts a hand to her head. 'You're the limit!'

I stand up and button up my jacket. 'Right. That's it.'

'Are you off?' says Rachel in some surprise.

'We are.'

'Where to?'

'The Dorchester, of course.'

Friday 7.30 p.m., the club, Mayfair

Noel is standing in the hallway, an earnest expression on his face.

'Now, please look after these plane tickets and remember that Sister Teresa will be expecting you the morning after you arrive in Colombo. The details are all in the itinerary I've given you.'

'That's all fine. I've booked the hotel and everything's under control.'

He nods slowly. 'My nephew will greet you on arrival. He'll take you to your hotel.'

'There's no need, honestly.'

'Yes, there is. It's Sri Lankan hospitality.' He smiles. 'And I wish you good luck with your fete in Mallorca. The orphanage will be so happy.'

'I do hope so. Mind you, I doubt we'll make much money from second-hand toys and books.'

'Every little helps,' he says magnanimously.

We shake hands and I head off into the drizzle outside. Not for the first time I'm fumbling in my handbag, wondering what on earth I've done with my dratted umbrella.

Friday 10 a.m., the office, Berkeley Street

Ed is sounding downbeat.

'Put it this way, if the BBC makes all these redundancies, I could be in the front line.'

'Why do you say that?'

He gives a sniff. 'Think how many years I've worked there. They probably want to employ some bright young things on lesser salaries.'

'Don't forget they'd have to pay you off.'

He sighs heavily. 'I can't imagine not working at the Beeb anymore. It's been my life.'

'Has your boss hinted that you might be for the chop?'

'Well, he's been giving me odd looks of late.'

'But everyone does, don't let that worry you. Even I give you odd looks and I've known you donkey's years.'

'Thanks.'

'Look, Ed, I have to go. We'll discuss this when you know more.'

'Are you off to a meeting?'

I dread mentioning the cattery again. 'Actually, I'm off to meet Catalina and Stefan at Paddington Station. We're visiting The Cat's Whiskers.'

He splutters into the phone. 'Not that place again! Don't tell me you've persuaded Catalina and her brother to go?'

'It's a fact-finding tour, to see how we could build such a structure in Sóller.'

He gives a snort. 'Words fail me.'

'Good. Speak to you later.'

I put the receiver down and look up to see Rachel standing in the doorway.

'Off to your cattery?'

I pick up my handbag. 'Yes. Let's catch up when I'm back home.'

She has a curious expression on her face. 'You're quite serious about this cattery lark, aren't you?'

'I think it's worth investigation,' I say cautiously.

'But what would happen to the business? I mean, I'm not sure I'd be happy if you were completely out of it.'

'There are loads of options. You could get a partner, or we could sell up.'

She furrows her brow.

'But that would be madness. The work's coming in fast and last night was a triumph. You couldn't exist without the buzz.'

'Last night was fantastic, but there are other things I want to do.'

'Such as?' she says crossly.

'Maybe start a cattery and grow vegetables…'

'Oh please!' she gives a cynical laugh.

'It's good to have a change.'

'As long as it's for the best.'

I head off out of the office, pulling my suitcase behind me.

'True, Rachel, but how do you know that until you've tried?'

Saturday 6 p.m., The Cat's Whiskers, Dorset

Catalina is sitting at Jessie's office desk tucking into an iced bun. She's spent a whole day working in the cattery with me and is pleased to have a break.

'Mmm, this tastes good. I like English cakes.'

Jessie stares out at the falling rain beyond the glass panes.

'Well, a cuppa and a cake always cheer me up on a day like this.'

We listen to the rain pattering on the corrugated roof above and shiver as a blast of cool air blows under the front door. Jesse sits next to me on the small sofa flicking through photos of some of her past inmates. She gives me a nudge.

'Ah, that's Snowy. He was lovely. Used to come here every summer until his owner died.'

'What happened to him?'

She wrinkles her nose. 'Apparently a nephew inherited him. Lived alone. You know the type.'

I'm not sure how to take this, but nod sagely.

'And what about this Siamese?'

'That's Tabitha. She was the German Ambassador's cat, but we're going back some years. She moved to Bavaria.'

Catalina gets up and comes over to us, bending to see the photos.

'How do you remember all their names?'

'I just do. It's like being a headmistress, I suppose. Been doing this for fifteen years now.'

Catalina takes a swig of tea from her mug. 'Do you think my brother will be OK with Willie? He can't speak much English.'

'"Yes" and "no" will be more than enough,' she says without humour.

The door springs open and a beaming Stefan enters with Willie. They're both wearing cagoules and wellies.

'Shut that door before we all freeze to death!' Jessie shouts at her husband.

He bangs the door behind him and claps his hands together.

'Stefan understands everything. He's a clever lad. I've gone through all the architectural plans and we've had a good tour round the site. Builders speak the same language, see? Don't need words.'

Catalina smirks at me. 'How did it go?' she asks Stefan in Mallorcan.

'*Bé. Molt bé.*'

'My brother says all is good.'

'Told you so. Now, all you have to do is take some photos of the place to show your mayor and later we can go for supper at the local pub.'

'Great!' exclaims Catalina. 'I love English pubs.'

'Not so fast,' chides Jessie. 'I need to explain about all the different cat food and diets there are. If Catalina's going to help at your cattery, she needs to learn all about that.'

Willie raises his eyes. 'Well, when you're ready, let us know. We'll be in the kitchen having a pint.'

Stefan gives me the thumbs up and follows his new best friend out into the rain.

'Typical men,' mutters Jessie. 'Now, where shall we begin?'

EIGHTEEN

FAREWELL TO A FRIEND

Snow has settled on the highest peaks of the Tramuntanas and, like warm white icing, dribbles down the mountainous slopes in huge dollops. Trickling insidiously into verdant pine glades, it soon transforms to ice, glazing rocks and stones with a transparent film that makes them slippery and treacherous underfoot. Down in the valley the air is clear, but the cold is palpable. In the orchards animals huddle together, their communal white breath rising like steam from a New York air vent while rats and mice burrow deep within stone walls, home to the *garriga* field snake and a burgeoning insect population. Tonight the sky is punctured with tiny stars that glimmer in the dark night. In the courtyard a layer of white ice has formed on the car and the windscreen resembles a mini ice rink. The Scotsman, dressed as a gangster in black trilby, old raincoat and a dark suit, fumbles with the ignition key. Ollie is dressed as a Death Eater from the *Harry Potter* books and has difficulty locating the back door of the car.

'Might be an idea to take your mask off first,' I proffer.

He finally stumbles upon the icy handle.

'If I take it off someone might recognise me.'

'We're not likely to see anyone about at this hour until we reach Fornalutx.'

He doesn't budge. I settle into the front seat, stowing my riding crop and helmet under my feet.

As the gate clanks open, our wall lights, created from old roof tiles, automatically spring to life, illuminating the front garden and courtyard. Normally, lizards cling to the tiles, but tonight there isn't a scaly limb in sight. We crunch along the stony track, the headlights illuminating Llamp's lonely, vacated run and Rafael's home which is cloaked in darkness. At Silvia and Pedro's *finca*, lights blaze above the olive green gates. I wonder if Margalida is dining with them tonight because when we reach her chalet the shutters are closed.

'Hang on Alan, I need to drop off some cakes for Margalida.'

'Go on, Florence Nightingale of the valley,' he says. 'Make it snappy.'

I jog up the steps to Margalida's door and leave the sandwich bag of chocolate cakes on the mat. Even if it should rain, the porch will protect them from getting wet. I bob back into the car.

'It's so cold out there. I hope they'll have heating on in the garage.'

'I'm sure they will. Anyway, a few drinks will warm us up.'

We set off along the quiet mountain roads, winding up towards this most traditional of Mallorcan villages for the annual carnival party. Last year I had given the mayor a jolt, dressing up as a geisha, so this time I've opted for a rather modest gymkhana outfit, having borrowed items from various local friends. As we arrive in the village, light fills the street and music thumps from the old underground garage where village festivities are often held. Various witches and ghouls are striding along the road from the little *plaça* and as we park the car four characters robed in black approach the vehicle.

'Who are they?' quizzes Ollie.

'Haven't a clue, but they seem to know us.'

'They're wearing traditional burkas. Now who'd be able to get their hands on such gear?' says the Scotsman.

'A Moslem?' says Ollie

'A seasoned traveller?' I suggest.

'Indeed, then it must be…'

He springs from the car. 'I know who you are! Veils up!'

They explode with laughter as they uncover their heads. Jack and Sarah, our Australian friends, give us a quick flash of their faces as Catalina and Ramon wrestle to lift up their hoods.

'It's not easy to wear these, you know,' Catalina complains. 'I would need to practise for a long time.'

'I picked them up when I was travelling in the Yemen,' says Jack. 'Thought they'd be just the ticket for tonight.'

'At least we can wear thermals underneath,' adds Sarah. 'And what the hell are you supposed to be? A flasher?'

Alan gives her an indignant look. 'Just watch.'

He pulls a violin case from the back shelf of the car, sticks a *puro* in his mouth and dons an old pair of shades.

'What do you think?'

'Whose violin did you steal?' mocks Jack.

'I borrowed it from Cristina's daughter, you know, at the Aimia Hotel. She's a budding violinist.'

'Well, don't for Christ's sake lose it,' he shouts, accentuating his Aussie twang.

All around us costumed characters are appearing out of the shadows. A team of Real Madrid look-alikes jog by and I notice that Stefan, Pere the plumber, and Llorenç are among them. They blow on their whistles and wave as they pass, disappearing into the bright garage interior.

'Come on you lot, let's get going.' Jack stumbles ahead of us with unseeing eyes followed by his three robed accomplices. Ollie follows blindly in his black cloak and mask behind them. I watch as their arms flail wildly about as they edge their way cautiously towards the steep slope leading to the mouth of the garage.

'It's worse than three blind mice,' sniggers the Scotsman. 'Go easy.'

His words miss their mark. A moment later, a blur of airborne black gowns rushes at speed down the slope amid banshee-like shrieks, until at last halted by the embrace of Juan, the village *batle*, who stands welcoming the arriving guests. He steadies himself, a small grin imprinted on his lips.

'Sometimes I wonder who's crazier, our resident Brits or resident Australians.'

'What about Mallorcans?' says Alan, pulling at the side of Catalina's mask.

Juan spreads his hands in agreement. 'You're right, Alan, she really does have to be the craziest of all!'

We arrive back at the house in the early hours. Ollie is asleep in the back of the car and Alan is singing some unrecognisable Scottish ballad.

'Well, that was some night!' he declares as he turns off the ignition.

'The costumes were fantastic this year but the garage was freezing,' I say as I exit the car with my riding crop and helmet.

He opens the passenger door and lifts Ollie onto his shoulder.

'If you'd danced you would have kept warm,' he replies.

I open the front door and turn on the lights. Ollie wakes up and sleepily makes his way to his room. 'Who won the competition in the end?' he asks from the doorway.

'Chicken Licken,' I say.

'Oh good,' he mutters and disappears into his room.

'Feel like a nightcap?' The Scotsman asks, bounding into the kitchen.

'Why not? It'll warm us up.'

We sit hugging glasses of *herbes*.

'So, who was the vampire with the golden cape?' I ask.

'That was Tolo from Banca March. I thought you knew.'

'It was not! Tolo wouldn't go as a vampire!'

'It was so, and the man dressed as Elvis Presley was Xavier from Colmado Sa Lluna.'

I thump my glass down. 'Elvis Presley? That wasn't Elvis Presley! Xavier was supposed to be Tom Jones. Honestly!'

Alan shakes his head. 'Well, if he wasn't Elvis Presley, why did he sing "All Shook Up"?'

I have to think about that. 'Probably because he was cold.'

The Scotsman rolls his head back and laughs. 'Don't be daft. Anyway, I suppose it doesn't really matter. It was great fun.'

'Another carnival and another year over. I can't believe it!'

He drains his glass. 'Imagine what we'll be saying in ten years time.'

'More to the point, will we have exhausted our costume supply by then?'

'Probably, but then we'll just have to go as ourselves. They'll never guess who we are!'

And with that we turn off the lights and head up the stairs for bed, Alan hugging a violin and a trilby and me a riding crop and a pink rosette.

I am on my way back from Palma, having dropped Ollie off at his school. With relief, I have left the overcrowded Cintura highway behind and am coursing along the less congested rural roads that peel off to Valdemossa, one-time retreat of Chopin and his companion, George Sands, and Deià, home of the poet, Robert Graves. The almond trees are bushy with blossom, their delicate pink flowers exuding a fragrance so pure that it is tempting to stop the car and run wildly through the orchards gathering up the fallen petals to drink in the intoxicating perfume. But I don't. Not today. Instead, I wind down the windows, stick on some music and revel in the freedom of an open road flanked on both sides by orchard after orchard of unremitting beauty. It is only beyond the Sóller tunnel that I catch up with local traffic; two hay carts, a concrete mixer and an elderly man wavering precariously on a stuttering *moto* immediately in front of me. At every roundabout, at every slip road, I will him to turn off, but no, my elderly outrider stubbornly pop-pops along, one minute ahead, the next at my side. I consider parking the car and jogging home given that we're now proceeding at such a funereal pace that the car can hardly cope in first gear. I reach my turning and with relief see him crawling like a disabled *centpeus* in the direction of the port.

At the mouth of the track I expect to see Margalida, but she is not in her garden and the house remains shuttered and still. Something's up. At the side of her chalet a lorry engine purrs as its driver connects the tank to a large pump drawing up water from a nearby well. The *agua portable* lorries are frequent visitors to our track especially in the summer months when these mountain dwellings, without their own water supply, rely heavily on such deliveries. The drivers know Margalida and always take time to chat with her and discuss local gossip. I call up to the driver.

'Have you seen Margalida?'

He shrugs. 'I don't know where she is. Maybe at Silvia's?'

I walk up the steps to her front door and pick up the chocolate cakes. Inside the transparent bag small droplets of

309

water have formed and minute flies, like black dots, cling to the plastic lining. I'm puzzled that they've been able to penetrate a sealed bag. With a sigh I take them with me, ready for the bin. I clamber back into the car and slowly level with Silvia's house. The cleaning lady is sweeping leaves in the front yard and comes over to greet me.

'The elderly senyora isn't well.'

'What's happened?'

'She had another fall but this time it shook her very badly. Silvia and the doctor think she should rest for a few days here.'

I nod in agreement. It's not the best news, but I'm relieved to know she's being well cared for.

I arrive back to find Alan reading the *Majorca Daily Bulletin* and nursing a cup of coffee at the kitchen table. Roaring flames crackle and hiss from the fireplace in the *entrada*.

'I'm glad you're back. Nancy just called and asked if I could pop round to pick up some stuff for Ollie. She's been clearing out some junk before the move.'

I put on the kettle and look out at the sky. 'I can't believe that she's going next month.'

He drains his cup. 'That's life, I'm afraid. Nothing stays the same forever.'

'A cheery thought.'

He puts an arm round my shoulders. 'Look, much as we'll miss Nancy, I think the change will do her good and she needs all year round warmth with her arthritis.'

'I suppose so.'

'OK, well I'll be off. I've got to pop by Pep and Juana's on the way back. He's got me some discounted chicken feed apparently.'

'It's one excitement after the other up here, isn't it?'

He laughs. 'Sure is.'

'You know Margalida's had another fall?'

'Don't tell me!'

'She's over at Silvia's recuperating. Lucky she didn't break anything.'

I pull the cakes from my handbag and dump them on the table.

'These won't be much use to her now.'

He gives me a sympathetic smile. 'Ah well, you can make her some more when she's back home.'

He strides off towards the car. I listen as the engine comes to life and he sets off up the drive. Leaning against a work surface with a cup of tea in hand, I contemplate some of the tasks I must get done today. First, I've got to fix a time with Catalina and Stefan to meet the mayor with the proposed cattery design, then call the owners of the overgrown orchard to discuss a sale. I've a pile of work to do for Rachel but it's not too urgent, which is fortunate because I've still a lot to organise for the fete next month. Various friends have offered to man stalls and make cakes and we've been deluged with old books and toys to sell on the day. I should feel positive that things are coming together, but I have a weird sense of foreboding. Absent-mindedly, I pick up the cakes and hurl them in the bin.

The stones make a grinding sound as I jog along the dark track past Rafael's house, and down towards Silvia's shadowy gate. There's not a sound in the valley and the screech owls are yet to appear for their habitual evening prowl about the skies. My body is shaking with cold despite warm running kit so I quicken my speed. Clinging to the ancient rock walls withered ivy tendrils and sharp twigs occasionally spring out like the gnarled fingers of a witch's hand, scraping my face and arms and caressing my hair. I shudder with the chill, cheerfully imagining my return run from the port, heading back home for a bowl of home-made vegetable soup by a dancing fire. I glimpse back at the *finca* which in the distance emits warm, amber light. Ollie will be in his room dawdling over his homework, and Alan pottering about the corral with a torch, trying to fix a broken fence. Margalida's chalet looms before me, its white facade stark in the blackness like an exposed and luminous bone. I arrive onto the lane and, panting, pause to set my sports watch. It is then that I hear it. A cry. I swivel round, the hairs on my neck stiffening. Someone is sobbing my name. The voice is weary, filled with anguish and despair. Frightened and trembling, I turn to see a man's silhouette back along the track. Like the light from a firefly, his cigarette burns a vivid orange tracing a slow pattern in the air as it is wafted this way and that in the impenetrable gloom.

'Who are you?' I shout, retracing my footsteps.

'It's Felipe.'

'Felipe?'

I am disorientated, not having seen Margalida's grandson for some months. As a busy architect and artist in Palma he rarely has time to pop up to the house when he's visiting his family. With increasing dread I draw nearer, not wanting to hear the words I know in my heart he will say.

'She's dead.' And then as if for reaffirmation, 'She's died.'

He attempts to stifle a tremendous sob. 'Just like that. Slipped away.'

I see his eyes dancing in the treacley night, wet with tears and shock. In her ninetieth year she may have been, but Margalida seemed eternal, the matriarch of the track, a hopelessly endearing and loveable friend and grandmother. I throw my arms around him in silence. In this grim moment all Spanish and Catalan words are lost. My mind is blank. I hear myself mumbling incoherently about the funeral. It will be tomorrow at eight. In Spain death is a stickler for punctuality. Bodies are whipped from the houses before they're practically cold and squirreled away to morgues for a quick stay before being buried or cremated. The hurriedness of it all seems strange and callous, but in hot countries it was born of necessity. The tradition still stands.

'She regarded you as a grandchild,' he is saying quietly.

My eyes well with tears. A flashback of images fill my head; Margalida at my gate with jacaranda flowers, Margalida in her kitchen poring over an antiquated photo album. I can see her as clearly as if she were with us now, standing in her Sunday best, her snowy hair teased into little waves, her trusty crucifix and walking stick glinting in the sunshine. It seems impossible to imagine her chalet unoccupied, her tabby cat bereft of its mistress. In truth, how can life ever be the same again around here?

Felipe is at the gate of his mother's house. He gives me a sorrowful wave and is gone. I stand on the track, unsure what to do. My body is shaking with the chill. A light rain begins to fall, tears shed from a helpless sky. In automaton state, I find myself sprinting, running faster, faster, down the track, out onto the open road, pounding the pavement until my limbs seem to pulsate with heat. I forget where I'm heading but my body carries me along, down to the roundabout and right onto the port road. A blur of lorries and cars race by, their flickering tail lights whispering in the falling rain *she's gone, she's gone*. And now I'm running parallel to a wild and fretful sea that coughs spume up onto the beach and curses the wind and rain. I drag myself on and on to the very end of the esplanade and, deluged by water and fighting for breath, crumple onto the floor and cry. And why am I crying? For Margalida, for loss and the fragility of life. For things we puny humans cannot control. In London, distraction, noise and frenetic living can so insidiously mask the senses, kill emotion and dissolve the fear of what might be, but here there's no escape. Life and death walk fearlessly hand in hand; every day, all around us, new life forms and old life bites the dust.

Wiping my eyes, I walk back onto the port road, the sea howling over my right shoulder. The rain has stopped and a light wind rustles the brown leaves of the trees, coaxing them to pirouette in small showers to the ground. Feebly, I begin to jog, the clothes sticking icily to my skin. Margalida is frowning and waggling a finger, '*You'll catch your death of cold running in the rain!*' I find myself laughing – laughing at what I have no idea. A tram rattles by, its bright lights momentarily casting a pale glow, the colour of straw, on the road. And then, with a loud toot, I see Gaspar, his thick thighs astride his *moto,* waving manically as he pootles slowly along. He flags me down and with great effort brings his bike to a shuddering halt. He dismounts and gives me a hug.

'You're all wet.'

'Yes. I got caught unawares.'

A small frown wriggles across his forehead. 'You look sad. Has something happened?'

I drop my head. 'My neighbour, Margalida, has died.'

He exhales deeply and shakes his head.

'Yes, I know.'

I wipe the tears from my eyes. 'How can you know already?'

Gaspar is slightly taken aback by my reproachful tone. And rightly so. Why should I seek exclusive first rights to such sad tidings?

'Of course, I knew she was unwell and then, when I popped by yesterday, her cleaner told me the news.'

'I see.'

He puts an arm around my shoulders. It feels as heavy as an iron rod.

'You know she lived a good, long life and had such strong faith. She never feared death.'

I wipe my eyes on my sleeve.

'She would want us to celebrate her life, not mourn her,' he says softly.

'Yes, of course.' I give an involuntary shiver.

He feels my cheek. 'It's like marble. Come on, let me drop you home.'

'We'll never both fit on your bike.'

'*Pues,*' he rubs the stubble on his chubby chin. 'You're not big. Come on. Let's try.'

Numbly, I attempt to straddle his bike from behind. It seems to buckle with our combined weight.

'There,' he says. '*No problema.*'

'Are you sure?'

'The worst that can happen is that we'll both fall off. No harm in that.'

I cling to his damp windsheeter as he starts the scratchy engine and hesitantly pulls out onto the long, dark road. There isn't another vehicle in sight. So slow are we that I imagine the poor old dilapidated bike might expire at any moment.

'*Bé?*' he yells cheerfully above the drone of the engine and the wind. Am I OK?

'*Bé!*' I shout back.

With his back to me, he gives the thumbs up and breaks into song. I see a tabby cat, surely not Margalida's, walking calmly along the tram tracks that follow the road all the way into town. It watches us impassively. Even at such a regal pace it seems to have taken the lead, leaving us trailing behind. *Errrr… crikey… pop-pop, errrr… crickey… pop-pop*, the frail bike seems to whine and splutter. I laugh. Gaspar laughs and the bike wobbles so precariously that I think his ominous prediction might come true. No harm in that. Somehow, we cling on even when the bike takes a sharp left, quivering like a whippet with the effort, white, acrid smoke billowing from behind. It sets us off laughing again. Howling uncontrollably, until the tears pour down our cheeks.

'*Bé?*' hoots Gaspar, his huge body overcome with mirth.

'*Bé,*' I reply.

The creaky old oak door of Santa Maria church, witness over the centuries to countless celebrations and calamities ushers in new life and shoos out the old with the swift efficiency of a housewife with a broom. It has welcomed penitents, snarling marauders and pirates hell-bent on its destruction, tremulous brides and wailing newborns and, last but not least, those who arrive in state, slumbering in a box on the shoulders of hefty pallbearers, to attend their very last mass.

We peer into the sombre belly of the church, dazed to see so many crammed into the pews. Huddles of men stand around the grey stone walls, hands loosely crossed in front of them as they pay their last respects to a woman well known and loved by them all. We close the door behind us, hoping its anguished moan will be drowned by the echoing mantra of the attendant priest. Heads swivel to see who the newcomers are. There's a rustle, a slight rippling of brows. No smiles. Formal in our London black, we appear alien, out of place among this simple gathering of local people dressed as if they were on their way home from work; maybe some of them are. Self-consciously, we tiptoe to the darker reaches of the church, solemn, keen to merge with the walls, the floor, the very fabric of the building. But then, like a blade of grass ignited in a breeze, a whisper runs the length of the pews, and suddenly a buxom lady tilts her head and turns.

'*Venga!*' she whispers, jolting her neighbours so hard that they are squeezed together like sausages in a frying pan. We creep over to the pew, thank the senyora, and take our seats. A few pews ahead of us, the instigator of the whisper, Enric, who owns the local grocery store, dares to hover above his seat, turns to give us a nod. We smile back. A friendly face in a blur of anonymous mourners. And so the service rattles on in Catalan, words that soar above our heads, but the tone is sincere and inclusive. I run my eyes over the walls, the nave of the church, and strain to see the priest in his inky black tunic. On the wall, gilt-framed paintings of the Stations of the Cross depict in stark, visual episodes the grim story of Christ's crucifixion, and there staring down at me with red-rimmed eyes is the Madonna herself in a shawl of blue, the colour of babies' eyes.

The service changes tempo. The pews rise en masse and make their way to the front of the church, forming a long silent snake of a queue. Uncertainly, we follow the senyora and, shuffling behind her, eventually spy in the distance Silvia, Pedro, Felipe and the rest of Margalida's family. They are separated, the men standing together, a forlorn line up on one side of the altar, the weeping female relatives on the other. My stomach knots. What do we say, and how will we be regarded, the only foreigners at this most poignant of gatherings? But Catalina has briefed us. The word 'Pesame' – it weighs on me – are all that is required. Is that enough? I want to say so much more. At last, we reach the line-up. Pedro takes my hand and smiles sadly.

'Pesame,' I say huskily, my mouth devoid of moisture.

Felipe, pale and gaunt, kisses my cheeks, his hand tightening on mine. Wordlessly, we walk on, acknowledging brothers and cousins, nephews and nieces. Silvia, her face chafed with crying, shakes her head and clasps me close, the lifeless, damp tissue in her hand wrinkled and twisted with use. Alan dabs a tear from his eye and Ollie, pinched with cold and silent, grasps my hand and together we return to our seats. We genuflect. Prayers are said and with hands raised high the priest makes the sign of the cross. Once again the old door stirs, yawning open to allow the cool night air to flood into our midst. The congregation spills into the courtyard of lemon and olive trees. Old friends greet one another, neighbours hug, animated voices rise into the stiff, cool air. In a corner, trying to ward off the chilly night, some frail elderly women grip their coats and jackets tightly about them while their husbands grapple for cigarettes and *puros* with shaky hands. As we take our leave, locals approach us, no longer anonymous, smiling, touching our coat sleeves sympathetically. Together we stand united in grief and also in celebration at the closure of an ordinary life.

Alan and I walk silently up the stony track, arm in arm, while Ollie skips along beside us, relieved to have escaped the confines of the church. Suspended in a velvet sky, a full moon smiles benignly, and drifting across the valley is the soft, insistent, tinkling sound of bells. The calling card of our woolly mountain sheep.

NINETEEN

NITTY GRITTY MATTERS

March has slipped in through the back door and unpacked its swag bag of blue skies, white clouds and soft breezes before we've had time to shake off our February woes. Birds are clamouring from the trees and baby fish, slivers of gold foil, dash about the pond in search of fast food – low flying insects. Ollie is at school and, having polished off my column for the *Majorca Daily Bulletin* upstairs, I amble into the front garden and head for the pond. Our musical frogs, newly returned from their long winter break, dart among the weeds and bulrushes while I stretch out on the rocky edge, catching the warm rays of the sun on my face. Even with eyes closed I can feel his presence, the haughty features surveying me with impatience.

'Miss me?'

As if in a trance, my eyes click open and there is Johnny, emblazoned in sunlight, his olive brown skin glistening with water as he puffs out his broad chest from atop a mossy rock.

'You're back. Did you have a good time?'

He blinks. 'You know how it is. Too many relatives pushing food down your neck. I don't wanna tell you how many bluebottles and midge mojitos I've knocked back in the last few months.'

'Life's for living.'

'Yeah, well just don't look at my waistline!'

It's true. He is somewhat tubbier, but he's got attitude. A sort of Orson Welles of the toad world.

'So, what's new?'

I shrug. 'It's been a bit bleak. Nancy Golding's just left for the States, Margalida died last month. Even Llamp's gone.'

He's chewing something, maybe a passing fly.

'Get over it.'

'Thanks for the sentiment.'

'What do you want me to say? Life's tough, but you gotta keep trucking. This island ain't Utopia, honey. It's real life.'

'I know that,' I snap.

He blows out his cheeks. 'That Margalida was a nice old dame, I admit, but she was ninety for Crissakes! You can't go on forever. Nothing stays the same.'

I fiddle with a stray tendril of ivy.

'So, what are you gonna do, just mope around feeling sorry for yourself? Pathetic!'

A sadistic thought strikes me. 'Remember my cattery idea?'

'Jeez, you're not still stuck on that track? Please!'

'As it happens we've got a meeting about buying that land today.'

'And where's the loot coming from, Miss Smarty Pants?'

'Well, that's a slight obstacle, but where there's a will…'

'Still on Planet Daydream, I see. Well, wake me up when you've had a reality transplant.'

He splashes into the water, casting ripples across its glassy surface.

Alan calls me from the house. 'Greedy George is on the blower.'

I groan and slump into the house. George is yelling into the receiver.

'Hi guv! Got you off your sun lounger?'

'No, my inflatable lilo.'

He's gurgling. 'Funnily enough, that's what I wanted to talk to you about.'

'Inflatables?'

'Sort of. I've come up with a whizzo idea. Havana Mediterranean, a range of leather beach products.'

'Excuse my ignorance, but doesn't leather blanch and dry up in sea water?'

'Well, Miss Sarcastic Fantastic, you're absolutely wrong. I've developed a new leather finish that makes it impregnable and soft as a baby's bum. I can do lilos, rubber rings...'

I'm in no mood for such lunacy at this time of the morning. Mad dogs, or rather frogs, and Englishman are supposed to strike at midday, aren't they? I've had both well before eleven.

'Ever struck you that rubber rings are made of rubber for a reason?'

'I know all that tosh, but they've got no style. Anyway, my leather sun loops have a rubber inner tube which makes them float.'

'Leather sun loops? You've really lost the plot this time.'

'Don't forget, guv, that I've made a cool few million on my pet gear. Who's laughing now?'

Whether I like to admit it or not, Greedy George is right. The madder the concept, the more it seems to sell.

'I'm thinking leather lilos, loungers, parasols. Sort of cool urban chic in the sun.'

'Why stop there? What about towels, buckets and spades and suncream?'

'Now you're just being silly.'

'OK, so when are you planning on launching all this?'

'That's the thing. I thought we could do a launch photo shoot near you in a couple of months. Be fab, guv! I come out with a crew and we get the whole thing wrapped up in Mallorca.'

Oh God. How can I allow it? Greedy George set loose on this poor, unsuspecting isle. Will it ever recover?

'But won't you need to develop the products first?'

'I've got some prototypes hot off the factory floor.'

He fills the void.

'And I can look over your cattery plans. Sort out a range of pet wear for the cat boutique.'

'What boutique?'

'The one we discussed.'

'Oh, not that again. I thought you were joking before.'

'Course I'm bloody not. I've already sketched a design for the shop and I've worked out what we can sell.'

'What on earth would possess me to do this?'

'Money?' he suggests.

'There's more to life.'

'Give me a break! You need filthy lucre just as much as the next mug,' he yells. 'Come on, what d'you say? We'd have a blast.'

'D'you know what, George? I'm going to get back right on my lilo and have a ponder about it all.'

'Great. Call me with some ideas on fab locations. Oh, and we'll need sun.'

'Oh, I'm sure you can whip up one of those with a few scraps of leather.'

He wheezes with laughter and then with a click the line's dead.

'On viu?'

Where do you live?

'Visc a Sóller.'

I live in Sóller.

That was easy enough. Now he'll hopefully move on to the next row.

Guillem flashes me with a Cheshire cat smile. He's still facing me.

'On treballes?'

The rest of the class, like an impatient firing squad, shift in their chairs to face me. Where do I work? Mallorca… London? That's far too difficult to explain in Catalan, for crying out loud. Find an easier option. Quickly, you dolt.

He's wiping his glasses. *'On treballes?'*

Some swot coughs impatiently behind me. It's the clever Swedish guy with the glasses. I know his superior cough.

'Er, en ca meva.' I stutter. At home.

The Swede tuts at my back.

'Treball a ca meva,' corrects Guillem. I work at my house.

'Molt bé.'

He pats my arm encouragingly and walks slowly past in search of a new victim. Julia elbows me in the ribs amid stifled giggles. She scribbles me a note in Spanish – *Has repasado para el examen?* Have you revised for the test? Bugger. No I haven't. This is my third exam, and having done reasonably OK in the second I'm annoyed that I'll fare less well this time. I'm ashamed to admit that I've missed a bunch of lessons with all my gallivanting to London. Ten minutes later, Guillem bounces cheerfully to the front desk and pulls out a sheaf of papers. There's a glint in his eye. 'This is just another little *examen* to see how much we've learned in the last few months,' he says winningly. A collective groan fills the room as he hands out the sheets. He looks at the clock then gives the word. Silence. The exam has officially begun.

Alan comes into the kitchen, washes soil from his hands and sighs. He has been planting *faves* all morning, the delicious baby broad beans that grow so effortlessly in our fertile valley.

'I've got the lettuces, artichokes and beans planted too, but the beetroot will have to wait till tomorrow.'

'Is your back stiff?'

'Just a touch.'

I put on the kettle. 'D'you want the good news or the bad news?'

He collapses onto a chair, casting a weary eye over my face.

'In whatever order.'

'The bad news is that Sabine Ricard just called. She's in town and intends popping round with Veronique.'

He hits his head on the table.

'The good news is that she can only stay a few minutes. Lunch party with her lump of a husband back in Santa Ponsa.'

'Thank God for that! What the hell does she want this time?'

'I don't know. She sounded hysterical though. She said it was too terrible to speak about on the phone.'

'She's probably broken a nail.'

'Don't be a meanie.'

He gets up and heads for the kitchen door. 'Sadly, I shall be otherwise engaged. I'm going to hide out in my *abajo*.'

'Coward.'

'Undeniably.'

'Ollie?' he bellows. 'Veronique alert!'

Fast feet scamper down the stairs. 'She's coming?'

'Any moment. Let's hide.'

'OK. I'll bring a packet of Top Trumps and some books.'

He races back up to his room, returning with a pile of booty.

'Thanks for the support, guys.'

'Don't mention it,' says Alan, as they jog across the patio. Ten minutes later there's frantic tooting at the front gate. I slope out to the porch, watching as Sabine draws up into the courtyard. Veronique jumps out to greet me. I'm puzzled to see that her hair has been pulled into a severe bun befitting an elderly matron, but that could be the influence of ballet.

'I can't stay long!' shrieks Sabine, crunching purposefully towards me across the gravel. 'We have had a nightmare!'

'Whatever's happened?'

She swings her handbag over her shoulder and, marching into the *entrada*, furtively looks around to check that we are alone.

'*Piojos!*' she whispers.

'Sorry?'

'Nits!'

She grabs Veronique's arm. Obediently the child flops her head forward like a ragdoll. 'Look. See anything?'

I shake my head. 'Not sure about the bun though.'

'Let me tell you,' she spits. 'that I spent five hours last night pulling nits from her hair. I nearly fainted.'

'Loads of kids get them. It's not a big deal.'

'You don't think? Never in my life have I seen these things. It's absolutely *dégueulasse*. In Paris, Veronique never had them. They don't exist in France.'

'That's silly, Sabine. Of course they do.'

'*Non, pas du tout!*'

Whenever Sabine is in high dudgeon, she breaks into her native French.

'Here, you must spray everything immediately. I bought you this.'

She pops a can out of her bag and begins waving it about in the *entrada*, and before I can stop her, the kitchen.

'Stop! I've got fresh bread on the table.'

She hovers by the fridge. 'Too late. What a stupid place to leave bread!'

Coughing on the noxious fumes, I snatch the offending can from her grip and rush out on to the front porch.

I read the label. 'This is Permetrine. It's horribly toxic.'

'Who cares? It zaps the little bastards.'

'Can I just point out that Ollie doesn't have any nits?'

She faces me belligerently. 'Maybe not now, but he will. That school must be crawling with them. I don't want him to give them to Veronique.'

'But any child could.'

'Exactly, so I will visit every parent in the class to warn them.'

'It's better just to inform the school on Monday and they'll put a note round. A good scalp rub with tea tree oil and alcohol for a week or so and Veronique will be fine.'

She seems disappointed. 'I thought you'd take this more seriously.'

'It's just a fact of life.'

'For me it is the straw that breaks the camel's back.'

'What do you mean?'

She gives a dramatic sniff. 'Michel and I are returning to France.'

We're sitting in the kitchen with Juan and Lucia, the couple who own the other half of our orchard.

'That's a lot of money,' says the Scotsman morosely. 'The amount's gone up since we last spoke.'

Juan gives a nonchalant shrug that seems to say *take it or leave it*.

Pep, like an astute poker player, flicks his ash away and raises a conciliatory hand.

'Maybe there's just been a little misunderstanding.'

Stefan, who has joined the meeting as joint negotiator with Pep, looks embarrassed and purses his lips together.

'It's a lot for us as it is,' growls Alan. 'This new figure would be impossible.'

Lucia seems anxious to compromise. 'When could you pay us?'

'In a few instalments over, say, a year,' says Pep nonchalantly. 'The bank would vouch for them. We could draw up a quick contract. Deposit now, the rest later.'

'How soon?' asks Juan.

'Tomorrow? We can sign it front of the *notario* for security,' Pep reassures.

A silence descends on the table. I squirm with embarrassment. This couple are immensely likeable. We were enjoying an incredibly warm and cheerful conversation with them until negotiations, rather like milk curdling, took a turn for the worse. Money really does close as much as open doors. A sheep cries from some far off field and Orlando stretches his body out across the kitchen tiles, oblivious to the tension building at the table. Pep is huddled over his notebook, inscrutable as ever while Alan and I study the fruit bowl. Stefan spreads his hands before him and appears to be counting his fingers.

'We'll do it.'

Everyone looks up, startled. Lucia has spoken.

'It's my parcel of land. We agree your price.'

There's visible relief on the faces of all the men. Smiles all round. I give Lucia a squeeze of the arm.

'Thank you.'

She gives me a wink. 'It's time.'

Handshakes and hugs are exchanged and finally they all leave, save Pep. We return to the table and exchange looks.

'You were a star,' I say to Pep.

'But what suddenly made Lucia change her mind?' quizzes Alan.

'I think she felt sorry for us,' I hazard.

'Not really,' says Pep. 'We Mallorcans are good negotiators. We like to push a deal to the limit but with a little gentle persuasion we're happy to compromise in the end.'

'*Poc a poc,*' I say.

He has a mischievous grin on his face. 'Yes, as we Mallorcans say, *poc a poc.*'

Catalina is sitting in the garden with Ollie weaving Scoubidous while I sift through a cardboard box full of Barbie dolls and old toys. We have been gearing up for the big day when local children will descend on our field to sample our interpretation of a traditional English fete. We intend to serve scones and jam, cucumber sandwiches and cups of tea, and are planning on doing an egg and spoon, sack and three-legged races among others.

'What a fantastic day,' I say, staring up into the sky.

Catalina runs a hand through her short hair and squints at the sun. 'Hey, Ollie, she's only saying that because she got a good mark in her Catalan exam this morning.'

'Yes,' he jeers. 'If you hadn't got a good mark, you'd be in a grumpy mood.'

'Actually, I'll have you know that I'm in a good mood because I've finished all my work for Rachel and I've just pulled off a full page interview in *The Times* for Daniella Popescu-Miller.'

'This is the vampire lady?' quizzes Catalina.

'The same.'

Ollie pushes his chair away from the table and potters over to me holding a clump of brightly coloured strings. 'Catalina and I have made fifty Scoubidou key rings and you can't even make one.'

'True, Scoubidous aren't my forte, but I am good at making muffins.'

'Yes,' says Catalina. 'At least she can cook.'

He shrugs and resumes his seat. 'Suppose so.'

Catalina gets up and stretches. 'Fancy a quick look at your new land?'

Now that we've acquired our small strip of terrain I like nothing better than pottering down into the field to admire it, despite its wild and woolly state. We stroll across the patio and descend the stone steps to the field. Catalina picks her way gingerly through the undergrowth and plucks a lemon from a tree. She sniffs the skin.

'These trees need pruning. You'll have a lot of work to do with this land.'

'In time.'

She rests her hand on the bark of a tree. 'How are you going to set up a cattery here with all your other work?'

'Well, I'll have to cut down on the office stuff. I'd prefer to keep up my journalism and just do some ad hoc projects for Rachel.'

'Would that be OK with her?'

I shrug. 'Probably not, but she'll get used to the idea. If it wasn't the cattery it would be something else. She knows I want to do other things.'

'I hope the cattery happens so we can work more together.'

'Segur!' I say, squeezing her arm. 'I couldn't do it without you.'

We suddenly hear a strange, deep hooting from inside the thicket and, exchanging mystified glances, venture forth. A few seconds later, on the only stretch of grass in the midst of bracken and wild bush, appears a male pheasant, it's magnificent, iridescent plumage glinting in the sun. We gasp.

'Precioso!' whispers Catalina.

Gorgeous it may be, but what's it doing here and where did it come from?

In answer to my furrowed brow, Catalina gives a little smile. 'There are wild pheasants all over the island but it's rare to see one so close up. It's a good omen for the cattery.'

'Do you think so?'

'Of course!' she says with conviction. 'Why else would it be here?'

Why else, indeed.

It's early morning and only the cats are stirring in the garden, stretching their long limbs in preparation for an assault on their food bowls. I close the bedroom windows since a chill is in the air, and tiptoe down the stairs to the *entrada*. The front door is gaping, testimony to our sloppy stance on home security. The Scotsman must have rolled up to bed long after me with little thought to the prowlers of the night waiting longingly for his moment of absent-mindedness. Before I even cross the *entrada*, two cats, unknown to me, hurtle up from the basement and skedaddle out onto the porch. The track is quiet and Rafael's house is shuttered. From his orchard comes the piercing sound of a baby lamb. I look inside the empty dog run, wishing that Llamp was curled up in the unoccupied kennel with his tartan blanket and chewed-up rubber toys. When I reach Margalida's chalet I walk into the garden and sit on the stone bench under her jacaranda tree. The leaves droop like tawny bats from the branches, for Margalida's beloved jacaranda blossoms are not yet in bloom. The house is asleep, its shutters clammed shut like heavy eyelids, and its door, a sealed mouth, no longer welcomes visitors. From nowhere I hear a cry and Margalida's tabby cat appears at my elbow. It sits like a Sphinx next to me, surveying the grass, the budding roses and jasmine clustering in the porch. It looks well fed so I imagine Silvia is caring for it. A gentle breeze ruffles the trees, and suddenly a shower of jacaranda leaves come twirling down, touching my face and hands and settling in my lap.

'Never fear, Margalida,' I whisper, 'I haven't forgotten you.'

There's the gnawing sound of a *moto* on the track and Jorge, the postman, appears. He turns off the engine and gives me a blindingly radiant smile.

'Catching up with Margalida?'

'Yes, sharing a few jokes.'

He sits down on the bench beside me.

'It's hard to believe she's gone but I keep telling myself that she had a wonderful long life.'

He smiles encouragingly. '*Si*, and slipped away so peacefully with all her family around her. She wouldn't want us to be sad. Life must go on.'

I give him a nod.

'Margalida told me how pleased she was that you'd moved to that *finca*. Growing vegetables, learning Catalan, being part of things here.'

'We can but try, Jorge.'

'You do OK,' he grins.

'I'm glad you're back in the valley. Where have you been these last weeks?'

'Oh, Argentina. To put some matters to rest.'

I notice that, with a touch of pathos, he fleetingly glances at the tiny 'R' on his right wrist. Curiosity gets the better of me.

'Does the letter "R" remind you of someone special?'

He flushes pink. '*Si*, she was my fiancée but not any more. I returned to Argentina but we split so now I will stay here in Mallorca and maybe find a nice Mallorcan girl.'

Lucky her, whoever she is.

'I will have to lose this,' he says, touching the little initial on his wrist. 'Unless I find a girlfriend called Rosa.'

I give him a shove. 'How cynical!'

'No, just practical,' he laughs. 'But now I must be off.'

'Where to?'

'To deliver the mail, of course!'

With a shake of his mane and a flash of his dazzling teeth, he mounts his bike and speeds off in a shaft of golden sunlight. No doubt when word gets round the valley a stream of local girls whose names begin with the magic letter 'R' will be lining up like would-be Cinderellas in the vain hope of claiming their Argentinean prince.

Salvador is strutting about the corral in furious indignation. Throwing our chickens some seed, I inadvertently shower some on his head. Such humiliation is hard to bear when you're leader of the pack. I apologise profusely but he points his beak in the air and stomps off, his harem following at a genteel and diplomatic pace behind. I could swear Minny and Della stifle a guffaw as they go. Alan beckons me over to the wilderness we have just purchased. I close the corral door behind me and follow him into the undergrowth.

'It's like an undiscovered Eden,' he says in wonderment. 'I've just unearthed a huge palm and several fruit trees.'

'Maybe we can start a jam-making business instead?' I proffer.

He gives a brittle laugh.

'Buying this land was the best thing we ever did. It means no one can build on top of us and we have a treasure trove of an orchard.'

'The small downside is that we have to find the funds to pay for it,' I reply.

'Admittedly, it's a hefty sum, but we'll manage it over time and if the cattery comes off...'

In the last few days we have learned from Stefan that a new planning law affecting orchards has been introduced which could put paid to dreams of building a cattery on our newly acquired land. The mayor is doing his best to find a solution, but with local bureaucracy that could take some time. However, we're used to the slow pace of things around here. With a little patience, everything comes together in time. *Poc a poc...*

'Senyor Bisbal's old troll of a chum has given me some specs for local land, but it's expensive and quite far away.'

Alan shakes his head. 'No, I don't think that's viable. Let's stick to our guns and if it doesn't happen we'll have to look at other options.'

'Such as?'

'I'm not sure, but something will turn up. It always does. Anyway, this will please you.' He unfolds a piece of paper from his pocket. 'Came in this morning so I printed it off for you.'

It is an email from Nancy Golding. She's arrived safely in LA, and has apparently found a beautiful sunny studio and flat near her daughter's home. Better still, she's coming back to visit in May.

'You see, things always work out in the end. You've just got to have a little faith.'

And with that, one side of the corral collapses, flat as a pancake, to the ground allowing Salvador and his chums to make a speedy break for freedom.

TWENTY

A HAPPY FETE

Catalina is singing as she turns into the drive. We are visiting our local Aladdin's Cave, the Cooperativa, which sits on a narrow country road en route to the picturesque villages of Biniaraix and Fornalutx. It is here that local farmers bring their harvests; olives, fruit and vegetables for sale. In the autumn it is tempting to dawdle outside the netted fences watching the olive production in progress, but in spring the mud-caked and battered machines lie dormant in the large concrete forecourt and attention is given over to the selection of oranges and lemons instead. Catalina screeches to a halt in the parking bay and leaps out of the car, leaving the door wide open. I scramble after her.

'Here comes trouble,' yells one of the farmers. 'What are you after today?'

'*Sacas!*' she yells.

He spits on the ground. What type of sacks, he wants to know. They're for *una cursa de sacs*, she replies. A sack race? The old man slaps his leg and titters.

'*Venga!*'

He beckons us into the deep interior of the building. Like a small air hangar, it is airy with a lofty roof but that's where the comparison ends. For piled high on its pitted concrete floors by the entrance are box upon box of animal feed, nuts, seeds, onions and shallots, tomatoes, potatoes and peppers. Inside, lining the walls above and running in rows the length of the building, are broad wooden shelves bulging with wine bottles and containers and buckets full of olives, herbs and flour. To one side, the entire floor seems to be covered in crates bursting with lemons and oranges. I stop to study them.

'We receive thousands of these,' he proffers.

'What do you do with them all?'

The man's eyebrows lift a fraction. '*Pues,* some go to local stores and restaurants, but many just go rotten. There isn't enough local demand.'

He's right. All of us living in the golden valley have lemons and oranges coming out of our ears. You can't give them away.

'What a waste,' I sigh.

He's momentarily distracted by a vision at the door. 'Maria!'

Catalina's aunt strides towards us. 'What's going on here?'

'These *locas* are doing sack races.'

Catalina and I greet her aunt who throws us a quizzical expression.

'Sack races?'

'We're going to hold a fiesta to raise money for an orphanage in Sri Lanka. We'll have all sort of races and stalls for kids.'

'At your house?' she says with surprise.

'It's what we call an English fete, Maria. We'll hold it in the field.'

'You're brave. Heavens know what the kids will do to Alan's plants and trees down there. And what about the weather?'

I point to the sky. 'I've had a word with you know who, and he says it will be a perfect day.'

She raises her eyes and slaps me on the arm. 'Good luck with it. I'm buying a few things and then must get back to Canantuna. We've got a booking for an anniversary party today. Thirty at one table!'

She scampers off while our patient farmer rustles in a deep box and draws out some empty hessian sacks. He thumps them against a wall and white powder rises like autumn mist into the air.

'They're flour sacks, but I've some almond ones too. How many d'you want?'

'Ten?' suggests Catalina.

He wanders off to some high shelves and after rummaging about, returns with a heap of old sacks.

'Here, have them.'

'How much can I give you?'

He walks out into the drive with us and shouts to a young man pulling crates of fruit from a van. 'How much for these? At least five hundred euros, I'd say.'

The other man laughs. 'At least.'

'*Molt gracies*,' I say.

'*De res*,' he replies. In other words, think nothing of it.

He packs them into the boot of Catalina's car, and with a smile presents us with some goodwill plums.

'Good luck with the fiesta. If you want some boxes of fruit on the day, just let us know.'

'A fete? Isn't that a rather British concept for Spain?'

'That's the fun of it, Ed. We're going to do races and have stalls and serve cucumber sandwiches and traditional cakes.'

'You're bonkers. Will anyone be helping you?'

'Lots of people. Pep and Juana, Catalina and some parents from Ollie's school and the football club.'

He takes a bite of something.

'Sorry, just munching an apple. I'm on a diet.'

'Yet another?'

'Well, Charlene thinks I'm slightly overweight.'

'Only slightly?'

'Oh, shut up!'

'So what's the verdict on the BBC?'

There's a pause.

'I have happy tidings. I'm not being made redundant.'

'Hallelujah!'

'They have asked me to move to a new department over in White City.'

'Is that so bad?'

'It'll be a long commute.'

'Oh.'

'Mind you, there is one compensation.'

'What's that?

'They have a fantastic staff canteen.'

A sky the colour of corn flowers, dotted with white puffs of cloud and a perfect yolk of a sun, unrolls like a canvass above us. The air is warm and down in our field children scream and race about. Small children jump and slide on an enormous bouncy castle, which is practically buffeting the corral. Salvador peeks round the corner of the chicken shed now and then like a veteran detective, shaking his feathers and observing the scene before him with mounting suspicion. Like a sports master, the Scotsman, lines up the umpteenth sack race of the day and blows his whistle. Children of all sizes and nationalities jump along the grass, lurching and falling while parents and visitors call out and cheer. Ollie, proud to have won an egg and spoon race, now sits at a stall with his friend Angel, doing a roaring trade selling plastic Scoubidou key rings and trinkets to his classmates and football chums. Having spent weeks weaving Scoubidous he's delighted to see his hard work has finally paid off. On the cake stall, Nina, the thirteen-year-old daughter of a friend from Deià, has proven to be a remarkable saleswoman having sold nearly everything.

'How much is that chocolate cake?' asks one of the budding Ronaldos from Ollie's football club.

'A euro,' she replies.

He hands over a two euro coin.

'I don't have much change. How about buying two?' says Nina sweetly.

And off he happily skips with cakes in both hands. Pep isn't faring so well on the Barbie doll stall.

'These bloody things. Look at them! Any decent woman would shoot herself to have a pair of tits like these.'

He twirls a Barbie doll in the air by its flaxen hair and flings it back on the table.

I tweak his nose. 'You're supposed to be encouraging the girls to buy them. Stop abusing the stock.'

'Can't I man the women's lingerie stall instead?'

'Well, you could if we had one.'

'OK, what about books?' he persists.

I look over and see that Juana and Vicky, a parent from Ollie's school, are shifting a good amount of second-hand stock.

'Right, you go to books and get Juana to run Barbie world.'

He gives me a little wink and, dragging on a *puro*, goes over to his wife and points in my direction. She pulls a face and bustles over.

'I hate these Barbie dolls too. How come you have so many?'

'Veronique gave us hundreds and a whole load of these strange looking creatures called Bratz.'

'Urgh!' she drops one back down in front of her. 'They're pretty hideous.' Then with a huge smile she begins hollering,

'Come and buy beautiful nearly new Barbies and Bratz – special discounts now.'

Within minutes little girls are clustering around her.

'You see, Pep, she's a natural,' I say, poking him in the ribs as I pass by.

He pulls out his tongue and tosses some coins into his tin. Catalina walks slowly down the steps with a tray of tea cups.

'We've practically finished washing up in the kitchen. Have you any more chocolate muffins?'

'I made at least fifty. They can't all be gone.'

'Oh yes they have! We've only a few cakes left and then I think we roll things up.'

I nod and skip up the steps. Two little German girls are sitting by the front door brandishing enormous carrier bags of toys and books.

'Have a good time?'

'The best. You'll do this every year?'

'Let's wait and see.'

Alan is calling through a loudhailer in the field.

'This is your last chance to buy. Hurry before the stands close.'

A surge of children descend on the stalls which run in a horseshoe around the field and orchard. Under a tree at a discreet distance from the hubbub Sarah, our Australian friend, is calling herself Gypsy Lee and wearing a colourful scarf and enormous gold hoop earrings. She swivels a crystal ball in her hands in an attempt to attract customers. She calls me over.

'You won't believe it, but I'm a natural psychic.'

'Really?'

'Yes, I just told some stuck up French woman that she'd be off to live in Paris soon and she said, '*Voilà!* It's true.'

'French, you say?'

'Yeah. Anyway, she told me that some time ago she'd found a crushed egg in her handbag and wondered what it could mean.

She's obviously a bit of a nut so I humoured her and said it meant that she shouldn't keep all her eggs in one basket.' She roars with laughter. 'She gasped and said I was a visionary. What do you think of that?'

'Beginners luck? I'll make a prediction too… was her name by any chance Sabine?'

She gives a yawn. 'I don't think she said.'

Pep plods over to me. 'Come, I want to introduce you to my brother-in-law.'

A tall be-suited man, his gelled dark hair glinting in the sun, politely extends a hand. 'I am Antoni. You speak Spanish?'

'I keep trying.'

He laughs. 'I hear that you may want to move your son to a Spanish school?'

My eyes drift to Pep. He nods encouragingly.

'We're thinking about it quite seriously, but it would have to be good academically and nearer to Sóller. The daily drive to Palma is a real slog.'

'I know. I've done it myself.'

'The fact is,' says Pep, 'that Antoni is going to be teaching at a new trilingual school in September. We're thinking of sending Angel there. It could be perfect for Ollie. Only a fifteen-minute drive.'

'Sounds very interesting. What's it called?'

He smiles. 'It has a very Mallorcan name, *Llaüt*, which means fishing boat.'

'Believe it or not, I've learned that word in my Catalan class,' I reply.

'You're doing Catalan classes? That's great!'

'Yes, but she can only order a coffee,' says Pep with a chuckle.

I give him a grimace. 'Ignore him. So, can we speak sometime?'

'Absolutely. Pep can set it up.'

He shakes my hand and heads off towards the bookstall.

'What do you think?'

'Worth a punt.'

Alan, aloft a wooden plinth, booms from the loudhailer. 'And the raffle winner is…'

There is applause as a small boy with a shock of black hair makes his way over to the plinth to receive an enormous Easter egg.

'And now,' Alan continues, 'If my wife could please join me.'

I squeeze through the merry throng to his side. 'How are we doing?'

'Fantastic! We've raised just about one thousand quid.'

'Yippee!'

I take the loudhailer from him and ask for silence. There's a hush.

'We want to thank you all for your brilliant efforts. Together we've raised about one thousand pounds for the orphanage. Enough to keep it going for at least a year.'

A huge cheer goes up.

'As you know, we'll be off next week to Sri Lanka to hand over the funds raised from today and the New York marathon. In total, we'll be donating more than three thousand euros – enough to make a real difference.'

As children and their parents whoop and clap, I see my neighbour, Rafael, waving from the courtyard. He makes his way down into the field, a Dalmatian at his side.

'This is Alberto!' he cries, giving me a hug and nearly knocking me off my feet. 'He's my new dog.'

I narrow my eyes at him. 'But will this one stay?'

'Sure, he no like chickens.'

'How can you be sure?'

He gives a knowing smile. 'Because, *mon amic*, he's vegetarian.'

Stefan is sitting at the kitchen table sipping at a cup of coffee.

'That coffee's good,' he says.

'Yes, the coffee's OK but the blinking machine's a pain to work,' Alan retorts.

Catalina taps his arm. 'It's very simple to use, you just get impatient with it like you do with your computer.'

Alan shrugs his shoulders. 'It's true. I'm not of the new technological age.'

'But you're a good gardener,' says Stefan brightly.

'So', says Catalina as she munches on a biscuit. 'What do you both think?'

What do we both think? The last month has been a roller coaster of activity. I have been frantic doing work for Rachel and arranging a photo shoot in Mallorca for Greedy George which will take place on my return from Sri Lanka, and in the meantime I've taken on some new writing assignments. Meanwhile, the Scotsman's been flat out with looking after Pep's flat bookings and doing another advert and we're both recovering from organising the fete. So I'm not worried by this latest news from Stefan that we need to submit more detailed architectural drawings to the mayor before the council can reach a final decision. The delay will give Alan and me a small breathing space.

'I suppose we just submit the new plans and sit tight until we hear back from the mayor.'

She turns to face me. 'As long as you're happy with that,'

'I think there'll be no problem with planning permission,' says Stefan. 'But things take time here.'

'Poc a poc,' says Alan dryly.

'Exactly,' says Catalina.

Having to wait for the town council to make a decision about the cattery will please Rachel. Much as she has come round to the idea of my eventually bowing out of the business, for now she still wants me around to handle key projects with her. For a time I'm happy with that and it will help pay the bills until other plans fall into place.

'When is your client George coming over?' Catalina suddenly asks.

'Next month.'

'Fantastic! You know I love it when he calls. He's so funny.'

'He can certainly reduce me to tears.'

'I'm dying to meet him,' she enthuses. 'Your clients are so interesting.'

'Deranged, more like it,' mumbles the Scotsman.

'Oh come on, you wouldn't want to give them all up. Your work's so exciting,' she says.

'Exciting?' I snort. 'Hardly. Mind you, it does have its amusing moments, I admit.'

'Anyway,' says Catalina. 'I'll help you when the cattery opens, so you don't need to give up consulting. Why not do both?'

Why not indeed? The point is, though, that it'll soon be time for a change, which I'm looking forward to. Still, there's no rush and for the moment I'm happy with my lot.

'So,' says Stefan, bringing us back to the discussion in hand. 'Can we just check theses final architectural drawings before I submit them?'

He spreads the plans across the table. On cue, there's a scratching at the kitchen door and Minky and Orlando's two heads bob into view through the glass pane.

'Ah, the rest of the planning committee,' says the Scotsman cheerfully, opening the door. 'Now we can officially begin.'

The house is shuttered and the cats have been shooed out of the house into brilliant sunshine. In the *entrada* our cases are lined up by the door.

'I hope Catalina will remember to feed the cats,' frets Ollie.

'Of course she will. Now, have we got everything?'

Alan is in the kitchen checking through passports and flight tickets.

'I think so. Let's head for the airport.'

Ollie picks up his rucksack packed tightly with small toys and tennis balls to give the children of the orphanage and walks out to the car. I take one of the cases and am just heading for the door when the telephone rings.

Alan groans. 'Leave it.'

'Should we?' I run into the kitchen and grab the receiver.

'Hello?'

It's Rachel.

'Immaculate timing. We were just leaving.'

She's breathless. 'I hope you have a great time in Sri Lanka.'

'Thanks, Rachel.'

'And I just wanted to let you know that Dannie's sent you a thousand pounds for the orphanage.'

'My God!'

'She's gone off to an Indian ashram for three weeks. It means that Mary Anne can actually go on a break with her son.'

'Fabulous news. Well, I'd better be going..'

'Just one thing.'

'What?'

She gives a little shriek, 'I've got some great news!'

'More?'

Alan is gesticulating for me to wind up the call.

'On the back of the Crown jewels event, you'll never guess who's approached us about doing their PR…'

She whispers the name into the receiver. I'm too stunned to respond.

'It would be insane to take on something, or rather someone, that big.'

'Just think, we'd have the world's press on our doorstep!'

'It would take over our lives, Rachel.'

'It would help pay for your orchard. In fact it would pay for your cattery,' she says slyly.

'Maybe.'

'Aren't you tempted?'

I smirk at the disembodied voice.

'Not today.'

'What about tomorrow?'

I laugh. 'OK, let's discuss it when I get back.'

'Great. Happy landings.'

The car rumbles out of the courtyard and along the track just as a rotund ball of wool clatters by, hell-bent on reaching our gate before it snaps shut. Another follows in hot pursuit. Ollie peers round anxiously from the back seat.

'They've done it! They've got into our garden.'

'Oh no!' I yell.

'The gate's closed.' Ollie giggles hysterically.

'It's too late to stop,' says Alan. 'We're not going to miss the plane for some damned ewes.'

We level with Rafael's *finca*. Alberto is pottering about the yard, examining his new home and wagging his tail.

'Do you think they belong to Rafael?' asks Ollie.

'He doesn't have any sheep now. Only lambs,' mutters the Scotsman.

'So maybe they were just a figment of our imagination?' I tease.

Alan turns left onto the lane, a smirk on his face.

'You mean phantom sheep?' says Ollie.

'Or maybe,' I add with a smile, 'It's simply the triumphant return of the vanishing duo. Ewe Number One and Ewe Number Two.'

A Lizard in my Luggage

MAYFAIR TO MALLORCA IN ONE EASY MOVE

ANNA NICHOLAS

A LIZARD IN MY LUGGAGE

Mayfair to Mallorca in One Easy Move

Anna Nicholas

ISBN: 978 84024 565 3   Paperback   £7.99

Anna, a PR consultant to Mayfair's ritziest and most glamorous, had always thought Mallorca was for the disco and beer-swilling fraternity. That was until her sister hired an au pair from a rural part of the island who said it was the most beautiful place on earth. On a visit, Anna impulsively decided to buy a ruined farmhouse.

Despite her fear of flying, she kept a foot in both camps and commuted to central London to manage her PR company. But she found herself drawn away from the bustle and stress of life in the fast lane towards a more tranquil existence.

Told with piquant humour, A Lizard in my Luggage explores Mallorca's fiestas and traditions, as well as the ups and downs of living in a rural retreat. It is about learning to appreciate the simple things and take risks in pursuit of real happiness. Most importantly, it shows that life can be lived between two places.

'A witty and devilishly intelligent foray into the highs and lows of a new life in Spain'   XPAT magazine

'A beautifully written and highly entertaining account of the upside of downshifting'   THE DAILY MIRROR

'If you thought that glitz and glamour don't mix with rural country living you must read this book. Anna tells her highly entertaining tale of commuting to London while living in her Mallorcan restoration project'   BELLA Online

SNOWBALL
ORANGES
ONE MALLORCAN WINTER

PETER KERR

SNOWBALL ORANGES
One Mallorcan Winter

Peter Kerr

ISBN: 978 84024 112 8   Paperback   £7.99

It's the stuff of dreams: a Scottish family giving up relative sanity and security to go and grow oranges for a living in a secluded valley in the mountains of the Mediterranean island of Mallorca. But dreams, as everyone knows, have a nasty habit of not turning out quite as intended. Being greeted by a freak snowstorm is only the first of many surprises and 'experiences', and it isn't long before they realise that they have been sold a bit of a lemon of an orange farm by the wily previous owners.

'*Peter Kerr writes with a combination of nice observation and gentle humour.*'   THE SUNDAY TIMES

'*Fabulously evocative*'   SPANISH HOMES magazine

'*It is a really funny read and had me laughing out loud on my journey to work*'   FAMILY CIRCLE

'*This should do for Spain what* A Year in Provence *did for France. A delightful, often hilarious account of a Scottish family who bought an orange farm on Mallorca*'   THE SUNDAY POST magazine

'*…an affectionate and amusing tale on Majorca and its inhabitants*'   THE SUNDAY EXPRESS

Spain
by the horns

A journey to the heart of a culture

TIM ELLIOTT

SPAIN BY THE HORNS

A Journey to the Heart of a Culture

Tim Elliott

ISBN: 978 84024 574 5   Paperback   £7.99

It all began when Tim read a newspaper story about a bullfighter who was spotted practising on the beach at dawn. Intrigued, Tim tracked him down, looking for an interview, but instead he was told about another bullfighter in Spain, Jesulín, a man described as 'perhaps one of the most controversial and ridiculously over the top characters you're likely to meet'.

Disillusioned with his current life and job, Tim went to Spain to find him. Criss-crossing a country synonymous with flamboyance, passion, spontaneity and adventure, Tim found himself in a world of ancient ritual and eccentric characters, on a quixotic quest through a land where no one was ever on time but where every vibrant second oozed with the promise of heat and excitement. The famous bullfighter, who filled arenas with adoring women, surely held the key to the heart of this fiery nation.

Funny, fast-paced and revealing, *Spain by the Horns* takes you below the surface of a nation on a journey to the heart of a culture.

'a witty and delightful read that slips you under the skin of Spain... A must-read if ever there was one'   XPAT magazine

www.summersdale.com